TOWNSHIP POLITICS

TOWNSHIP POLITICS

Civic Struggles
for a New South Africa

Mzwanele Mayekiso

Edited by Patrick Bond
Foreword by Mel King

Ⓜ
Monthly Review Press
New York

Distribution of this book in South Africa has been made possible
with the generous support of the Holland Committee on Southern Africa,
Amsterdam, The Netherlands.

Library of Congress Cataloguing-in-Publication Data
Mayekiso, Mzwanele.
Township politics : civic struggles for a new South Africa / Mzwanele Mayekiso.
        p.   cm.
    ISBN 0-85345-966-5 (cloth : alk. paper) : $30.00. — ISBN 0-85345-965-7
(paper : alk. paper) : $15.00
    1. Social conflict—South Africa—Alexandra. 2. Social movements—
South Africa—Alexandra. 3. Alexandra (South Africa)—Politics and government.
I. Title.
    HN801.A95M39   1995
    303.6'09682'100dc20   95-33985
                                                                          CIP

Monthly Review Press
122 West 27th Street
New York, NY 10001

Manufactured in the United States of America

10 9 8 7 6 5 4 3 2 1

Contents

Foreword
Mel King

Mzwanele Mayekiso's book describes the evolution and growth of the civic movement in South Africa in the 1980s and 1990s. The author uses developments in Alexandra township as a starting point to lead the readers Into the story of the civic movement as a whole. In so doing, he shares the lessons learned by the members of the South African National Civic Organization (SANCO) during the struggles to overcome apartheid. He also discusses the dilemmas and problems that lie ahead as the organization continues focusses on the redevelopment of South Africa after apartheid.

Readers in the United States, particularly those of us concerned about community building and networking, can benefit in a number of ways from Mayekiso's work. In the first place, Mayekiso argues for the validity of local experience and knowledge in all development initiatives. While he admits that we cannot uncritically translate from the local to the global level, he believes that the role of the civics—their experiences with mass mobilization, democracy building, addressing local grievances, and building new institutions can and should be shared with comrades in other societies. In particular, readers in the United States will see many parallels between the struggles of the civics in South Africa and those of community organizations and community development corporations in our own country. Mayekiso knows that SANCO has to transform itself in order to be an effective participant in the country's future development. He knows that the organization has to move from being a successful protest movement challenging the authoritarian apartheid regime to a movement that supports physical, economic, and social development. SANCO's struggle to become an effective service provider and advocate, while working within the framework of a political system, forms the heart of this book.

Readers in the United States will find it interesting to compare their experiences with American community development organizations as they follow the South African civics' transformation from being outsider organizations protesting governmental negligence and abuse of power to becoming insider organizations working within a governmental process. I am personally most familiar with the CDCs, or Community Development Corporations, that were founded in a number of cities in the United States in the 1970s. The CDCs were designed to be community-controlled institutions that would provide housing and economic development for those who were not being served—or were being under-served—by mainstream institutions. Many of the CDCs found that they were replacing the old bureaucracies, but without having the financial resources to fulfill their commitments. Others found themselves becoming property managers and housing developers, rapidly moving away from their mission to serve the community's broader needs and concerns. SANCO will undoubtedly face this dilemma soon, and I believe—as does Mayekiso—that it can only be overcome through community education and participation; this has, unfortunately, been largely neglected by the CDCs.

Building on his understanding of the events unfolding in Alexandra, Mayekiso places the role of civic movement in the struggle against apartheid in historical perspective, allowing us to understand the civics' active and passive resistance as a model for cultural survival. He links the growth of SANCO with the struggle to create a nonracist South Africa, demonstrating the power of community-based strategies of organizing and protest.

There are some obvious parallels between the civics' struggles in South Africa and those of the civil rights movement in the United States. Yet there are some interesting differences as well. Mayekiso points out that although there were different interpretations of, and values ascribed to, the civic movement by different parts of the political spectrum, the civics were more representative of the community's needs and interests than other entities and were therefore more useful for challenging both class divisions and the state in the fight for better housing, health care, education, and other services. This is very different from the union movement in the United States, which addresses similar issues but which is, in many instances, detached from the struggle against racism.

Mayekiso raises several interesting issues that are pertinent to events unfolding both in South Africa and in other nations throughout the world. The transfer of power in South Africa has been a long and difficult process. Unlike other countries that have overthrown the scourge of colonialism and oppression through violent means, South Africa has undergone a radical transformation while the physical and institutional infrastructure created by the previous government remains firmly in place. In order to be successful in the long run, the new government must use this infrastructure to fashion a democracy that can involve all the people. The civics have the potential to play a major role in the creation and development of that democracy.

As local institutions that support community development, the civics face the task of bringing diverse groups and interests together. SANCO must cut across party lines, as well as bridge tribal and ideological differences, if it is to work on issues that are affect the community and country. It can look toward Mandela's own blueprint for action as a source for inspiration—an inclusive philosophy that has been successful in bringing diverse groups of people together to focus their collective energies on formulating strategies, plans, and approaches to national development. Such a strategy of "complementary holism" allows for diverse groups to work together while maintaining their own autonomy. A powerful example of the short-term success of this model is the Rainbow Coalition, which has allowed different oppressed groups to struggle together to attain a society that is liberating for all, all the while retaining their separate identities.

SANCO's model of community education and participation is not a passive one, where experts tell everyone else what is wrong and then recommend solutions. On the contrary, SANCO's model is one of participation, where well-informed people are guided to think critically about problems that affect them and participate actively in the creation of solutions. For this approach to be successful, however, I believe that SANCO must be convinced of the capacity of all the people. It must stop using terms such as "lost generation" and define people, particularly youth, as both deserving and meaningful participants in the country's development.

It is heartening to note that Mayekiso has given serious consideration to the role of youth and of women in the country's development. I too believe that a successful youth-adult alliance is necessary for any community development initiative to be successful, as is a holistic approach that does not ignore the concerns of any oppressed group. In addition, struggles to build communities in the United States need to be chronicled in the same way that Mayekiso has chronicled the struggles in Alexandra. His analysis and concerns about the role of community organizing as part of the larger political struggle need to be explored and extended in the context of similar struggles in the United States.

Any community development effort is fundamentally a struggle for minds and for land. When Mandela was in prison struggling for the freedom of the land, his mind was still free and open to possibilities, supported by a vision of a nonracist South Africa. The civics can play a vital role in helping those whose bodies are free but whose minds are in jail to see the light. The civics have the potential to develop the critical thinking skills of the people they represent, and can serve as a model for community-based development that can be duplicated in other parts of the world.

Like Dr. Martin Luther King, Jr., who asked, "Where do we go from here: chaos or community?" SANCO must now ask where and how it wants to lead its constituency at this critical juncture. The test will be to see if it can exercise leadership and support the development of an inclusive, participatory democracy.

Mzwanele Mayekiso is convinced that an international body devoted to linking civic associations is necessary. He reaches out to citizens of the United States interested in linking communities worldwide in on-going struggles for social justice and democracy. Advances in technology, particularly the emergence and success of electronic communications, have the ability to foster alliances that cross national boundaries, making such a vision of community-based development ever more possible.

Preface

I have long contemplated writing a book about my experiences as a young South African during the 1980s and early 1990s, an extraordinary period of social turbulence, economic crisis, and far- reaching political change. I played a small role in shaping these developments in Alexandra township, and in interpreting them to my comrades across the nation and in other parts of the world. As the reader will see in this book, townships are places that are in many respects unique, and Alexandra was a formidable place for me to hone my politics. In South Africa the very word township conjures up images of Alexandra.

But this book comes not from any desire for attention as an individual (my long spell being in the eye of the then-police state, as well as the media and the public, was quite enough for anyone, and I am now content to be a low-profile student again). It comes because as fashions change and many of our best civic movement cadres leave the movement for new opportunities in government, we need to renew our thinking about civic action. To do so, however, means we must look backward.

Examining township politics during the mid-1980s uprisings and during our struggles for economic and political democracy in the early 1990s requires me to try to set straight a record that has become twisted over time. Dubious journalists and the pamphleteers of conservative political parties and big business think-tanks are not the only ones to blame. Distorted paintings of our movement have also emerged from the groves of academia. These scholars, as I try to show in the pages below, often missed the point

11

entirely, perhaps because of their distance from the realities of the townships, perhaps because of their own theoretical biases or political agendas.

As an insider facing generally hostile outside interpretations, I have considered it my challenge to provide a frank, up-to-date account of some of our civic, youth, and political struggles. Of greatest importance is showing the linkages within social movement organizing. I hope that I have achieved this by covering nearly all facets of our civic work in Alexandra: our early organizing, the campaigns against the army and police that verged on military maneuvers, our efforts to maintain perspective even while in prison, the critiques we leveled against capitalist development plans, the campaigns against local apartheid puppets, negotiations for a democratic future and more equitable development, the visions we constructed of our own commu- nity- controlled development projects, and the continuing attempt to make the civic movement more equitable along class, gender, and generational lines.

South Africa's civics have taken the idea of independent civil society a long way, possibly as far as any social movement in the world. The trend toward increasingly independent institutions of civil society is something that confronts all of us, in every society. But there are progressive and reactionary ways of considering this phenomenon. For instance, if we put all activities in the realm of civil society, the concept loses real meaning. Worse, we run the risk of following the agenda of imperialist development agencies and foreign ministries, namely, to shrink the size and scope of third world governments and to force community organizations to take up state respon- sibilities with inadequate resources.

What is needed to combat this powerful trend is a far more class- conscious perspective on civil society, one that highlights those strategies and instruments of the working class that are crucial to social, political, and economic progress. Thus in my analysis, our struggle against apartheid flows directly into our struggle against capitalist exploitation. South Africa's liberation movement was, after all, made up activists convinced that we were fighting for national, gender, and class emancipation. This required us to develop and maintain critiques of apartheid, patriarchy, and capital- ism.

But since the victorious election of April 1994, as inequality has become somewhat easier to redress on racial and gender lines, we need to take a closer look at social relations and class structure. After all, the most recent income distribution data show that over the past couple of decades South Africa has become one of the most unequal countries in the world. In the midst of its own crisis of profitability, big capital has countered this dangerous situation by locating its political interests strategically. How has the democratic movement addressed this thorny situation, and how will it do so in the future? Some of our strategies are described in the book, and even if our battles against banks and big business were not conclusive, they hold many lessons for our future movement toward socialism. Most importantly, to link our community struggles to the traditional struggle for socialism requires us to consider carefully the new politics of what I call working-class civil society.

In doing so, contradictions within our communities and within the civic movement rise to the surface, and I have tried not to disguise these (which would, in any case, be impossible in the case of Alexandra). Can, for example, township civics represent poor and working people and the small but important black middle class at the same time? Can we represent people with homes as well as the homeless? Can we confront the diverse issues that divide people and that cross-cut our various identities? (No one, after all, is simply and solely a proletarian, a mother, a township resident, a young person, a black South African. We are often many of these, and this fact shapes the way we think, act, speak, and relate to others.) Can we overcome leadership styles that are sometimes not as conducive to democratic practice as we might want, and as our movement requires?

It is a tall order, one that we work at haltingly, yet with growing conviction. Civics, after all, emerged not because of apartheid or the Black Local Authorities. They emerged because of the daily struggles of residents who, even in a democratic society, will continue to need civics to represent their interests on socioeconomic (and hence political) issues in a nonpartisan way.

The future of the civics depends to a great extent on our strategies as we adapt to the changed circumstance of the coming years. In the past, the enemy was very clear. Now the situation is different, very gelatinous (as I like to call it). Indeed, there is even the possibility of co-option by the state and the death of our social movement.

This is the theme with which many analysts have concluded studies of urban social movements. In *City and the Grassroots*, for instance, Manuel Castells argued that social movements are transitory because they often succeed in their immediate objectives, only to lose momentum, cadreship, and ideological clarity. Nevertheless, he wrote, social movements do

> produce new historical meaning—in the twilight zone of pretending to build within walls of a local community a new society they know to be unattainable. And they do so by nurturing the embryos of tomorrow's social movements within the local Utopias that urban movements have constructed in order never to surrender to barbarism.

But this historical meaning can, I believe, project far into the future. I am confident of this because I have seen reflections of South Africa's experience in other places, particularly the better community organizations in the United States and the mass urban movements of Latin America. And others—including Andre Gunder Frank—agree that social movements can be more durable and inclined toward socialist politics than Castells believed. In his contribution to *Transforming the Revolution,* he wrote optimistically about the movements' potential:

> In seeking and organizing to change society in smaller, immediate but doable steps, which did not require state power, the utopian socialists were perhaps much more realistic than the scientific ones—and they were more akin then to the social movements of our time than the "scientific" socialists of the intervening century. What is more, many utopian socialists proposed and pursued social changes and particularly different gender relations, which were subsequently increasingly abandoned or forgotten by scientific socialists.... The real transition to a "socialist" alternative to the present world economy, society, and polity, therefore, may be much more in the hands of the social movements. Not only must they intervene for the sake of survival to save as many people as possible from any threatening abyss. We must also look to the social movements as the most active agents to forge new links, which can transform the world in new directions.

I would be careful not to overstate the case, and not to claim that the urban movements I know are proto-socialist in nature. But their other democratic and popular characteristics are not in question. This is corroborated by James Petras and Morris Morley, who argue that over the past two decades, South Africa's civic movement, along with the mass movements of many other countries,

emerged to break the bonds of authoritarian politics and the constraints of police state regimes, to overcome the passivity and paralysis
of the traditional opposition, and to forge a new political reality. What
makes these social movements different from those in the past is that
they are independent of traditional party-electoral political machines.
They are led and directed by grassroots leaders. Policy is constantly
debated in democratic popular assemblies. The strong ties to local
communities and the intense but profoundly democratic political life
has enabled these new social movements to mobilize previously
unorganized strata: the unemployed, young women, squatters, indig-
enous peoples. The new social movements combine with and tran-
scend the action of organized labor movements; street action surges
beyond the wage issues toward enlarging the areas of freedom for
people to act and realize their human dignity.

Realizing human dignity in South Africa has never been easy for
blacks—or whites. Were it not for the instruments of working-class civil
society I have been associated with, and the many progressive leaders,
cadres, and commentators I have come to know within these, my own
personal development would have been far slower and more uneven. My
political growth within the ANC/SACP culture has helped me to make
meaningful contributions to civil society, and hence to use my energy in the
civic struggles for a New South Africa. The book, therefore, is not a polemic
(though some may read it this way), but instead represents the next stage of
my own attempt to augment my organizing interests with intellectual
arguments. I hope that it will at the same time help the ordinary civic activist
to understand some of our traditions.

For it is with the ordinary citizens of our cities, towns, and villages that I
rest my greatest hopes and expectations. Their role in South Africa and
elsewhere has been inspiring, and it is in the whole rather than in the sum
of the actions of a few leaders that change is accomplished. For those of
you who were active with me in Alexandra, I hope that my accounting does
this period justice. The aim is not to praise or attack individual personalities,
of course, but instead to offer a contribution to both the intellectual and the
practical struggles over township politics. The success of my contribution will
therefore rest on the controversies and critical commentaries it foments.

Thanks must go to those who helped introduce me to—and worked with me within—organizations such as the ACO and SANCO. In particular, I want to thank my older brother Moss, presently an ANC Member of Parliament, formerly a trade union and civic leader whose inspiration in building working-class civil society has been unparalleled. Debates, disagreements, and decision-making with Moss, especially during the most intense periods of civic struggle in Alexandra, taught me more than any formal education could, and this is reflected in many places throughout the book.

There are so many other comrades who were also there—too many to do justice to in a short list of acknowledgments. But I cannot ignore the influence of Richard Mdakane, friend and comrade and co-treason trialist; Langa Zita, my one-time housemate and one of the critical young analysts of the contemporary political situation; Penrose Ntlonti and Sandi Mgidlana at SANCO headquarters; my brother (and SACP activist) Mzonke and my sister Nobantu; my parents and indeed the whole Mayekiso family.

It was impossible to finish this project without the critical support these friends and comrades extended. I thank the many people who have, over the years, helped me shape into a book my speeches at rallies, rough notes made in prison, and my articles from popular and academic periodicals. I must mention some of my publishers—*Africa South and East, African Communist, Alexandra Times, Multinational Monitor, Red Pepper, Southern Africa Report, Southern African Review of Books, Times Literary Supplement, Urban Forum, Work in Progress*—as well as the extremely valuable advice and support I have received over the years from Solomon and Jenny Dunjwa-Blajberg in Rio de Janeiro, Sergej Debrouwer and the Committee for Southern Africa in Amsterdam (which has provided a subsidy for township civic readers of this book), Roland Fett at the Third World House in Germany, and especially Hilary Wainwright in Britain. And in the United States, there were so many people, including comrades from our sister-city of Chicago (Slim Coleman, Michael Friedberg, Joan Gerig, Lisa January, Judith Scully, and Helen Shiller); Susan Lowes and Michael Tanzer of Monthly Review Press; Chester Hartman of the Poverty and Race Research Action Council; Tom Angotti, Ron Shiffman, and Ayse Yonder at the Pratt Institute; my fellow planner and community organizer Becky Himlin of the University of Maryland; and a comrade whom I consider among the most loyal of friends and allies, Patrick Bond, my editor throughout this project.

To all of you, I say Huntshu! Nang'ams'ontozakuthi! — Thank you, comrades! Civic struggles will continue!

PART 1
A WELCOME TO ALEXANDRA

1
Alexandra as Freedom Dawned
(early 1990s)

*Welcome to Alexandra Township, just north of Johannesburg. To start
this book, I will provide a walking tour of the township as it appeared in the
early 1990s, just prior to our transition to democracy. First I want to describe
the township, then I want to try to explain and analyze some of the things
we will see.*

View from the street

You always remember your first sight of Alexandra Township, it is so
striking. Visitors expect to see many high-rise buildings, since around
350,000 people live in this small area of less than two square miles.

Instead, you are immediately surprised as you leave the Pan Africa taxi
rank on the outskirts of Alex. You must dodge cows, goats, horses, chickens,
and mangy dogs that no owner would claim, all roaming the streets,
scavenging in litter pits for food. But you quickly conclude that this is not,
by any means, a rural scene.

Alex is unlike any city in the world. No South African township is as
densely populated, as well developed politically, as decimated by unemployment and economic despair, or as socially tense.

If you have come from the Wynberg suburb into Alexandra, you will have
seen the main commercial area on First Avenue. The taxi rank is central,
with thousands of people going to and fro, except when there is a taxi war
in progress. There are some major shops such as Sales House, OK, and

Checkers, but commerce is also controlled by smaller shops owned by Indians and some whites.

The prices charged here are higher than in downtown Johannesburg, due to the ability of shop owners to exploit customers who must otherwise pay an expensive taxi for a trip to buy cheaper goods. Hawkers outside the shops have slightly better prices. A few African-owned shops are on the Alexandra side of First Avenue.

There is also a good deal of industry on the outskirts of Alexandra. Marlboro, Wynberg, and Bramley View are filled with small factories. And there are white residential areas nearby as well, separated from Alexandra by a buffer strip of small industry in Bramley View and Kew, as well as by open fields.

The most interesting things happen within the township. Take a walk through these streets with me and you will understand more about these contradictions. It is always wise to have a guide on your visits to Alex, if you are an outsider. When I first came here from the Transkei, when I was in my late teens, my sister Nobantu showed me around. Things have become much more complicated since the early 1980s.

This is obvious when you talk to the people of Alexandra. Looking to your right, you find small groups of unemployed youth. They often spend time gambling with dice and cards, with some winning or losing up to R1,000 a day. By the way, if you have a lucky streak and win that much and then try to walk away, it might cost you your life. Some of the players stole their families' savings to play this game, and do not take losing well.

As an outsider, there is a fair chance you will be mugged if you walk these streets carelessly. Thugs carry knives, and guns are now becoming the fashion. Ordinary criminals have begun a virtual arms race here. One result is that you will quickly learn of the organized gangs that operate here.

Not all our street-life economic activity is criminal, of course. The informal sector is buzzing. Coming up this road here is comrade Tsediso, who is unemployed, a school drop-out, and now a peanut seller. He sells these nuts in little packets the size of your palm for R1,50.

Tsediso takes in about R30 each day, and in the early hours of the next morning he must spend R15 of that getting more nuts. Tsediso starts selling to workers near a factory at 6 a.m., moves his stall around the township during the day, looking for concentrations of people, and ends up at night near the factory gate. Twelve hours is not unusual, as Tsediso manages one

Kids playing in the street, Old Alexandra. East Bank is in the background. *Photo: Helen Shiller.*

sale every half hour. It is tragic that a person must spend time in such a manner.

The R15 profit Tsediso brings home must feed eight people. He barely survives. Other vendors are competing for Alex residents' scarce money. Some sell the heads of sheep, and also the internal organs. Very little goes to waste here, since people are so desperate.

There is a small crowd of youngsters, even though it is still school hours. Some are also regulars at the shebeen, the equivalent of a corner tavern, but located within a house. Some youngsters are to be found in houses and shacks, seduced into having sexual relations with adults who have money. It is not formal prostitution, but just reflects how the social fabric has decayed.

Further along this road is a garbage dump. Homeless people are living there, moving around the township scavenging for food in dustbins. They are social rejects, and must live as human garbage in these conditions with makeshift cardboard covers or even just in the open.

But we must be careful, and not just about muggers: a kombi (minibus) taxi is approaching fast. These taxis can be very dangerous, racing through the streets to beat the competition. Transport is the best example of the success of the informal sector, the experts say. There is no railway linking Alex to Johannesburg, and the bus company went bankrupt. Transport is a big issue, and the entire community now depends on taxis.

A trip from here to Johannesburg and back costs R3,40, which is a large amount for people who earn less than R1,000 per month. Worse, they must still wait as long as two hours during the morning and evening rush hours for space in a kombi. The kombi that nearly ran us down belongs to Alexandra United Taxi Association. The other main association is the Alexandra-Randburg-Midrand-Sandton Taxi Association. Their politics are different, but their drivers are just as crazy. You must pray if you are a passenger, or even just crossing the road.

And for quite some time, you also had to pray if you went anywhere near Roosevelt Street, one of our main arteries. Not even the taxis used this street. Why, you ask? Look up the hill, and you see the answer: that brown, military-style barracks. That's Madala Hostel, the oldest hostel in the township, and therefore called Old Man's Hostel, or M1.

There was a good chance of being a sniper victim if you proceeded along Roosevelt near the hostel; it was best never to go closer than a few hundred meters. The life-long community residents who used to live next to the hostel, in what we call Beirut, were forced to move to churches and community halls and even the offices of the hated Alexandra Town Council. That is a sad story we will have to spend time clarifying later in the book.

There is a women's hostel, however, which is safe to visit. The 2,800 women in this prison-like structure live in overcrowded conditions, four or five women in tiny rooms with no space for relaxation. They cannot have their husbands or children even visiting them here. Life is hard, but they keep their spirits up.

For women elsewhere in the township, life is also very hard. They must get up earlier than anyone to take care of the family and go to work. Their pay is nowhere near the man's, for even the same job. They come home at night, clean up, cook, do laundry, and prepare the children for bed. The man of the house is usually out visiting friends, or sitting in the corner, relaxing and reading a newspaper.

Outside, the streets are dangerous. I think it is time to move into a shebeen nearby. In fact, every third house in Alex is a shebeen and there are many types of alcoholic drinks to chose from. Some shebeens specialize in jazz music, some disco, and some funk. The music in this one, rap from the United

Two women in a room for four to six in the main women's hostel. The occupants, each of whom pays rent, are typically unrelated—so the lack of privacy makes tension within the rooms common. *Photo: Anna Zieminski, author's collection.*

The Jukskei River. A popular dump site for white-owned companies, the river has been found to contain a variety of toxic chemicals, as well as rubble. *Photo: Helen Shiller.*

States, is extremely popular. But it is too loud for us to carry on the conversation for long.

Out on the road again, we must cross the little river that divides Alexandra, called the Jukskei. Children play there when it is hot. The water is filthy, a health hazard. The river banks are not well kept, and indeed they sometimes collapse when people walk on them. You can see that the shacks built right up to the edge of the banks are in severe danger of falling into the water, which they sometimes do. If, on the other hand, you visit the same Jukskei River in Sandton, you will see how clean it is and how the banks are well fortified.

Crossing the bridge, we come to the part of Alexandra called the East Bank. The homes here are very fancy, and were built when my comrades and I were safely locked away in prison, facing charges of high treason—I will return to that story later. On the surface, it is a pretty sight, but not all is well here, and the residents of the East Bank are confused.

For ordinary people with no way to get decent accommodation in Old Alexandra, the East Bank seemed to offer an escape. Talk to my friend Sizwe, who stays in that typical R80,000 East Bank house there, and you will see that his feelings are now somewhat elitist. He thinks he is a better person than those who must still stay in the overcrowded rooms in the old part of the township. Sizwe thinks that the old township has no culture; I think he has lost his sense of community.

It is a shame, because today Sizwe is struggling hard to make his monthly housing loan (bond) repayment. He will need our help soon, once he skips a month and the foreclosure notice comes. But you see that Sizwe seems to be happy, thinking that life is rosy since he is away from Old Alex.

If you look beyond these nice houses, further to the east, you can see an enormous field, which we call the Far East Bank. The grass gently sways in the breeze. In the distance is the highway that circles Johannesburg, and beyond that even more vacant land, owned by the chemical giant AECI, a subsidiary of the Anglo American Corporation.

If you look closely, you see that the soil is not so good. The first people who thought about living here were whites, but they rejected this area for that reason. On the East Bank you can see the cracks in some of the houses. The soil across the highway, on the AECI land, is said to be polluted with the company's chemical waste. Our people suffer from land hunger, and when they are told of the poor soil and the problems with the AECI land, their frustrations rise to the boil.

A typical multifamily unit in Old Alexandra. This house probably shelters between fifteen and twenty families, one family per room. *Photo: Helen Shiller.*

A typical East Bank house for a professional or other upper-income family. *Photo: Helen Shiller.*

The Far East Bank looks like a mirage in the desert, and many people are anxious to have a properly-built house there, made with strong foundations on the shifting ground. But they have only been offered what is called "site-and-service," which means people must actually build their own houses bit by bit. Our own position in the civic association is that sufficient resources for housing must be provided to all the people of Alexandra. We see housing as a right, not a privilege, and if we are successful maybe one day you will visit and see that a healthy community has been built.

Back across the Jukskei in Old Alex, we must now visit some friends of mine. The family of Nokuzola, a young woman, includes eight people staying in one room, in a four-room house. The house stands on a plot of land (the "yard") with fifteen families, one communal tap, one washing line, and three buckets where people urinate and defecate (this is termed "night soil"). She will tell us of the problems that come with overcrowding, such as suspicion, mistrust, and conflicts with the neighbors. Next door, Nokuzola says, lives a witch who casts spells on families so that they suffer perpetually.

As you can smell, night-soil buckets are often not well attended. On some days, workers leave them in the streets until noon. The stench is unforgettable, and the buckets are a health hazard. With such overcrowding, you understand why we hear so many people shouting at each other. The resources are scarce, the needs are great.

Many of these tin-roofed, plywood-walled shacks were built quickly, with no planning. They will decay under the pressure of heavy rain and wind in the summer. Each shack is attached to the next, so when one catches fire, the whole area burns. This happens often, especially in winter. It is no place to call home. The choking smoke from fires and from paraffin oil for lighting and cooking makes it very dirty at night, which is why Alex is called "Dark City." It was not long ago that we had no electricity or street lighting at all.

Trees were plentiful once, and helped to keep the air cleaner. But people are desperate, and are chopping the trees down mercilessly, which degrades the environment even further. In addition, Alex has been used as a dumping ground for toxic waste.

There is electricity in the homes of a few people, but only those who have enough money to pay the R800 hook-up fee (the new pre-paid meters cost even more, around R3,000). Looking up, you see these flimsy wires connected to electricity poles. This is the work of unemployed technicians, who are paid up to R200 to get this illegal, and free, source of electricity.

A spaza shop in Old Alexandra carrying a variety of essentials. Many of these kiosks are run right next to their owners' homes. *Photo: Helen Shiller.*

And then there is the harsh lighting set up on very high poles, which gives us the feel of a military camp at night.

Let's keep walking. These shack areas we're passing have little kiosks known as "spaza shops" interspersed throughout. This is another informal sector activity, where people can earn a few rand without a license, selling sugar, the staple corn meal, bread, rice, matches, and other essentials. Over there is a typical "corner shop," which is a real shop with a license. Prices are more expensive in both kinds of shops than in Johannesburg. Some of the owners have begun to climb the ladder, but with such intense competition between them, and because of robberies, the owners are not really prospering.

With no recreational facilities, children must compete with the farm animals and cars for street space. We are now walking comfortably on a tarred surface. But this is new, only placed over the dirt road in the last couple of years. Even now, you can see that the roadbed was so poorly constructed that it is cracking.

Until recently, the deep soil erosion and ruts in these streets made them safer for children's play, since cars could only travel in starts and stops, negotiating painfully through the canyons. When the rains came, however, the roads became rivers, dangerous for the youngest children, many of whom know what it is to be swept by a flash flood all the way into the Jukskei.

During heavy rains, the mud could be impenetrable. Losing your balance in that mud meant that going out in good clothes was sure to lead to embarrassment at your destination. After the rains stopped, huge potholes in the streets captured stagnant, stinking water, sure to result in the spread of disease.

Alex has only one decent clinic to serve the entire population. The nearest hospital that we are allowed to go to is in Thembisa, which is sixty kilometers away if you must travel there by taxi. Meanwhile, they are shutting down a white hospital just four kilometers away.

Life is very different if you go just three kilometers to the west. It is unbelievable, but there you find one of the richest suburbs in all of Africa, even the southern hemisphere. Sandton is a dream to the blacks of Alexandra, in terms of living standards, a place to raise a family in peace and quiet.

And if you look into the distance you will see Sandton City, the high-rise, luxury office, and shopping center. Our people travel there to work as security guards, cleaners, or menial laborers. They see the wealth all day. At night, the confusion and despair of Alexandra welcome them back. It is a tragic tale of two cities.

A popular joke in Alex is that when Harry Oppenheimer, former boss of Anglo American Corporation, flew in an airplane over Alex, he thought it was an old, disused scrapyard for junk cars, set in the middle of a beautiful suburban scene dotted with swimming pools and leafy trees, and immediately thought about redeveloping the scrapyard for profit. As one *Star* newspaper report has it, "Approaching Alexandra by air shocks the sense more than it would on the ground. One moment you are gliding over large beautiful homes set in lush gardens amid tennis courts, stables and sparkling swimming pools, then the earth below you suddenly turns brown and scabrous as if it had died."

It may seem like an abandoned pile of junk to the very rich, but life in Alexandra is always vibrant at the street level. If you return to Alex on a weekend, what you see in the backyards will amaze you. Each ethnic group reverts to traditional cultural recreation. The Pedi people come out with their beautiful dances, as many people watch in admiration. The Zulu people have their dances too, as do the Xhosa. And you can go from one to the other, enjoying the richness of African culture. Then you can visit a stokvel, or burial society, which offers a mix of saving money and socializing.

The churches are also very well attended on Sundays. But from the Catholic church to sects such as the Zionists, it is older people who are the loyal core of churchgoers. They pray, sometimes with great energy, running in circles in small, unventilated areas. But you can feel the tension between the mainstream churches and the sects. And there is a real class difference between churchgoers, which you can see from the quality of the clothing and the way they walk to church.

Alexandra is a very splintered place, you see. What nearly everyone shares, though, is a sense of insecurity. It is difficult to see this at first glance, because of the tradition of hiding the problems. But once you meet people and gain their trust, you hear more and more of the problems that poor and working-class South Africans must face.

Describing these problems is one thing. We must also try to *explain* them.

Looking below surface-level

Let us back up and consider exactly what is going on here. There are good intellectual studies of Alexandra (including two sociology dissertations by Philip Tourikis and Mike Sarakinsky from the University of the Witwatersrand), and also some questionable academic studies of community politics here, as I describe later. But let us take a first, simple look at some of the things that we have seen on the surface and try to explain their roots.

First, what are those cows doing in the streets? Alex is a township, to be sure, but there are very strong linkages to the rural areas. Most people have relatives in the homelands or other rural areas, and travel to and fro. Some of those who settled in Alexandra try to maintain a rural way of life, and value livestock as a means of accumulating wealth. Some of those who buy livestock do so in order to perform traditional rituals, such as communicating with ancestors through animal sacrifice. The traditional African healers ("izangoma") are still popular, and when new healers have been trained, blood must flow to thank the ancestors.

That explains the goats and cows, which seem out of place on first glance. It's interesting that no one ever seems to steal livestock, even when it runs free, whereas theft in shops and homes is widespread. There are no controls over livestock, so you see goats and cows wandering all over Alexandra.

A primary school in Khayelitsha township, Cape Town. Crowded classrooms are common throughout South Africa. *Photo © 1992 Eric Miller, Impact Visuals.*

What about the kids in the streets? These young boys and girls are completely frustrated with the schooling, because Bantu education is still the system. There are not enough teachers, textbooks, chalks, or paper. The schools cannot be considered institutions of learning, but are more like military barracks, and the most they attempt is social control. But they are not very effective, as you can see from the large number of truants.

Next, we must consider why the streets are unsafe. Why do you see so much gambling, and why do you run the risk of being mugged? The answer is straightforward. It relates mainly to the apartheid economy which does not absorb labor any more, even during the so-called economic recovery that began in late 1993. Under these conditions, it has been difficult to set up community institutions to control the streets.

Economically, things are very bad. Whereas back in the early 1960s, about 80 percent of those who came into the South African job market found formal employment, by the early 1990s that figure had dropped to 10 percent, according to official statistics. That is, only one in ten of those who finish school are able to get a job these days. This steady fall in the ability of the mainstream economy to employ our people explains the situation Tsediso finds himself in.

The situation has become even worse recently because of three things. One is the longest economic recession in South Africa's history, which began in early 1989 and lasted through the early 1990s. This recession was partly due to the mismanagement of the economy under white minority rule, and partly because capitalist economies, here and internationally, periodically face long, deep crises.

Another factor is the sudden increase in the population of Alexandra. Many people were coming to Alex even before P.W. Botha, the former apartheid state president, dropped Influx Control (the "Pass Laws") in 1986. In the late 1980s, the floodgate was opened. The high cost of land and housing, and the continuation of Group Areas Act restrictions until 1991, meant that all the townships in the Johannesburg area were subject to massive overcrowding. Because of affordability problems, we expect this situation to continue into the foreseeable future.

It just goes to show how, despite the fact that apartheid was rigorously planned, its ending has been unplanned and chaotic. The free market has been the main force in determining where people must live and what jobs are available. And that is the main reason for the mess that now exists.

A third factor is the legacy of apartheid's repression. At one point, you see, the streets were safe. That was a brief moment in early 1986, when our "organs of people's power" were in operation—I will have much more to say about them later, too. Since then, we have tried to bring back the spirit of early 1986, but another problem has prevented the organs of people's power from operating properly. Key activists were assassinated, and there were periodic massacres of ordinary citizens. In short, we faced a concerted effort to liquidate our organizations and our politics.

Finally, the influence of gangs must be considered. This is not new, for in Alexandra we have a rich and tragic history of criminal gangs, including the well-known Msomi and Spoiler gangs of the 1950s. Msomi was founded to look after the interests of the community, but without political conscious-ness, it became instead a vehicle for bribery and corruption. The thuggery that emerged created its own logic. The Spoilers simply followed that pattern of thuggery and turf wars, aiming not at community power but at profits.

This led to many smaller gangs, comprised of dejected thugs from Msomi, or new gangs (like the Americans), which aimed to boost egos where Msomi or Spoilers could not. Some of these gangs died off because the leaders killed each other or became vulnerable to certain types of police harassment. New gangs then took their place.

The streets are unsafe, therefore, for several reasons. But at least what were once muddy roads are now paved streets. To understand why the apartheid regime offered some limited resources for the upgrade requires going back to why Alex in 1986 was considered an "oil spot," a place that needed some money dropped in, like oil on troubled waters, simply to quiet the unrest. We will cover that in depth, in Part 2 of the book.

In fact, however, the old regime's upgrading was not quality work. Potholes are already appearing in these new streets. The Development Bank of Southern Africa, which did some of the work, responds by saying that the lack of garbage removal and drainage means highly corrosive fluids are constantly washing down the roads. Of course, we say, but that is all your fault, for propping up a town council that is no use, and for not doing proper engineering. Consulting with the local people, through the civic association or even its street committee, might have helped avoid these and many other problems.

But it is not just the Development Bank work that is substandard. Even expensive houses on the East Bank, like Sizwe's, are experiencing severe problems. Cracks are appearing in the foundations because of the poor soil, and this is tempting residents who were once aloof to consider joining the civic in order to get change.

So you can see that the upgrading of Alexandra has created as many problems as it solved. In general, the National Party strategy was to paper over the widening cracks in the system. The strategy was designed to whitewash our minds, to confuse us into thinking the apartheid state was addressing our needs. This was a strategy that some analysts called "winning hearts and minds," or WHAM!

It was a strategy aimed first and foremost at diminishing the power of the activists in a township. Naturally, all residents want a working infrastructure of roads, water, and sewage. Yet the apartheid upgrading was top-down, void of community participation and control. And the oil-spot mentality meant that the upgrading was done with the short-term pacification of the residents in mind first, and profits for the big companies next.

One thing the apartheid regime did not feel responsible for was transportation. The state initially failed to put in a railway line because it planned that Alexandra would be "removed" from the rich northern suburbs. Only in 1979 was this plan finally dispensed with, but there was still no railroad. Instead, a private bus service was the main form of transport. Then, in the 1980s, the taxi industry boomed, as government billboards claimed that

"Free Enterprise Is Working," using the taxi driver as the example of the successful entrepreneur.

But within a few years a new crisis emerged, due to lack of planning and regulation. Too many taxi drivers are now competing for passengers during off-peak hours, yet there are always too few taxis available during rush hour. The taxi owners cannot afford the banks' high financing charges any more. Many are going bankrupt. Passengers are paying higher fares. Under pressure from the owners, drivers are driving much faster, causing accidents. Taxi associations are at war with one another.

The next question you might ask concerns the hostels we saw on the hill. Why did these suddenly become the base from which Inkatha (the semi-fascistic political party under the command of Zulu leader Gatsha Buthelezi) launched murderous attacks on the community?

The simple answer is that this was a response, in late 1990, to the challenge that progressive community activists posed to the local town council, then run by Mayor Prince Mokoena. His failure to gain control of development on the Far East Bank land in February 1991 was the last straw. Within a week, Mokoena had organized Inkatha killers to replace many hostel dwellers.

As a result, our own civic structures in the two male hostels were destroyed. This declaration of war against the civic association was a last gasp for Mokoena, but did not succeed in saving his political career. Inkatha's offensive did, however, lead to the death of nearly a hundred people in March 1991 alone, and many more after that. I will explain this in more depth later in the book.

The next question concerns women's oppression. To explain the various forms of domination requires addressing women's exploitation at the workplace and by apartheid's legal structures. Why do men make this worse by dominating women at home? It is part of the man's response to his own exploitation, which he in turn displaces to the woman by requiring her to help in his own reproduction.

But this is not the whole story. Even where there is no formal exploitation of men, for example, in rural areas where peasants simply produce enough to live by and a bit more to trade with, the same types of relations exist. The women must still cook, feed children, do laundry, and clean, even after a hard day's work in the fields. The question of women's oppression runs very deep, and must be taken up bit by bit.

Across South Africa, increasing incidents of family violence—child abuse, wifebeating, incest, and even murder—reflect all sorts of problems that go far beyond the culture or race or ethnicity of the attackers and victims. Take the case in the *Star* newspaper of 28 April 1992. A twelve-year-old was in such a hopeless situation that he broke into a factory, where he was spotted and shot dead by the owner. But this was a white boy, Johannes Victor, who lived in a working-class area just south of Johannesburg. His parents were unemployed, and had been cut off from a small welfare stipend six months earlier and told to "get a job." Johannes's father was a sickly sixty-year-old and his mother an uneducated, unemployed woman. The mother acknowledged, very sadly, that she was too busy looking after her own problems to sort out why her young son was intent on self-destruction. The violence that was spawned in this family was the product of neglect, which itself was a byproduct of the operation of the economic system.

Families often break up in the black community as well, or become violent, sometimes due to extramarital relations. Aside from the serious threat of spreading AIDS and other sexually transmitted diseases, extramarital affairs undermine relationships. Rape is another feature of the power that men have over women, and it is the most vile form of sexism. We cannot run from this, as it is so rife. But rape is yet another symptom of a deep-seated frustration in our society, and we must take pains to understand it in these terms.

Our people's courts were important instruments for dealing with rape and other crimes by locating them within a social context. As I describe later in the book, these courts were initiated by youth, but they drew deeply upon African tradition.

But tradition does not always have such a strong hold on our daily lives, as witnessed by the modern music we hear in the shebeens. To me, culture expresses what people are actually experiencing at a given point in time. People express their pain, or their happiness, through music.

The traditional dances, and even churches (for the elderly), reflect, on the one hand, loyalty to tradition. But on the other hand, our Sunday afternoon stokvels, or shebeens, where people go and become stinking drunk, also represent a necessary outlet for the socioeconomic tensions that are growing in Alexandra. With the unemployment crisis so severe, these outlets offer a means of escape.

Drugs are a more dangerous form of escapism. In Alexandra there is plenty of dacha (marijuana), mandrax pills, and even cocaine. Crack is our worst nightmare, judging by its effect on some sections of inner city communities in the United States. When I was in Chicago and New York, it was easy to understand the effect of drugs on African-American communities, as well as their lure: there is simply no other economy in the ghetto.

As an alternative to escapism and economic exploitation, we in the civic movement advocate activism. A good example is our effort to address the housing crisis. There was, from early on, a large private housing stock in Alexandra. The reason for that goes back to 1912, when blacks could still own land. In 1913 the Land Act prohibited this, but left Alexandra and a few other townships as exceptions because of grandfather clauses. There were even white Johannesburg bankers making housing loans in Alex during the 1940s and 1950s.

But the overcrowding, the uncertainty about the township's future, and the desire of owners to collect rent meant that over the years many people moved into backyard shacks. So today, with the privatization of housing, there are conflicts about who has rights to remain living in yards with both a house and a large collection of shacks. Our Alexandra Civic Organization (ACO) has struggled to find a means to reconcile these claims.

Site-and-service was the apartheid regime's vision for the future. It is a means of providing a family with a plot, some rudimentary services (such as water), and a title deed that can, in theory, allow a bank to make a loan (using the deed as security). As many as half the people in South Africa must settle for serviced sites instead of proper houses.

In this situation it is clear that the regime abdicated its duty to provide and subsidize housing for working-class people and tried instead to get the private sector to take over. The private sector initially saw the move as an opportunity to make a quick profit. The government's Independent Development Trust even doled out R750 million for this purpose over a two-year period. Some developers call it the "above-ground gold mine," since so many sites were easily serviced, without the problems usually associated with building actual housing.

The for-profit private sector also gained because workers who have site-and-service can then be given much lower wages, because they bear more of the burden for constructing their houses, in comparison to workers who pay the going rate for real housing and thus require higher wages to make payments on a loan. In essence, the site-and-service approach lowers the costs of reproducing labor, and that is why it has been so popular with corporate think-tanks and international financial institutions since the 1970s.

The civics are against this whole approach. We see housing first and foremost as a right, not a privilege. But the attitude of the Botha and de Klerk regimes, in advocating site-and-service, was to sanction shack cities. There was certainly enough money in the government budget to pay for these houses at a subsidized rate, although apartheid bureaucrats were not interested in finding or applying the funds to black housing shortages.

The same was true for electricity. We must ask why Eskom, the state-owned producer of electricity, has been shutting down 15 percent of its power plants and firing tens of thousands of workers at the very time that people in the townships need electricity most. Eskom overestimated the strength of the economy throughout the 1980s, and borrowed too much abroad. Now Eskom will only provide electricity in the townships using a system of pre-paid meters. This system atomizes consumers, because it means they pay individually for electricity. It therefore denies communities any collective say over electricity use and design. Something must be done about electricity, partly because the most important environmental issue is township pollution due to coal and wood fires.

We can see there are enormous problems in Alexandra, and we have tried to understand them. As we leave Alexandra, it is useful to pass by the main cemetery, which in many ways sums up our situation. Between the industrial complex of Marlboro and the filthy Jukskei River, there is a large plot of unkept land with tall grass. This is where most of our people are buried. Yet the housing crisis is so bad that the Alexandra Council decided that respect for the dead is a luxury only whites can afford. And so shacks are beginning to take over one part of the area, with Council approval, on top of gravestones. At one point, vandals came in to desecrate these stones, and they were left in that condition for weeks.

The vandalized graveyard is one scene that stays in the minds of most visitors. But visitors can leave. For the people of Alexandra, the graveyard-cum-shack settlement is a constant reminder that we are simply third-class citizens. In other communities, the cemetery is a place where, in times of personal agony, people can go to talk to, or think about, their ancestors. A new, non-racial local government of Alexandra will hopefully care for these cultural shrines, rather than see them abused because of an unwillingness to tackle the housing crisis.

We must remember this apartheid scene of disdain for the dead. But now we turn to scenes of my youth, so that you as the reader will understand the background and biases of your tour guide.

2
My Pre-Alexandra Years
(1964-1985)

In telling the story of township politics in South Africa, there is no way to be purely objective. It is impossible for me to separate myself from my background and traditions, world view, political baggage, emotions, and aspirations. While many commentators on black South Africa, especially those based in the universities, attempt to gain objectivity through such scientific means as polling, documentation, and airing "all" points of view (as if they were equally valid), even this exercise is not value-free. It is only fair, therefore, to describe the formative experiences that color the window through which I analyze, in the next chapters, at the situation in Alexandra.

Family

I was born and raised in a homeland, the Transkei, in the vicinity of the trading center Cala. There are about 100,000 people living in that general area. Askeaton is the village in which I was raised, fifteen minutes by car from Cala. Cala is in an arid southwestern part of the homeland, and most of the economic activity there is based on small farming.

Our family, like so many millions of others, was forced into the apartheid migrant labor system. My parents were not formally educated, and my father was an ordinary laborer for the railways, working in Cape Town, a day's journey from Askeaton. He could only return home for three weeks a year. Unions did not exist, and so when he retired (I was ten years old) there were no benefits and no retirement fund.

As for my mother, she had no paying job, but of course her work was the most important: unpaid labor raising a large family. As children, we therefore grew very close to my mother. I have six brothers and two sisters still living. Moss, my eldest brother, was born in 1948; the youngest, Mzonke, was born in 1968; and I was born in 1964. Four sisters didn't survive: they died in their infancy. My father's sister lived with us, and other family members also depended on us for subsistence. The extended family relationships were very strong, and they remain so today.

For example, we were very close to my mother's mother. In fact, my grandfather had two wives, so we learned early on about some of the problems that polygamy causes. My grandmother was known to us as "Kuye" (similar to the Afrikaans "kooi," or cow, a nickname that reflects a motherly, humble creature). She had a large impact on us through communicating oral history, notwithstanding her lack of formal education. One important story from her childhood was of her responsibility for herding livestock, as the only child in the family then capable. That showed her that there was no difference between the two sexes, and this understanding made sharing a husband harder.

Kuye was a feminist in the traditional mold, and she raised these issues clearly, though not in a rebellious way. The other wife of my grandfather sometimes claimed that Kuye was a witch. This was a result of economic problems, and the consequent difficulties they faced sharing very scarce resources. My grandmother had six children, and the other wife also had six children. Since my grandfather had to visit them in their separate houses, some distance apart, polygamy was not a good tradition for us, I believe. The husband has a duty to provide love more directly, and polygamy was especially hard to accept under circumstances of economic deprivation. But in spite of such hardships we were a close family.

Just a walking distance away from Askeaton was Bumbana. That was my family's traditional home, but official policy was to relocate people from their ancestral areas in order to move them closer together. The point, it seemed, was social control. Bumbana was simply made to disappear, and today its run-down houses are used as a camp for cattle. My father had moved there from Cofimvaba, the area that produced Chris Hani of the South African Communist Party and Clarence Makwetu of the Pan Africanist Congress (PAC), as well as Matanzima, Transkei's puppet ruler.

My family, December 1993. In order of seniority from left to right: my father Zenzile, my mother Ellen (Nodambile), Moss, Thamsanqa, Mzwamadoda, Nobantu, Nonzwakazi, me, and Mzwonke. Not present: Andile. *Author's photo.*

In a typical tragedy of the apartheid system, my father's father had been swallowed by the mining industry in the Northern Cape. He simply never returned home. Then my father's brothers died. With such misfortunes, my father believed that the family was bewitched in Cofimvaba. So as a result of that he moved to Bumbana, where he met my mother, before being moved to Askeaton.

Apartheid

My father was taken from us by the forces of the racist migrant labor economy. But like many young rural blacks, I only gradually became aware of apartheid. At one time, there were plenty of whites in the Transkei who had trading posts, but after the homeland's so-called independence in 1976, many left for East London and ran their rural shops as absentee landlords. Cala was actually a place that once, long ago, had several white traders and ordinary white residents. But the only white in the village of Askeaton (until recently) was Basil L. Baxter, and even he lived most of the time in East London.

Baxter was well respected in Askeaton. Thanks to his monopoly, the B.L. Baxter Trading Store was lucrative, so he was friendly to us, and he spoke Xhosa. We even played with Baxter's kids. Our early experience with apartheid was therefore indirect, and it came more through the puppet ruler, Mantanzima, than through contact with whites. The apartheid system has sometimes been more dangerous through its black puppets than through those who benefit from their white skins. That realization was important for the development of our anti-apartheid politics.

But we did ask our parents about Baxter. Who was he and why was he different? Those are normal questions for young children. My parents responded with memories that had been passed down through generations through word of mouth. Their story was historically accurate, and focused on the eight Xhosa wars in the early and mid-nineteenth century. They explained Baxter in those terms so that we understood things in a social, not just personal, way.

Historically, Xhosa kings and people fought courageously against the white settlers but were physically subdued. The settlers then took livestock from the people, who were also forced to pay high taxes for whatever the settlers didn't want: land, oxen, huts, and so forth. People were tamed in this process of economic exploitation, and this left a political vacuum.

In addition to the traders, the other whites who came were missionaries. My parents came under their influence. My father was extremely devoted, my mother a little less so. But my parents were also objective about it. They both maintained their own Xhosa culture while trying to take what they could from Christianity. Many Africans have been able to do this throughout history, often without the missionaries fully realizing it.

Yet the history of the missionaries left me with a very bad taste, and when I was ten years old I made the decision to drop my first name, Gideon. My African name Mzwanele means, roughly, the house is full, which reflects the fact that I was the seventh born in the family. My father felt, at the time, that the clan name would continue, and he was satisfied. But without family planning, four more kids were born, three of whom died in infancy.

Ethnic traditions

Apartheid, capitalism, colonialism, and missionaries all attempted to use the ethnic backgrounds of blacks to divide and conquer. Coming from the Libombo Mountains, our family clan moved between several kingdoms: the Thembus, the Pondos, and the Gcalekas. Qocwa was our own clan name; we were a clan known for skill both with iron smelting and with weaponry such as spears and sticks.

In researching his history of the Xhosa people, *The House of Phalo*, Jeff Peires interviewed a clan elder, M. Kantolo, in the Kentani District, who explained how the amaQocwa immigrated to the area from as far north as Natal and what later became Swaziland. According to Kantolo's oral history, the Qocwa became trusted councilors of the Xhosa king. But a plot was launched to get rid of the lead Qocwa councilor. As a cattle disease spread, the Qocwa leader was framed. A diviner was bribed to say that the Qocwa was responsible for killing the cattle, an accusation that was tantamount to a death sentence.

There is still a great deal of research needed to understand the history of the Qocwa, especially in Cala, which has received no attention from historians. However, in a personal letter, Peires wrote the following: "In precolonial times, present-day Cala was inhabited by chiefs who owed allegiance to the Thembu kings, but were not themselves of the Thembu royal line. When Ngangelizwe, through his own cruelty and stupidity, invited the British to occupy Thembuland, these chiefs were not consulted. As a result they found themselves under colonial rule without ever having agreed to it. They therefore engaged in a major rebellion, in 1880, together with some chiefs from other districts such as Dalasile of Engcobo."

The rebellion was put down, and in 1882 there was a colonial land commission. This created in Cala a large class of wealthy peasants, who were notable for their progressive farming and also for their political resistance to white domination.

In general, the polity of the Xhosa was not well organized, since power was decentralized. Peires gave me this explanation: "I would strongly relate decentralization to the question of democracy. On the ideological side, the people had the right to overthrow a greedy chief. On the material side, one should not forget that land was a free good, like water, in the early days. There was a shortage of people, not a shortage of land. The chief could not control the people through the process of land allocation, as is the case today. Chiefs encouraged people to join them by promising to behave democratically and generously."

Peires may well be right, but there are other factors to consider. It might be argued that the same situation existed in what is now Natal, where the chiefs could be overthrown and where land was in plentiful supply. Yet King Shaka of the Zulus used undemocratic, cruel means to centralize the African peoples in his area. (Historian Julian Cobbing, however, explains what has been called Shaka's *Mfecane* expansion in terms, first, of colonial mythologies, and second, of slave trade pressures from the north, in what is now Maputo, and early colonial expansion from the south.)

Other factors may also have played a role in the development of the Cape. What with the colonial conquests, there may have been limited capacity for a single cruel and ambitious king to warmonger with the aim of creating a unified nation. In addition, economic factors (like pastoral agriculture) may not have required a highly centralized kingdom.

Traditional culture and the means by which people identify with one another were also often attacked by the colonial powers, while many traditions that persevered under colonialism are dying out under modern capitalism. For example, when Xhosa boys are eighteen, they make the transition to manhood, in a lengthy process that we call *ukuya entabeni* or *ukoluka*. But with the development of a labor market, some of these traditions have become threatened. If you go away for the six weeks required to pass into manhood, your job may not be there upon return. Nevertheless, the feasts and other rituals connected to *ukoluka* are important to many people. Another tradition that has survived is *imbeleko*, which is the introduction of a newborn child to society. In sum, culture is not static but adapts to new circumstances. As for me, I passed into manhood in 1983, while at school.

Childhood fun and hardships

All told, it was a very peaceful lifestyle in Askeaton, with none of the hostile elements that you find in the cities. One of our tasks was hunting for rabbits, wild goats, and the like. We had dogs and used knobkerries, axes, and spears. I was still young and was not very effective, but it was a great adventure. Even snakes were good targets. We roasted one huge snake, a very poisonous puffadder, over a *braai* (barbecue) and ate the flesh, avoiding the poisonous bones. We then took the bitter liquid from the snake's gallbladder and poured a few drops down our throats. The mythology behind this tradition was that we would become very brave warriors. In a fight, when we hit someone, they would become poisoned and suffer serious swelling.

The main recreation for the village boys was stickfighting. There were games where we faced boys from another village. You held two sticks, your hands covered in cloth. One was for protection, one for attack. It was a dangerous game, and sometimes people were killed. But it was enjoyed by the village people because of the traditions involved, and the successful players were "big fish in a small pond."

I didn't play that game, I simply fought without sticks. I left Askeaton before there was a demand on me to prove myself in stickfighting, when I was still young. In any case, since our family is Christian, some of my brothers avoided the fighting. With Moss away as a student at school, we were slightly urbanized. My other brothers then began going to Cape Town, as my father said they must come and go to work. That made us a bit different.

For example, one December in the early 1970s, my father and brothers had come home. A crowd of village boys—perhaps one hundred—soon arrived at our house to challenge my brothers to stickfight, but my brothers were away with friends. My father was confronted with this gang, and men from the village came to protect him. The boys were beaten badly, as many of them were drunk. The family reputation was enhanced. It was that sort of place.

Even without such incidents, on a day-to-day basis life could be harsh. Subsistence living involved getting water from far away. We dug furrows to help irrigate the gardens, although this was impossible in the larger maize fields. Like much of the Transkei, Askeaton had very poor soil, and the produce was not good. On top of that, the people of the area were mainly overworked women, along with elderly people, children, and people who were injured. The migrant system churns up men and spits them out again, considering them useless when they can no longer work.

Through this system, the women developed a sort of matriarchy, even though the bigger system was patriarchal. The women controlled the household. At harvest time, my mother would sell the maize, as well as some fruits from our small orchard. She did well compared to many people in the area. And sometimes my father would send R60 a month, maybe even R100 in a good month. My father was unable to save for himself, though, and lived hand to mouth.

How do we put this into perspective? In some of these respects, my childhood background is typical of the distorted apartheid system. With the complication of migrant labor, I do not know if it is correct to call our family a peasant family. Since the men in the cities sent money, there was a semi-proletarian edge to our existence. We were in the middle of two "modes of production," as Marx might say.

Of course, with that meager amount of money, it was difficult to actually become consumers of commodities. Like most people, we had an account with Baxter's shop in Askeaton. We crossed the Indwana River to go there every day. Even if we had no money, we would go to see if there was any mail for us. But when there was money, we bought paraffin, bread, candles, and occasionally a chicken. Baxter gave us credit, sometimes up to R100, but that depended on our situation.

So capital was not circulating in any obvious form. Instead, we were kept in our places according to a well-organized Bantustan system of control, with a hierarchy of informers and bureaucrats and chieftainships and *indunas*. We had to pay a hut tax and a dog tax, which forced my father and brothers and other relatives and neighbors to keep feeding into the migrant labor system.

Without industry or much commerce in the area to create a demand for skilled workers, the school system was quite undeveloped. I was at a junior secondary school in Askeaton from the age of eight. When the river flooded, we couldn't go to school. And I was also forced to take turns going to school, sharing with my older brother Andile. Some days he went to school while I went to the mountains to herd our small flock of sheep and goats. After a while the sheep were stolen and the goats were sold, so we were left with nothing.

There were always these ups and downs in our lives. Sometimes we had no food at night, just water. That had a profound impact on my life, in the sense that when I later moved to King Williamstown I could really feel and understand the differences between classes of haves and have-nots.

Student politics

When I was twelve years old I failed my school exams because of taking turns with Andile. During that year, 1976, my father's cousin Willy demanded that I stay with him in the nearby homeland of the Ciskei. Willy was a successful businessman with a cash-and-carry store, restaurant, and bottle store. That was in Zwelitsha, a township that served as a labor pool for the textile factory in the white city of King Williamstown.

This was soon after my father was forced into retirement, and so his cousin said my father should give up one of the boys, since my father was having trouble supporting them all. Why me, of all my siblings? I have asked myself that question many times, but am still not sure. Maybe it is because I did not like the domestic work. I preferred to be outdoors.

However, going to Zwelitsha in late 1976 changed my life. Life there was hard at first, because the township was very different from Cala. I had to learn new things, and the world began to open up. Tarred roads, tapped water, and fluorescent lights were all new. Boys of my age never had to go to look after livestock. I tried on nice shoes for the first time, borrowed from my cousins.

I felt isolated for a while, and had to act as if I were already an adult. It was another world. I missed the youthful adventures and the growing experiences of being with my peer group.

Although the world broadened for me in some ways, the problem was that I was trapped behind the counter at Willy's shop, serving customers, making money. Willy's children and I were anxious to learn more about the world, but after school we were forced to go to work. Even when my father and siblings came to visit, there was no time or privacy to have fun with them.

That was a momentous year, 1976. Students in Soweto protested Afrikaans as the medium of education, and quickly broadened that to condemn the entire apartheid system in their great uprising on 16 June 1976. But in 1976, my first political encounters took the form of participation in the debates about education that were going on across the country. Many high school students, even in King Williamstown, were arrested. Some fled the country. In 1977 I repeated my exams with no problems, but there was no time to write final exams due to the student uprisings.

Things became more complicated still. My uncle Willy was a close collaborator of chief minister Lennox Sebe, and belonged to the Ciskei National Independence Party. Willy headed a group of five hundred vigilantes in that area, with knobkerries, sjamboks, pangas, and even guns. These "Green Berets" were well-trained by my uncle.

The Green Berets would go to the three high schools and the training college where the uprisings were coming from. They would beat up students, arrest them, and bring them to our home. I remember one student whose ear was cut off. Willy even interrogated him at home, blood dripping from his head.

My uncle was hated in the community, and this meant I was isolated. That affected me psychologically, and changed my attitude. These vigilantes were using government cars, and one day when the uprisings were strong, parents complained that Green Berets were killing the kids. White soldiers were brought in. The white soldiers, however, were no better, as they fraternized with the Green Berets.

In September 1977 the family complex of shops was attacked by students. We saw the students preparing the attack. When we reported this to Willy, he simply dismissed it. At 7 p.m. there was an attack, timed to coincide with the Green Berets' suppertime. It was telling that Sebe did nothing to help my uncle, and that too had an impact on my understanding of the apartheid regime's politics.

I was compelled to become politically active. I explained my story to the students one day. I told them I had no power over my uncle, and after that the students welcomed me back into their fold. I argued in front of 500 students that I was not in agreement with my uncle.

The next couple of years included sporadic boycotts. I became very active in school politics. Teachers were not of good quality, and class boycotts were called throughout. The activism, especially around the commemoration of the death of Steve Biko, attracted the police and Sebe's security forces.

At Thembalabantu High School, we organized support for those students who were caught by the regime. We attended meetings at night, which introduced me to the world of underground work. We were in small cells of disciplined cadres. As students we had to raise money, and I was elected to the finance committee. But my uncle Willy discovered this when one of his servants discovered the money and took it to him. I had a discussion with him then, and told him the truth. There was no going back, I told him. Diplomatically, he accepted it, and told me that he was not against the struggle.

As a result of the student politics and unrest, I failed the first form, and repeated it in 1981. This was the time that Ciskei tried to become "independent." I was becoming a liability to Uncle Willy, and he forced me to return to Askeaton.

I accepted this, partly because I thought it would mean more freedom. Coming home was interesting. The disparities between the two settings were extreme, especially the lack of young people and the boredom of those older people sitting around in Askeaton. It is said that "you can't go home again." This was true for me, as I felt alienated from the old ways of doing things. So that year, 1981, in December, I left for Johannesburg for the first time.

The reason I made that first trip was that my older sister Nobantu arrived and invited me for a holiday. She and Moss were both active in the Metal and Allied Workers Union. For me, it was interesting to come and, for the first time, to see the skyscrapers, busy people, and fast action of the city lifestyle. It was a life that was worth experiencing. The fact that my other brothers were there made it easier. Two of my other brothers, Mzwamadoda and Thamsanqa, and another sister, Nomzwakazi, were also living in Alexandra, so there were six of us there. For that month I moved around, trying to understand how things worked.

I then went back to the Transkei with Nobantu. In my former school near Askeaton they would not admit me, since the Ciskei students had such a radical reputation. Moss was also home on holiday, and took me to a mission school whose principal he knew, ten kilometers away from Askeaton. My brother Andile was also there, so I enrolled in the next class. It was a change of lifestyle, since I had so far to walk, again crossing a river. There was not much in the way of student politics at that school, and ideas like class boycotts, the fight against Bantu education, and so forth were not well known. I was frustrated, but helped challenge the teachers on corporal punishment and other issues.

During the holidays I was able to deal with the relative boredom and inactivity in the rural areas by briefly escaping to Alexandra. The frantic political and social activity there made me feel more and more at home. With my brother Moss, I went to a number of meetings of metalworkers and of Alexandra residents. I tried to increase my capability in political arguments and in my use of class analysis.

I also had my first brush with formal apartheid law: the hated Pass Laws, to be precise. This was during a trip in December 1982, on the way to a meeting in the East Rand with Moss. Moss was then branch secretary of the metalworkers' union. I was to meet Moss one morning at Johannesburg's Park Station, and took the taxi to North Street. During the walk across to the station, I was accosted by three black men, who I first guessed were just lumpenproletarian guys trying to mug me. I prepared for a fight with my rudimentary karate, but they pulled guns, announced that they were police, and were joined by a white cop. "Where is your pass," they demanded. Students had special passes issued by their schools, but I had left mine in the Transkei. They didn't believe me, of course, and I ended up in Hillbrow's Fort Prison.

Some of the people I was arrested with bribed the police to be released. I had no money, and spent the night there. The petty criminals and thugs at the Fort Prison searched us that night, and pinched everything of value. They beat up one Pass Law offender who resisted. Moss, meanwhile, had waited fruitlessly at Park Station and then prowled the city streets in search of a waylaid younger brother.

The next day I was moved to a Johannesburg court. As my eyes filled with tears because of the anger I felt, I suddenly looked up and discovered that my brothers were there. They were relieved as well, having searched all the police stations the day before. I appeared before the magistrate and was given release only after paying R150 bail. Two months later, when my case came up, I was acquitted, but the lessons stayed with me: the waste of time and energy, the humiliation, all because of my skin color. Millions who were arrested for pass violations also learned those lessons.

And the lesson from the apartheid prison was just as vivid. These jails are not for rehabilitation, but for social control through a form of psychological torture. Anyone spending time in the Fort Prison would think twice about violating the Pass Laws again. As I was released, thanks to my family, my heart went out to those who had no money for bail, who had to spend more days in prison on such senseless grounds.

Still, I continued to return to Alexandra periodically. The experience did not deter me from politics in the big city, but it did make me street smart. And it hardened my resolve to challenge apartheid at every opportunity. The regime probably did not have that in mind as a side effect of their psychological war, but for many this was the logical reaction.

In 1983, after finishing secondary education at Seplan Mission, I went to Matanzima High School. That was thirty kilometers from Askeaton, which forced me to get a place to stay near the school, along with Nomzwakazi, who returned from Alex.

Challenging Mantanzima's rule

Matanzima High School produced several leaders, including Chris Hani, Moss, and others. The school bore the name of the oppressive Transkei leader, but the tradition of resistance was strong. By that time there was a lull in student politics, because Matanzima's rule was so heavy. Students were seriously oppressed. The Matanzima Student Society, a small group that I started in 1984, attacked a new R8 fee that was to be used for renovating the school. The group was underground, given the lack of above-ground opportunities. We started writing pamphlets, plastering them around the school. We wrote anonymous letters protesting to the principal. We challenged the uniform code, given the poverty of many students. We tried to organize students not to pay that fee. The authorities had a tough time, but finally identified those students not paying. Student Society members were the last to pay.

The next year, 1985, our world view opened up much more. The Student Society linked with other schools in the region, as far away as Umtata. That year political protest exploded in the Transkei. The authority of teachers was challenged across the region. In August, with the entire country turning to boycotts, demonstrations, and "ungovernability," Matanzima called for a day of prayer. In our schools we wrote more pamphlets against the prayer day and many of us boycotted the prayers. Then came Steve Biko's memorial day, in September, and we called for another boycott.

We wanted to bring all activities to a standstill, beginning at 10 in the morning. Our pamphlets were printed, this time, on the school machine, thanks to our relationship with one of the staffpeople. She was very helpful, allowing us to get the keys to the school office. We took the typewriter away, and along with a stencil, worked all night. We made 10,000 pamphlets which we distributed that night. We renamed our school Mandela High School with paint. Our underground was a hardworking group of young comrades linked to other cells throughout the Transkei.

We also visited dormitories to request that students wear black and white in mourning for Biko. All the students observed this, and the pamphlets had a great effect. It was a great day, and it scared the reactionary teachers enormously. Seeing such a well-coordinated protest, the teachers failed to come to classes, and at break all students gathered at the main hall at Matanzima. This was happening all over the Transkei.

At 10 a.m. we began to sing the African national anthem and other freedom songs. Political talks began. A Students Representative Council was mooted for the school. Bantu education was criticized.

Then the police arrived. Students were beat up, and fled. One student nearly died. I was singled out by one teacher as the leader. I was in a classroom and refused to come out to meet the police, so the police entered and interrogated me. I was alleged to be a paid troublemaker working for the banned African National Congress (ANC) and South African Communist Party (SACP) throughout the Transkei. The other students were warned not to follow me.

Students were radicalized by this experience. The teacher who fingered me as the leader was then targeted by the students. His resignation was demanded, and he stopped coming to school. Inspectors from Umtata came and called me aside, warning me to end my political activism.

Meanwhile, links with other student groups were getting stronger, and we pushed to have a full stay-away day throughout the Transkei. On 22 September, a University of Transkei student leader, Batandwa Ndondo, was killed in cold blood by the Transkei security police. They came to his home in Cala pretending to be University of Transkei students and took him away. When he was in the police bus he realized he was being kidnapped. He escaped out the window, but the police drew their guns and killed him, in full view of Cala residents.

After this killing, the underground leadership advised me to leave the area. The threat had become very severe. School officials were now warning the parents of students about the dangers of activism. I avoided telling my own parents, and instead got Nobantu to be my guardian. All of us were addressed by a Transkei government representative. The government representative alleged that one student in particular was helping to coordinate the unrest across the Transkei. The government representative was jeered by the students. I came to the meeting clandestinely, and met my sister. She insisted that we leave Cala then, immediately. We drove straight to Alexandra, not even stopping in Askeaton.

The irony was that I was on very good terms with the authorities, because I was a good student and an example to the school. Even inspectors from outside were impressed with my work. I was the principal's favorite student. She never knew that I was a leader of the movement there.

I met with people from the South African Council of Churches, who advised me to return to Cala in order to gather information. They said they would protect me, and wrote letters to Matanzima. I was told that Matanzima wrote back saying that I was safe. I went back for final year exams. Without having had a chance to study, I didn't pass. That was the last of school. I then went straight to Johannesburg. Shortly afterward, Alexandra exploded with activity.

The war zone into which I was quickly immersed is the subject of Part 2.

PART 2
ALEXANDRA AT WAR

3
Alexandra Awakening
(1985-1986)

It is useful, I believe, to think about the awakening of our democratic movement and how it happened. This was an awakening in more than one sense of the word. For it was about a personal period of growth and commitment-building, as well as an introduction to a whole community's attempt to fight apartheid and to develop a coherent political perspective. This is a personal recollection of a complex series of events that took placed during what proved to be a watershed period not only in my life and in my own search for social justice: the tumultuous events of 1985-1986 raised the consciousness of an entire township.

The political setting

Back to Johannesburg, with its long, tall buildings, fast traffic, and multitudes of people. In December 1985 I made the move for good.

The next six months were absolutely crucial to the development of politics in the township, as well as in all South Africa. My own role grew during the period, to the point where I joined the leadership of the Planning Committee of the Alexandra Action Committee, the most strategic committee in the township, responsible for everything from organizing to workshops to boycotts to analysis of the changing political situation.

But let me back up a bit. Alexandra had changed during the period between my early 1980s holiday visits and late 1985. A bus boycott had been launched in 1984, and eventually the PUTCO (Public Utility Transportation Company) bus company withdrew from the township, until it returned in July 1985. The Town Council was not considered legitimate by most of the people living in the township, but the councilors, who were all dishonest puppets of the regime, were becoming both more bold in their operations and more corrupt.

In January 1985, the Council had tried, unsuccessfully, to incorporate Kew and Wynberg into Alexandra, to give business licenses to three councilors' families, to establish a R700,000 police force, and to build a multimillion rand center and international hotel. Earlier, the self-interested Sandton Council had rejected attempts by Alexandra officials to expand the township in that direction.

Popular protests were halting most of these initiatives. The town clerk had to withdraw a 100 percent rent increase in early 1985. Calls were frequently made for councilors to resign. The houses of the mayor and town clerk were attacked several times. Youth activists were repeatedly locked up and marches held for their release. Alexandra Youth Congress (AYCO) leaders were detained under the first State of Emergency in mid-1985 and the Congress of South African Students (COSAS) was banned. One eleven-year-old boy, Fanie Goduka, was detained for fifty-seven days before finally being released.

These were not just over local issues. The funeral of ANC guerilla Vincent Tshabalala, killed during a February 1985 shoot-out with police, attracted 3,000 people, and PUTCO buses were burned afterward. The Congress of South African Trade Unions (COSATU) was launched nationally in November. And the year's upsurge in militant activism culminated with the United Democratic Front (UDF) "Black Christmas" campaign to boycott shops.

So this was the situation when I arrived in Alex in December. Transformation from being a rural student leader to an urban community activist was easy only because of the conditions that existed at both national and local levels at that very time. These include the rent boycotts, detentions, States of Emergency, and the like. Many leading Alexandra youth activists were detained in 1985, which affected the conditions in which a new kind of civic politics emerged at that time.

It was actually not hard to adapt to these conditions. The experiences organizing in the Eastern Cape helped enormously, because of the combination of my political independence, which let me assess for myself the situation there and what role I would play, and organizational discipline. I knew how to operate at levels ranging from below-ground sensitive organizing, to above-ground polemics against the regime.

That was most striking was that there was no real conflict between the political goals of leading activists in the Eastern Cape and in Alexandra, although I felt the Cape was more militant than the Transvaal. The difference that is important is the overwhelming urban character of the struggle in Alexandra. I was helped in understanding this difference by the fact that I went regularly with my brother Moss to trade union meetings of metal workers. When one first comes into an urban setting, away from the rigid, patriarchal rural lifestyle, one begins to understand better what it means to be in the proletariat. There is much more of a focus on issues of working conditions, wages, and the problems that workers have with bosses, and much less concern with traditional customs and hierarchies.

Experiences with Moss sharpened my political outlook and strengthened my analysis and commitment to the working-class struggle and to socialism. In the Eastern Cape student movement, we had always had visions of free health care, free schooling, and so forth. But as students we had debated issues like workers' control of the means of production without much understanding. In Alexandra, staying at the same house as Moss led to much deeper discussions and debates over the role of the liberation movement in the struggle for socialism. Moss and such comrades as Sipho Kubeka of the Paper, Printing and Allied Workers Union helped open my eyes to trade union politics. The kind of socialist organizing project discussed in the union movement—especially by intellectuals associated with the Federation of South African Trade Unions (FOSATU)—was centered on the shopfloor, and was actually opposed to community struggles. (On the other hand, there were other trade unionists—for example, in the South African Allied Workers Union—who did attempt to reach out to communities, and later FOSATU's successors in COSATU reversed the older animosity to community struggles.) All of these approaches led us, in Alexandra, to consider issues of socialist transformation more carefully. These were often heated debates, but at the same time very healthy. The debates also moved outside our four walls, and many other activists were brought in.

The youth scene

Politically, I quickly felt at home. Socially, however, there was a huge difference between the Transkei and Alexandra. Life was faster, crime was much worse, and I had to learn to be tough and street smart.

One evening, for example, I was driving in an old car with my brother Thamsanqa. I was learning to drive, and so took over the wheel on the way back from a shebeen. With Thami navigating, I made a very sharp turn, nearly collided with a pole, and then came to a halt. Some thugs immediately arrived, and Thami decided he had better take over. The thugs, however, attacked Thami with a chain and took the car keys. We managed to fight them off, but they ran away still holding the keys. That was one reflection of how tough Alexandra could be even in the early and mid-1980s.

At that point the struggle became everything for us. Even having girlfriends was not a big priority, though I believe relationships are a vital part of one's development. On weekends we would move from place to place: from the soccer stadium, we would go to halls to hear choral music. The variety of things to do in Alexandra might surprise the outsider. My main area of interest was karate. This, and soccer, boxing, tennis, and even golf (but just caddying), filled the days when politics was slow. Musically, the stokvels and shebeens allowed us to keep up-to-date on the latest tunes.

The youth collected in the thousands in discos, shebeens, gangs, and various lumpenproletarian scenes. They were unorganized, and trying to prove to society that they had something to show they actually existed. In reality, they had no future, except as victims of gang wars, muggings, occasional killings, and alcoholism. These all testified to the pure alienation of the youth.

Because of my student activism, I did not fall under the influence of the various forms of youth escapism. Looking back on it, the indoctrination of struggle politics made me rather purist. Had the situation been different, with no apartheid and with sufficient resources, I probably would have learned to appreciate life more.

My own outgoingness was therefore structured to relate mainly to politics, especially organizing the youth. I had failed my exams again in late 1985, and had no money to further my education or skills, and found that the labor market had no use for people without education.

I also understood the conflicts that occur between those of different generations. In the rural areas, youngsters take orders from their elders without question. When you are young and have ideas about how to change society, that is not an acceptable situation.

With time, of course, the relationship between old and young matures, as we learn from one another. When I was in King Williamstown, I was befriended by comrades old enough to be my father, and political respect for that generation was an important bond.

In the mid-1980s, the youth were extremely militant, and we made no apologies for it. As a poor youth activist, I was confined to Alexandra, denied employment, and always faced violence from the regime. All of us were conscious that had our skin been lighter, a whole series of opportunities would have existed: rugby, climbing in the mountains, social adventures. We dreamed of such things, but in reality, they were very far away. I am still bitter about apartheid, for robbing a portion of my youth.

However, our organizing, and our long-term concerns, were not only about ending apartheid, but about *development*, especially of the mind. We were already beginning to think about the postapartheid situation, even in early 1986. One issue, for example, was that witchcraft was increasing in stature as the crisis deepened. When people are unemployed and desperately poor, they look for any kind of explanation of their situation, no matter how far-fetched it may be. So we could see that witchcraft was developing from being more than a form of escapism, and was now sowing confusion. We youth activists knew that we had to address the socioeconomic issues in a material, not mystical, way.

The more advanced activists recognized the untapped energy of the youth. Already mobilized into gangs of various sorts, the youth began to identify with a real struggle. Anti-crime campaigns were started in order to flush out antisocial elements. By early 1986, for the first time in the history of Alexandra, people could sigh with relief at the lack of crime. Women could walk alone, workers never worried about being mugged.

Origins of the Alexandra Action Committee

How, then, was the township's most popular community organization, the Alexandra Action Committee (AAC), formed? Just before I arrived, the youth leaders began a series of discussions with Moss, with other leading residents, and with other youth and students. The goal was to set up a proper civic organization that related well to the national liberation struggle. This occurred following ANC leader Oliver Tambo's January 1985 call to make South Africa ungovernable, which was passed on and amplified through our underground networks, and which had a profound impact on politics.

There were, however, two rather different precedents for civic struggles in Alexandra, which have rarely been reported on. First, there was the Alexandra Residents' Association (ARA), a grouping influenced by Richard Harvey, a wealthy white Trotskyist from the Hyde Park suburb of Johannesburg.

The ARA was founded in 1984, arising from the Ditshwantsho tsa Rona ("Our Images") study group. The group had a cultural focus, and created impressive videos, photography, and a militant newsletter called *Izwi Lase Township* ("Voice of the Township"). Yet Harvey's role in Alexandra was controversial. As a self-styled revolutionary, yet also as a very wealthy white man (a South African version of Friedrich Engels?), it was apparently his goal to infiltrate ideas into Johannesburg's townships.

Many of these were useful ideas, and the ARA did many admirable things. When ambitious redevelopment plans in Alex were underway during the early 1980s, the ARA organized against removals, correctly predicting that once families were moved into short-term accommodation (which mainly took the form of abandoned buses), they would never see their plots again. In this task they were extremely effective. They also won cuts in rental charges, and they developed many strong positions on issues such as housing, which have been taken forward in much the same form by the civic movement more recently.

Politically, however, the problem in the ARA approach to community was defining people as "workers," not as "residents." Thus, their definition of the working class was too narrow. They were isolated from the youth and students, and distanced themselves from what in effect had become the most powerful motor of the struggle. ARA once had some of its members affiliated with AYCO, but after a falling-out with some members over adoption of the Freedom Charter (which the ARA opposed), they took to ridiculing the youth in their literature. The ARA labelled our politics as "populist." This ignored the dialectical connection between the youth and their parents, the workers.

At one point in early March 1986, the ARA wanted to form a united front with the AAC, but the AAC had to reject that. In fact, Harvey once tried to recruit me, when I was on an early visit to Alexandra. He invited me to a discussion group where the Trotskyist perspective was explained. It was very purist, and with so little space for the women's congress, students, and youth, it was clear that this was not my home. In the end, Harvey's approach didn't succeed, and in spite of having very hard workers, the ARA decayed under grassroots pressure in early 1986 and was asked to dissolve so that Alex would have a single, united civic.

There was a second precedent for the AAC in Alexandra. But unlike the ARA, the Alexandra Civic Association (ACA), led by Mike Beea, had no up-front ideology. We must consider Beea with care, for as Marx remarked in *Capital*, "Individuals are dealt with here only in so far as they are the personifications of economic categories, the bearers of particular class-relations and interest." Beea, we will see, tried to represent the class interests of Alexandra's property owners. He represented a conservative element of the township, an element which fared well in some other places, but not in Alexandra. Beea had neither a coherent ideology, nor, in the end, a social base.

Beea actually started the ACA (then called the Alexandra Action Com- mittee) in 1981 as a means of contesting the first Black Local Authority elections, but he lost to Rev. Sam Buti's Save Alexandra Party. Beea's politics changed from collaborationist to oppositional in 1983, when he sat out the second round of local apartheid elections. He was even anxious to go back again to electoral politics in 1988, but then wisely reconsidered.

Many people considered the ACA simply a collection of opportunists. What was important, however, was that Beea, the ACA, and conservative civic associations elsewhere have survived for many years precisely because they have weak (or nonexistent) structures on the ground. With irregular meetings, democracy becomes a foreign concept, and individuals can pursue their own agendas. The AAC finally judged the ACA to be impossible to reform because of this.

By late 1985, as activists matured and political activism was intensified, these precedents for civic struggles were no longer acceptable. Attempts were made to democratize the ACA, but they did not work, because Beea was not interested. After the initial discussions between youth leaders and Moss on the need for a democratic civic in December 1985, general meetings were held in streets, where yard committees were formed.

Pre-launch organizing

In late 1985 and early 1986, over a two-month period, we canvassed opinions and discussed what the issues meant. The mutual respect between the residents involved in AAC organizing and student/youth activists remained strong. The activists all embraced class-oriented, non-racial politics.

For example, one of the catalysts for a new organization was the regime's attempt to relocate the so-called colored people of Alexandra to Rabie Ridge in Midrand. John Grant, an autoworker who lived on the same block as Moss, thought initially about forming a colored group to fight the removal. Instead, Moss suggested that this and other issues should be raised by a democratic, mass-based organization. The goal was to have workers understand their role within the community, leading the political struggles against apartheid and capitalism, but working hand-in-glove with other community formations on housing, education, transport, health, and the like.

This required education at several different levels. At the time, the role of big business in Alexandra was somewhat mysterious to the youth and unemployed people. We sometimes saw capitalism in its liberal paternalistic form. The *Star* newspaper's pathetic "Alexandra Uplift Program," for example, was supported by South African Breweries, Anglo American, De Beers, and the Urban Foundation. An insulting book, *I Love Alexandra*, was written and paid for by Anglo/De Beers, Barclays Bank (now FNB), Cummins Diesel, Blue Circle, Edgars, Nedbank, OK, PG Industries, Toyota, Volkskas, Pepkor, and a few other major firms. There was a liberal foundation called the Alexandra Development Fund, which built middle-income housing financed by the Perm building society, FNB, and Nedbank. Barlow Rand helped fund the Alexandra Enterprise Center as "a breeding ground for our future black manufacturers and industrialists." The Premier Group donated R100,000 to Alex programs, and FNB financed an old age home.

None of this made much of a difference to us. For approximately 200,000 people of Alex (in 1986), there were still just 10,000 houses, and most of these were old apartheid models. From 1980 to 1986, just 250 new houses were built (only 140 by the private sector, most of which were elite models built by a developer, Schachat Cullum). There were 450 housing units in walk-up apartment buildings built by 1986, mainly with government money.

Even if big capital had some charitable characteristics in Alexandra, the terrible material conditions that people suffered were conducive to our organizing, which was heavily influenced by socialist principles. By the time that Alexandra exploded into violence, in February 1986, we were having great success with grassroots structure building. We conducted general meetings in ten of the major streets of Alexandra, often with a thousand or more people. These were popular because for the first time they allowed people to have input into the formation of yard committees. Each of the ten long streets then went about forming yard committees. Were it not for the violent interruptions that occurred in subsequent weeks, we would have democratically organized all twenty-two of Alexandra's major roads in this manner.

We also had several meetings inside the three migrant labor hostels in January, and faced no resistance. There had previously been minor out-breaks of animosity between long-term community residents and hostel dwellers, less on ethnic grounds than because of class and urban versus rural tensions. The hostel dwellers felt resentful about the squalid conditions they lived in, and the apartheid division between migrant worker and permanent urban resident was still a factor.

But the arrival of the AAC refined the relationship, to bring the hostel dwellers into the heart of the Alexandra community. The hostel committees were in growing sympathy with other residents. During the police massacre that occurred the next month, many hostel dwellers came forward in support of the AAC position, our first indication that they felt part and parcel of the community struggle.

I would later sleep in the hostels, on many occasions, when trying to dodge the security police. And we had an education program to get the community to accept the hostel dwellers in brotherhood. The success of this approach was becoming clear, and ran against the government's divide-and-conquer strategy.

Word on the new organizing tactics spread throughout the township, into neighboring factories, and throughout Johannesburg, reaching as far as KwaNdebele and the Orange Free State. We even pushed for an organiz-ing drive in the neighboring Indian areas. Our approach was well-re-spected, even if among the youth there remained some controversy.

Youth ideology in flux

The direction of youth politics during this period is interesting. At its founding, the AAC consisted of individual community mem-bers, youth, and students. Initially, students believed they could drive the revolution, leaving their parents to come behind. How-ever, we argued that the parents must be alongside in the lead-ership. The AAC was our effort to engage and involve the parents actively in trying to resolve issues raised by their children. Highly energetic youth played a major role in organizing parents into the street-wide general meetings, to introduce the ideas of yard committees. This was done on a house-to-house basis, with a disciplined attitude.

But going back to when I arrived in late 1985, we faced a situation where many student and youth activists were already imprisoned. COSAS gave way to the Alexandra Students' Congress (ASCO), which had the same politics as COSAS. AYCO represented the youth, working and unemployed, who had left school.

When the AYCO executive members were released from prison in early 1986, they challenged our new strategies aimed at gathering unemployed youth into the civic movement. This caused dissent within the youth movement about the AYCO leadership. Some activists felt that even though they had served in prison, executive members were elitist and not close enough to ground-level struggle as it evolved. This reflected a growing sense of sophistication about issues of democracy and accountability in youth politics.

Since the AYCO executive members were not in Alexandra when the new strategies emerged, they campaigned against the AAC approach, as well as the earlier youth camp organizing of AYCO. In addition to personality cults and jealousy, their hostility was based on a feeling that Moss had "ultra-left" tendencies. The AYCO executive members were confused, however, about how to locate Moss in view of his rejection of the far-left Alexandra Residents' Association. Ultimately, the AYCO executive members isolated themselves from the youth on the ground, and were rejected in what amounted to a *de facto* coup.

But for a couple of months there was confusion throughout the youth movement. The old executive committee discouraged meetings in the various areas, including yard committees, during the period from March to May 1986. Some of the old leadership then worked closely with Mike Beea, and championed his ACA in the newspaper *Speak* as late as May 1986, even after a resolution, taken in a large workshop of leaders from many Alexandra organizations in April, that the ACA should disband.

There is a whole chapter in our history yet to be written about ideological struggles during the mid-1980s. The tradition of ANC ideology was overwhelming. Through the UDF, the "Charterist" ideology (left-popular demands flowing from the Freedom Charter) ruled then, and continued to for many years. But that tradition had its problems, including intolerance. I was an example of this myself, during the time I was a student leader, as I could not tolerate people from the black-consciousness Azanian People's Organization and the Pan Africanist Congress. We needed to develop a culture of tolerance in Alexandra. We needed to view everyone with a new set of glasses, and respect their ideological points of view. Recognizing the need to discuss everyone's point of view seriously, instead of worshipping individual leaders who in some cases are more interested in building personality cults, is perhaps the greatest political development since the mid-1980s.

The AAC attempted to develop this culture of tolerance from an early stage. We already had the seeds of the new politics of independent civil society growing in the AAC, in which all residents were welcome no matter their political ideology (this was partly the point of collapsing the other two civics into the AAC in April). We knew that, above all, consultation with people in the community is crucial, and that required dropping ideological blinkers. Otherwise, every political group would form their own civic structure, which would be more divisive and destructive.

Repression begins

The Security Police identified our organizing as a major threat, of course. It was the main barrier to their "oilspot" solution to Alexandra's problems: a combination of repression and upgrading. This was based on "low-intensity warfare," a theory used unsuccessfully by the United States against the people of Vietnam, before that became a bloody war and defeat of imperialism. In many Latin American countries too, the similar "Brazilian option" was used to deal with the democratic opposition.

Yet police strategies were not effective during the first half of 1986. For example, it seemed as if police viewed crime as a means of dampening the spirits of the people, to create a spirit of helplessness and despondency in a community. Criminals were regularly arrested only to be released the next day on flimsy grounds. This, in our view, was yet another form of psychological warfare. Our grassroots organizing activities worked effectively against this strategy, as many criminal activities within the township subsided as the organizing progressed.

The solution for the cops was to kill key activists. One of our comrades, Richard Padi, was murdered by municipal police on New Year's Eve of 1986. The anger of the community built up, as the role of the police in the community became clearer: to wage war against community leaders. Resentment grew, and the Alexandra Council, which controlled the municipal police, took much of the heat.

Under pressure, the Council and police began passing the buck on their own responsibilities, telling residents that if they had problems they should go to the comrades. It was a clever way of frustrating the community, because of course the AAC had no resources or formal powers to deal with official issues like licensing or welfare.

However, the people were now stiffening their resolve. Alexandra's mayor was the once-popular Sam Buti, whose Save Alexandra Party helped to win the formal reprieve for Alex in 1979, when there was still a threat that our township would become a hostel city. But Buti was now definitely seen as an enemy. Despite the fact that he began to use ANC rhetoric a bit and call for Nelson Mandela's release, he and others were considered co-opted puppets of apartheid and were isolated socially.

It was time for a real alternative to Council and the two moribund civics. The AAC began its series of mass street general meetings in early February 1986. In our view, the AAC would serve as an interim committee that would channel township energy until a democratic civic was launched. Activists were sent deep down to yard level to explain how the AAC was developing.

On 1 February, the next high-profile murder—of Michael Diradeng, an ordinary seventeen-year-old unknown in the political activist scene—became the catalyst for the famous Alexandra Six Day War. During the course of an argument, Diradeng was killed outside a Jazz Stores supermarket just outside Alex by a security guard, who later received merely a five-year sentence. Another young life was lost. It was the last straw.

The youth groups were furious, and in response organized a mass funeral for 15 February. Indeed, youth from across the Johannesburg region joined us to pay homage to Diradeng. We gathered to talk of our frustrations, and of the uncaring way in which young lives are seen by the system. The police response was brutal. A night vigil of 10,000 people, mainly youth, was bombed with tear gas over and over.

The next day we tried to negotiate with the police to end the harassment. This was my first direct experience with the authorities in Alex. We negotiated that the funeral would go ahead. Moss was to be the master of ceremonies at the Alexandra Stadium. The funeral procession, which was initially blocked from moving to the cemetery, was then allowed to move. Even the most angry of the youth paid attention to us as we spoke, and followed our directions to conduct ourselves with dignity.

But then, as a crowd of 40,000 was returning from the cemetery to the Diradeng home for a traditional hand-washing ceremony, they came under tear gas attack by provocateur police. The youth responded with a barrage of stones, petrol bombs, and so forth. A dozen white- and Indian-owned shops on the outskirts of Alexandra were the subject of looting that night, as the anger bubbled to the surface. In fear, the police left the township, and instead guarded the outskirts. Every weapon at the community's disposal was gathered. Trenches were dug to prevent police infiltration. A war had truly begun.

The Six Day War

From 15 February, the people of Alexandra began to revolt in a manner unprecedented in our history. But the existing organizations were not capable of channelling this into a lasting movement. So it was that on 17 February 1986, the AAC was officially founded in Sarah Mthembu's house on 31 7th Avenue. The street meetings had built sufficient consciousness and consensus, we believed, so that when the Six Day War broke out, the launch of the AAC was crucial for channeling the anger constructively and for coordinating activism. Minutes of the first AAC meeting include the following entry:

People at the General Meetings decided to have a proper structure which is going to unite the people from the Yard/Block and Street and to have the Acting Committee to facilitate the organizing of the Yards/Blocks and Streets Committee.

People asked about the Alex Civic Association and Alex Residents Association. People raised the issue that the ARA and ACA were not satisfying the community since they had no proper structures and therefore they felt there should be another organization to cater to their problems.

Problems raised at the General Meetings: high rentals, especially at new houses, bad houses with no repairs, bad roads with dongas, poor electrification, dirty toilets with no sewerage system, poor old houses and overcrowding, bucket system, demolition of houses and shacks with no suitable accommodation being provided, high rate of crime, unemployment caused by retrenchment with no new job creation, very high prices, very low standard of living resulting in starvation, very high PUTCO fares and taxi fares, PUTCO buses stopping at Pan Africa with broken windows, poor education causing boycotts, student demands not met, police occupation of school and township, some teachers and principals not cooperative to the students' demands, liaison committees. Peri-urban police harassing residents, councilors and the impimpis, influx-control hostel system, apartheid, and the killings of youth and residents by members of the army and the police.

Before getting into these issues, the AAC had to quickly turn its attention to violence in the street. Dozens of people were being arrested, including Moss and John Grant. At midnight on the night of 17 February, a convoy of security police came to 27 7th Avenue, the Mayekiso household. They searched the place and took some books. A notorious black policeman named Alex, who was known as being exceptionally trigger happy, told Moss, "You Xhosas, you are making problems for the government," and led him away for a three-week lock-up.

A crowd of 30,000 people jammed the stadium and demanded that the security forces withdraw immediately. In order to persuade the angry residents to leave, Bishop Tutu had to agree that the South African Council of Churches would bring their demands to the regime. Meanwhile, wounded people were being arrested at the clinic.

The killings became frequent, as the police began making raids into Alex. Their R-1 rifles peeked out of hippo portholes. Residents, in contrast, were armed only with stones. On one occasion a comrade was shot and fell. We rescued him, but saw that he was shot in the eye and was bleeding profusely. We had to take him to the 7th Avenue house, since the clinic was now under police scrutiny. Private doctors and nurses in the township were mobilized. The situation was bad, and we secretly had to move him to a hospital in Johannesburg, pretending he did not come from the riot zone of Alexandra.

It had rapidly become difficult for the AAC to actually organize. In order to evade the security police, our meetings were held at several places on 7th Avenue, even though the official AAC headquarters was 27 7th Avenue (the Mayekiso home).

Dozens of people were killed during the Six Day War. No one knows exactly how many (although the police said only seventeen). Some corpses simply disappeared. The police went to the families of the deceased, and tried to persuade them to bury their dead in the homelands. The police also dug communal graves on the outskirts of Alexandra, and as far away as Tembisa, where they put many of the Alexandra dead.

The people were so angry that at one mass meeting at the stadium on 21 February, their frustration at the continuing violence led them even to boo Bishop

Tutu, who was reporting back after negotiating with the police. The next day the police banned a Soweto memorial service for Alexandra youth.

The AAC and other organizations in the community tried to respond to each of these horrors in turn. The youth were especially active in the defense. The AAC also began to consider how to ensure that a mass funeral would be safe from further police hostility.

A test of leadership

The Six Day War was a crucial period of awakening for Alexandra. But it was also one for me personally, since for the first time I was faced with the responsibility of acting as a community leader, through the youth structures. As the crisis deepened, it was there that my arguments had to be as eloquent as possible, and that my ideas about organizing were adopted by the youth.

In general, there was a collective approach taken to organizing yard and street committees. Being an activist means having flexibility in these respects. Before going to a large crowd of comrades, we would work out the right approach.

Nevertheless, sometimes it is crucial to take leadership on the spur of the moment, as if by instinct. For example, one morning at the height of the Six Day War, I ran into a crowd of young comrades. Singing revolutionary songs about how the police were sellouts, they were leading a black policeman who was clearly about to be "necklaced." A tire was being prepared, with petrol, to hang around his neck.

The comrades said they were ready to get revenge on this particular policeman, who on the one hand had sided with the white minority regime to kill their friends over the previous days, yet who on the other hand would come home to his house on the very street where grieving was taking place. This was a logical reaction, in some ways, yet there was something else the comrades failed to consider seriously. Apartheid and unemployment force people to become policemen, I told them. If you are weak-minded, joining the police force as a means of employment looks attractive.

It was crucial to win this argument within a matter of a few minutes. I requested that the comrades consider asking the policeman whether he was prepared to resign from this job. They did, and he responded enthusiastically: yes, as from now, I am resigning. The comrades replied: if you have resigned, we want all of your police kit, including gun and uniform. The policeman readily agreed.

I went back to the house of the policeman, though I was concerned that arrests might follow and that as a lead activist I might be charged with kidnapping and taken out of action. Everything the man had that was connected to the police force was turned over to the comrades, who in turn wanted to give me the gun, the bullets, handcuffs, baton. They also wanted to exorcise the police part of the ex-policeman, so they took the uniform and kit, doused them with petrol, set a bonfire, and began the raised-knee "toyi-toyi" dance. The comrades celebrated the winning of one of the police over to their side. The policeman thanked me profusely, but I've never seen him again since that time.

The event, and others like it, showed that not only as an activist, but as an activist-politician, I had a role to play in developing political principles and analyses. We are not fighting individuals, but rather the system. And it showed that the credentials and leadership built up through the civic and youth struggles were now becoming more generally accepted.

After the war

As the Six Day War came to an end, funeral arrangements were made for the many victims. At first, a Funeral Coordinating Committee was formed by the ACA and black consciousness organizations, without consulting any of the other mass-based organizations. Mike Beea tried, with this maneuver, to stage a political coup.

The AAC, AYCO, ASCO, and the Alexandra Women's Organization all went to a Funeral Coordinating Committee meeting, and interrupted the proceedings in order to try to lay the basis for a non-party political funeral. This led to the creation of the Alexandra Crisis Committee, which had as chair Rev. Mofokeng from the Methodist Church, and which included all organizations which wanted to participate. (Trade unionist Sipho Kubheka and I were representatives of the AAC.)

Problems arose immediately. Crisis Committee subcommittees worked on burials, media, and finances. Beea manipulated the Crisis Committee by taking over the subcommittees, and the finance subcommittee could not account for the funds raised. As a result, the AAC charged that there was corruption and lack of democracy, and withdrew. The Crisis Committee carried out the mass burial on 5 March, but could not account for its funds, and then disbanded. Beea became even more unpopular because of that scandal.

A military patrol in a Cape Town township, 1985. Trucks such as these were a common sight in Alex during—and several years after—the Six Day War. *Photo: Dave Hartman, Impact Visuals.*

In spite of such problems, there were around 60,000 people in attendance at the mass funeral on 5 March. The whole township was mourning. Winnie Mandela and Albertina Sisulu were present, along with many other high-ranking political activists, church leaders, and trade union officials. The press was officially banned from covering the event, due to provisions in the first State of Emergency which had been imposed in June 1985.

The mood was one of deep anger, but speakers appealed to the youth to organize further rather than respond by fighting. Many placards in the crowd appealed to Rev. Allen Boesak (then patron of the UDF) to get weapons, and to the ANC to bring in its military wing, *Umkhonto we Sizwe* ("Spear of the Nation"), to defend the community. Many youths were so radicalized by the Six Day War that they left South Africa in search of military training.

The AAC position, made available through thousands of pamphlets, was that organizing should be stepped up. We explained how yard committees should function. After the first mass funeral, the AAC resolved to set up a fail-safe procedure for fundraising for the burials, one that could not be hijacked.

The AAC also began to deal with reports of excessive disciplining in the newly-formed "people's courts." Minutes from a 9 March AAC meeting called for "research on the people's courts' control and operation." The meeting resolved that the residents should be encouraged to discuss minor disputes and problems themselves, in their yards, and that corporal punishment should never be used. "People should mediate, and educate people about the causes of their disputes and problems and discourage misbehaviour."

This demonstrates how seriously the AAC took the role of these new structures, and how much responsibility was felt for ensuring that they operated effectively. The AAC also began to envision playing a role in community development. Notes from 11 March record that residents reporting from their yard committees wanted the AAC "to encourage people who are not employed to buy in bulk, and to sell their stuffs collectively ... to provide after-school care center ... to give family housing to the hostel dwellers ... and to make people govern themselves."

At that meeting, research was begun on the problem of illiteracy, and the AAC also agreed to "encourage unemployed workers' cooperatives and other self-help projects." As for turning hostels into housing, the AAC "is not in the position to solve this problem. It was decided that as soon as the structures are finished and the community organization inaugurated, it should take the matter to the Authorities."

This work was an early step in the AAC's attempt to respond to the needs reverberating from the grassroots with a popular, developmental program. Sadly, the work had barely begun before the continuing waves of state violence washed away our efforts.

4
The Advent of People's Power
(1986)

*Our most heady period of township organizing was the few months in
early 1986 when we could really claim that apartheid rule was being
displaced, street by street, by our own form of self-government. It was a
liberating experience, though it did not last for long.*

The theory and practice of "ungovernability"

We had adopted principles for challenging the system which can be summed
up in the idea of "ungovernability." But the strategy did not stop there, for it led
to the vision of building "organs of people's power" in the township.

The stage of ungovernability was a new political epoch. *"Make South
Africa Ungovernable!"* was a call that fit in very well with the thinking of the
oppressed. It accurately reflected the mood, and the activities, already
underway in the townships. Successful politicians make calls that derive from
the realities on the ground, not from some utopian idea of how to conduct
politics. And, in fact, by the time the ANC National Executive Committee
had made the call for ungovernability in early 1985, the frustrations of the
people were already more than evident.

The ANC's surrogate in many ways was the United Democratic Front, a
broad multi-class, non-racial coalition that coordinated the national protest
campaigns against apartheid. On the relationship between community
struggles and the UDF in the mid-1980s, Mark Swilling, in his book *Roots
of Transition*, has got it right:

The driving force of black resistance that immobilized the coercive and reformist actions of the state emanated from below as communities responded to their abysmal local living conditions. The result was the development of and expansion of local struggles and organizations throughout the country. As these local struggles and organizations coalesced, the UDF played a critical role in articulating common national demands for the dismantling of the apartheid state. In so doing, the black communities were drawn into a movement predicated on the notion that the transfer of political power to the representatives of the majority was a precondition for the realization of basic economic demands such as decent shelter, cheap transport, proper health care, adequate education, the right to occupy land and the right to a decent and steady income.

(I must mention here the fact that the AAC was viewed with some caution within certain UDF circles. This was in part due to the role of Moss, a trade unionist known for his socialist politics. And it was in part due to the ACA's informal affiliation to the UDF, supported by the earlier generation AYCO executive. However, when a few UDF leaders began considering the ACA's Mike Beea as an ally of the progressive forces, this proved controversial, and we began to suspect some in the UDF hierarchy were out of touch with the realities on the ground. Some said this was partly a function of emerging personality cults.)

Throughout the UDF, ungovernability became the catchword. The analysis, at least in Alexandra, was sober and clear. We said that it was not only crucial to shut down the existing state apparatus. Within the decay of the old apartheid order, brought on by ungovernability, we also knew that there was great need to plant the seeds of a new approach. We would seek out, through discipline, democracy, and accountability, the alternatives to apartheid. This involved assessing how much power we had to challenge the very basis of the regime, and to build new organs of people's power such as the embryonic structures of the AAC, people's courts, and economic and political development institutions.

Ungovernability was not an easy approach to sustain. We had a major community leadership workshop, on 13 April 1986, where a key question was raised: had ungovernability reached the point where people were actually ungovernable by their own organizations?

For example, some unruly youth regularly visited township shops, and extorted the shopkeepers for food. Car hijackings occurred against what were called "targets"—nearby industries and some whites who drove near Alexandra—were occurring at a rapid rate. Seventy cars were stolen in one week alone in mid-March 1986. Some of the cars owned by certain companies were burned in the township, as a sort of political protest act. These actions were drawing more and more police into Alex, and therefore dampening our ability to organize.

There were youth involved in these semi-criminal activities who were homeless. They had come from outside Alexandra to be present at the Diradeng funeral, and never returned home because they were compelled by the struggle underway in Alex. The argument of these youth was that they were weakening the apartheid economy. Industries were targets; some factories were even burnt down. The value of property near Alexandra quickly fell by 10 percent as the protests grew in strength, according to newspaper reports. White people were fleeing Lombardy East, and many shops and factories closed down and boarded their windows. And then some of the unruly youths turned their activities inward against the community.

The reality of the situation, unfortunately, is that as long as there is unemployment and alienation built into the society, unruliness will exist, even in times of disciplined protest like in 1986. However, we also noticed the opposite phenomenon: as our organization was becoming increasingly successful in Alex during that period, other types of crime in the community, such as family violence, rape, muggings, and murders, were reduced to a minimum.

The National Democratic Struggle

The youth branch meetings were strong on political analysis. The following are my own crude, rough notes, which were the basis for discussions at the 7th Avenue AYCO branch in early 1986.

1. Class inequality and class division

Our society in South Africa is divided into two major classes, the bourgeoisie and the working class. The two classes have got interests that are contradictory to each other. It is important for anyone who is involved in the struggle for liberation against apartheid and capitalism to know and understand the functions of the present society. South Africa is a capitalist country where the minority class dominates the majority class. The bourgeoisie own all the means of production, i.e., land, machinery, and capital.

2. The ruling class has persuasive methods:
2.1 Religion
Since the coming of the missionaries during the colonial era, religion has been used by the oppressor to keep the oppressed people loyal, inferior, and subservient. Religion addresses itself to life after death, whereas it ignores the present social problems caused by the unequal distribution of wealth and political oppression. Thus religion helps in taming the working class and serves in retaining the control of the ruling class over them.

2.2 Education (Bantu Education)
The education system in South Africa is at its very roots unequal and reproduces inequality because education has gone from bad to worse. It denies the black majority opportunities enjoyed by the minority white group. It has served in promoting tribalism and racism in the urban areas. You still find schools belonging to specific ethnic groupings and there are separate schools for white and black children. And we regard this educational system as a weapon by the ruling class to control and dominate the oppressed and exploited class.

2.3 Culture
Our culture, which should have been promoted and developed by the government, has been ignored, undermined and regarded as backward, inferior and uncivilized. Whereas, we regard it as the culture that portrays our feelings in relation to the problems and happiness in our surroundings. We expressed our feelings through our songs, poems, music, dance, and art, etc. In its place, the ruling class and its government have imposed the kind of culture that promotes their values and ideas. These values and ideas have corrupted and made our society a violent one, and have also caused a lack of morals within our society through their music, media, and films. This new culture has rendered our people subservient and individualistic.

2.4 Sport
Sport should promote good relations among the people and also should develop our people both physically and mentally. We believe that a healthy body which is both physically and mentally prepared is creative. They've suppressed and denied us the opportunity to develop and promote some of our sports, like hunting, fishing, stick fighting, African Mrabamraba, etc. Today they have introduced sports that we have always appreciated, and they have used them to promote a sense of competitiveness and a means of accumulating wealth. Sports are no longer taken as a form of entertainment, e.g., soccer. Therefore, sport has been used by the ruling class and its government to

make people self-centered and individualistic. The people ignore the present problems existing within their surroundings.

2.5 Media

Media has been used to promote and develop values and ideas of the ruling class through videos, radios, press, books, TV, films, and other publications. The types of ideas and values that are propagated are mostly those that make people have higher expectations.

3. The ruling class also has repressive methods:

3.1 Parliamentary system

They have denied us voting rights and as a result they are passing laws that are in favor of the ruling class and which we see as promoting their interests.

3.2 Army and police

The army is there to protect the interests of the ruling class and in times of crisis they are being called to help the police in the maintenance of law and order. They have occupied the townships and they (the army) can be sent to quell labor unrest as happened in 1922. The police are serving as law enforcing agents, because if a law has been passed by parliament, they see to it that that law is adhered to. During unrest situations like factory strikes for higher wages and other labor-related problems, and school boycotts, they come in to maintain law and order. We have no problem with the army and police but now they side with the ruling class in suppressing the working class.

3.3 Courts

The role of the court is to administer justice so as to ensure harmonious, peaceful and good relationships between man and man. Here in South Africa, courts have been seen as protecting the interests of the oppressor. We put forward this example because in South Africa courts are entrenching apartheid.

3.4 Law

In democratic societies law is something that is decided upon by the people to protect them against inhuman behaviour and to develop their way of life. In South Africa laws have been made by the ruling minority class to control and dominate the lives of the oppressed and exploited class.

3.5 Prison

We regard prisons as centers for reeducation and rehabilitation, but in South Africa they serve as camps where the offenders come out hardened criminals and more dangerous to the society. They also serve as concentration camps for the opponents of apartheid.

4. Apartheid

We have mentioned class inequality and class division, and that economic and political power is vested in the hands of the ruling minority group. Unlike other capitalist countries, South Africa has another tool, which is apartheid and which has successfully divided people into tribal and racial groupings. The apartheid system was redesigned by the late Dr H.F. Verwoerd by introducing Bantu education, extending passes to women and the passing of the Separate Development Act, the tightening of Influx Control, the introduction of the Bantustan policy, etc. It is apartheid that is responsible for the present crisis, like the underdevelopment of our townships, introduction of Bantu education, and many unjust laws.

5. Nation
Because of apartheid, our nation has been divided into different national groups and tribes. So we don't have a nation, and it is through the national democratic struggle that we hope to build a nation.

6. Democracy
In South Africa we know that there is no democracy; our people have no right to vote or be voted into parliament and government structures. The majority of the people have no voting rights; the authorities claim that they have a right to vote in the homelands, a claim rejected by the people. We are now fighting for the restoration of democracy to the people. The guiding document of that democracy is the Freedom Charter, which our organization, the Alexandra Youth Congress, has adopted.

7. Kind of society
The kind of society we are fighting for is a non-racial and democratic society in a free and united South Africa, as envisaged in the Freedom Charter.

Demands for people's power

The police killings continued apace. Several had occurred in March, leading to more mass rallies and funerals. On 11 April, 1,670 troops conducted a massive "invasion" of Alex, as the *Star* put it, yet arrested a total of just eighteen people on charges of possessing dagga or stolen goods, or driving without a license. The raid was, as Moss put it, another futile attempt by the Botha regime to frustrate, harass, and intimidate the people of Alexandra.

The security forces gave out a pamphlet which said, "Are you tired of being harassed? The police need information concerning people who are: Preventing your children's education. About people who are keeping you from work. About people who stop you buying where you like. Let us protect you." The cops told Alex taxi operators not to operate on Saturday, "in order to keep people at home." If a resident wanted to leave Alex, up to six body searches were required.

The next day, one of the leading apartheid public relations officials, Deputy Information Minister Louis Nel, pronounced, "I want to congratulate security forces who acted in a restrained, calm, and friendly manner." Nel said newspapers were waging a propaganda campaign against the cops by reporting that Alex was "besieged," "sealed off," and that the situation was "tense" and "simmering." It was beginning to feel like George Orwell's *1984*.

While several councilors resigned in the aftermath of the Six Day War, others were using the threat of eviction to try to force residents to pay rent. At that stage, in April, the rent boycott meant the Council's monthly rent income dropped to R44,000 (from R156,000 in late 1985), and in June it fell to R19,000. This was a serious problem for the state, which stepped up its harassment. The police even broke up an AYCO congress on 12 April, dispersing a crowd of more than 1,000 youth, who left in a disciplined manner.

But our responses also continued to put the regime on the defensive. The community-wide workshop held on 13 April at the Ihusong Centre was of historical significance for the people of Alexandra, and indeed South Africa, as it identified and heightened the main contradictions in the system. The workshop dealt with a wide variety of issues in the township, and helped us to assess the strategies and tactics to date. It was the success of the resolutions of that workshop that led to a subsequent police massacre.

More than a hundred leaders from a variety of local organizations attended. The organizations included the Chamber of Commerce, Traders' Association, Taxi Association, Ministers' Fraternal, Wynberg Traders' Association (an Indian group), the AAC, AYCO, ASCO, the Alexandra Women's Organization, ARA, ACA, and four other youth groups from the youth camps in the township.

The youth side was overrepresented because of its strong role in the development of people's power up to then. The youth offered very dynamic politics at that time. The AYCO executive had one set of views, generally against the AAC and the existence of the youth camps. With such a large gathering, divergent opinions were to be heard on all issues, and debates were heated.

The workshop was aimed at education on issues such as police violence, rent and housing, the upcoming consumer boycott, transport, health, and education. We asked hard questions about whether our strategies for making Alexandra ungovernable, and building youth camps, AAC yard committees, block committees, street committees, people's courts, and so forth, were actually working. And we adopted a variety of resolutions which represented early attempts to develop a "dual power" structure, by which we meant that certain institutions normally under the arm of the repressive state could be liberated and made to work in ordinary people's interests, outside state control.

Resolutions on building people's power

The following resolutions were agreed to on 13 April after six workshop commissions met and came up with quite different ideas about how the Alexandra popular struggles should proceed:

1) All progressive organizations should engage themselves in a program of building popular organizational structures, which are yard, block, street, and Action Committees by the end of April 1986.

2) There should be one civic body to ensure proper coordination of campaigns in the township.

3) AYCO should be the coordinating body of the youth groups to ensure proper education and training for their engagement in local and national campaigns.

i) Proper training should be given to the youth in order to bring about a qualitative growth of our popular organizational structures.

ii) To ensure democratic decision-making and implementation.

After much discussion, the workshop also set out a clear series of demands:

Realizing that our township is still under forced police and army occupation and continued detentions as well as the existence of unfavorable conditions and unpopular structures, we therefore resolve to launch:

1. RENT BOYCOTT
We demand

a) Rent we can afford and its suspension so long as recession prevails.

b) Proper electrification of our township.

c) An end to forced removal from our houses to undesirable housing.

d) Dissolution of the Town Council. All councilors, junior and senior, and their employees must resign.

e) Troops and the police out of the township. Resignation of police.

f) The immediate recognition of students' demands: People's Education.

g) The recovery of missing corpses and people.

h) Comfortable houses which we can afford.

i) Unconditional withdrawal of charges and release of all political prisoners and detainees like Nelson Mandela, M. Ngidi, Boyce Buhale, Carry Seahlolo, and others.

j) Unbanning of COSAS, ANC, and other political organizations.

k) Dismantling of the entire apartheid regime and the establishment of a democratic People's government founded by all democratic and progressive forces.

2. LOCAL CONSUMER BOYCOTT

a) Jazz Stores until it is closed down.

b) Portuguese stores until they stop maltreating their workers and customers.

c) Hazel's shop and shebeen until it is closed down.

d) Joe's garage and Chicken Lickin' until it is closed down.

e) All Councilors' businesses until they resign and join the struggle immediately.

f) Freddy's shop and his businesses until troops are out of the township.

g) Benny Goldberg indefinitely.

h) Droog Dry Cleaners until it closes down.

i) Mielie's shebeen until further investigation.

j) Mashido garage until it closes down.

k) Johnny's shebeen until it closes down.

l) All white businesses except chemists and garages which are not mentioned above.

3. BOYCOTT OF REACTIONARY PAPERS LIKE:

a) *Sowetan*

b) *Citizen*

4. BOYCOTT OF METAL BOX PRODUCTS: LIQUOR AND COLD-DRINK CANS

5. CAMPAIGN FOR NON-PARTICIPATION, TO ISOLATE ALL COLLABORATORS SOCIALLY

a) Business people are not to serve the police, Councilors and other collaborators in their shops, taxis and shebeens.

b) Do not board the same bus with police and other collaborators.

c) Everyone must terminate personal relationships with police and other collaborators.

d) All the students who attend the multi-racial, boarding, and homeland schools must come back to their local schools immediately.

e) All police and Councilors' families must stop rendering public services, like teaching, social work and others.

f) Collaborators, especially Mr. Buti and Mr. Makhubiri, must stop addressing church gatherings. To ensure genuine and active participation and avoid misdirected victimization of councilors and police who resign, they will be invited to a public meeting to fully clarify their positions to the satisfaction of all people.

Boycotts and non-participation

The 13 April workshop developed a strategy of social isolation of the collaborators, through boycotts against their stores and demands that their friends and even families break relationships with them, which together amounted to one of the most sophisticated popular campaigns in the history of South Africa.

The key targets were the Black Local Authority Councilors, the police and their families, teachers who worked with the police, and others judged to be collaborators. The town clerk, Arthur Magerman, resigned nearly immediately, citing the absolute rejection of the Council by the people. Other councilors also resigned.

The Alexandra mayor, Sam Buti, was a priest, and we called upon people in his parish to not allow him to preach. Buti's response was desperate. He wrote an article in the *Star* declaring, "What I and my Council want is to build a town without competing with black political organizations. We are not stooges, but we need the people to tell us what to do. The inference that I am the servant of the white government and a sellout who gives credibility to apartheid is wrong."

At this point Buti revealed that he had visited Nelson Mandela in prison, but this just increased our anger. Moss announced, "He is trying to confuse people, and he is degrading our leader. We are also very surprised that he was allowed to see Comrade Mandela, when so many activists have tried to see him and have been refused permission by the state." Moss called on ANC leaders to boycott a reported visit that Buti planned to make to Lusaka.

Buti was not alone in facing the community's wrath. If police officers or a councilor boarded a bus with people from the community, they were forced off. As Alex residents grew sick of oppression, policemen were even rejected by their girlfriends. Those who were married found the marriage to be at the breaking-point.

The shops boycott, which began on 21 April, required rapid education of the people, and pamphlets were circulated to all the yard committees as well as shops. The shopkeepers approached the AAC to try to break it. Those shopkeepers who came to apologize and make amends for their crimes were taken off the boycott list.

Some newspapers commented on how well-organized the boycott was. One businessperson was quoted as saying, "Those who defied the enforcers were advised not to do it again and given pamphlets listing the names of the shops which should be boycotted. There has been no physical violence against those defying the boycott."

In fact, this was perhaps the most powerful, efficient means of challenging state organs ever attempted at the grassroots level in South Africa. The Alexandra Council completely collapsed, as Buti and his last four councilors resigned on 22 April. It was the fourth such council collapse in South Africa, following Kwa Nobuhle and Lingelihle in the Eastern Cape and No Nzwakazi in the Northern Cape. But that night, vigilantes, including off-duty police, were brought in for revenge.

Vigilantes

On the evening of 22 April, following the resignation of councilors, the vigilante attack began. I was at a meeting in a house belonging to my neighbor Sarah Mthembu, a site of one of the people's courts (31 7th Avenue). Across the road, John Grant, his wife Jezebel, and their seven children were relaxing in their house.

Suddenly, we heard gun shots outside, and petrol bombs were hurled at Sarah's small house by a crowd of fifty men carrying pangas, knives, and guns. As Sarah later testified, "Bricks were thrown at our house. We found the house was burning. We tried to get through the windows but the men shot at us. We looked through the window and saw a Hippo. The Hippo's number plate was DZ394D. Then cops at the Hippo told us to move from the area." Youth activist Colin Ntohla was shot twice and killed as white men in the Hippo looked on, witnesses reported.

Jezebel Grant described the scene to the press: men wearing the light blue shirts and dark blue trousers of the police uniform petrol-bombed

Sarah's house and then smashed and burned the Grants' car before starting on their house. "I could not see their faces because they were wearing balaclavas and scarves. My husband axed out the glass of a small side window and we put the children out of the house to safety." But John was detained by the police.

Huddled in Sarah's burning house and not anxious to face the police, I had just one escape route: jumping out of a tiny window in the back. I crawled into the alley, and found myself on top of a dead body. The police Hippo was following the vigilantes, giving support. This is the closest I have ever come to losing my life in the struggle.

We ran across several streets, and regrouped elsewhere, raised the alarm, and began to defend the area. But the attack was simultaneous, happening all over, especially at the homes of activists. Sixty homes were petrol-bombed, and thirteen were fully gutted. ACA leaders were also targeted, and Mike Beea's wife was beaten up. A group of sixty men even took a baseball bat to a woman escaping from the house of another activist. The vigilantes all escaped, and according to the police, nine of our community lost their lives that night. Our people say the actual figure was at least seventeen, with dozens more injured.

By all accounts, even in the mainstream newspapers, the vigilantes were off-duty policemen. It later emerged from the seemingly unedited Wynberg police station operations register that black policemen wanted to launch a march into the township at 7:30 p.m. because one of their colleagues had been robbed. Within half an hour, another police patrol described scenes of mayhem across the township, including "a group of seventy to eighty-eight people, possibly black policemen."

Tougher community defense

That night, our street committee system went into action. A stay-away was called for the next day, and we worked through the night to get the word out. A crowd of nearly 50,000 came to the stadium. The streets were barricaded. This was the height of people's power. We controlled the township, but we did so in the context of defending residents from vigilante terror. It was a new form of state terrorism—a form we would come to know very well in future years. The police and army were learning to do to us what they had done in Angola and Mozambique in the late 1970s and tried in Zimbabwe in the early 1980s: arming and motivating groups of blacks who would do their bidding, militarily, against the progressive forces.

The crowd at the stadium that day roared approval for the boycott to continue. Speaker after speaker called on the community to form self-defense units. The UDF soon announced this was to be a new national strategy. Among the tactics that emerged was the "tank trap," which was a two-meter deep hole covered with sticks, leaves, and dirt.

The hostel dwellers were, once again, supportive, since we considered them part and parcel of the struggles underway in early 1986. During March and April we had reached agreement with the hostel dwellers, through AAC structures which had emerged inside the hostels, to convert the ghastly buildings into family units. At that time hostel dwellers asked us serious questions about this. There were those, after all, who had no desire to bring wives and children from secure rural areas to the city. The solution decided upon was to maintain some single rooms, but to upgrade them so that one person, not six, would stay there.

There was an agreement to move ahead on this. At a rally on 23 April, Moss called on the hostel dwellers to build shacks in the townships and to bring their families to stay. The shacks mushroomed over the next few weeks, and Alexandra Council attempts to evict the new shack dwellers from the hostel were met with the defiant answer, "Moss told us to build shacks, and we are not moving."

These kinds of harmonious relations between community and hostels could have developed further. (I have never seen this part of our struggle reported upon, either in the press or by academics.) However, a new round of repression intervened.

At the 23 April rally, the army arrived and sealed off Alexandra, and police confronted the departing crowds. More shootings, more injured residents. For the first time, our side used AK-47s to retaliate, and a white cop was shot in the stomach. The army then set up a permanent camp in the stadium and erected searchlights that combed the township throughout the night. Helicopters hovered above our heads. Police attacked, haphazardly, killing Richard Mdakane's brother Zephaniah in a gun battle at 3:30 a.m. on 28 April.

But by 29 April, it was clear, as Moss put it at a press conference, that the AAC controlled the township. The yard committees had mushroomed. The AAC was now a household name. A second Alexandra Crisis Committee was convened to run a mass funeral, but this time it was dominated by the AAC (and now there were no financial scandals).

This status was a result of the sophisticated system of organizing we used. We engaged issues ranging from political repression to socioeconomic exploitation. There was no other system like it in the history of Alexandra. In effect, we had established an overwhelming "common sense" consensus around our goals, strategies, tactics, and rhetoric. We had achieved political hegemony.

AAC hegemony

The mass funeral of 15 May was remarkable in that it was banned twice. The magistrate finally agreed to allow the funeral, but with the restriction that the services for each of the victims could not occur in the same place at the same time. The AAC agreed to this, but somehow at the point when the burial was to take place, all the coffins were indeed gathered together in the same church. There were thousands of people inside and outside the church, and the police could not alter this new development. We told them that we simply could not live by the words of a white magistrate who did not know our culture. A little later a group of 300 whites from the Johannesburg Democratic Action Committee defied police orders and drove into Alex to leave wreaths at the graves. Our people cheered when the white visitors said they wanted to be seen as our comrades, not just sympathizers.

Amidst the carnage of state violence, there were a few victories. After the Alex Council fell apart under people's power pressure, the central state was forced to appoint a white administrator, Steve Burger. The community was not consulted, but nevertheless it was clear to Burger that he had no hope of running Alexandra without understanding the new power relations. The AAC called Burger for a meeting, and sent a delegation to tell him he was not welcome. We also met with Sandton officials to tell them much the same.

The days of top-down development were over, we said. The AAC considered ourselves as much the mandated representatives of the people as anyone, and would serve in this capacity until a formal civic launch could be held with elections. We set a deadline for several weeks later, in July, to both launch the civic association and then meet again with Burger.

This is more than a bit of history. It reflects a maturing politics as well. In many analyses, the civics are seen as having evolved from "politics of protest" to "politics of development" only after 2 February 1990, when the ANC and other organizations were unbanned. That is clearly false. The failure of many commentators (especially academics) to understand the profoundly *developmental* nature of the AAC is addressed in the next chapter.

In fact, our civic launch never happened, because two weeks later most of the AAC leadership was detained. This followed a pattern in which our every attempt to stabilize the civic structure in the community through normal elections and through activism on bread-and-butter issues was derailed. We were developmental in our approach, but each time we were close to establishing a full democratic organization we were interrupted by brute repression.

The first time had been just as the Six Day War began. The second time was to have been 28 April, a date the AAC had chosen for a launch and democratic elections of the new executive. Instead there was the massacre of 22 April. On 26 May, street committees met to talk about a new date for the launch, and assess whether the AAC had a fresh mandate until July. But our discussions were interrupted by a new series of crackdowns, which I will return to in Chapter 6.

People's courts

The origins of people's justice are to be found in African forms of government. Justice was practiced in *Lekgotla* (Sesotho) and *Inkundla* (Xhosa), where chiefs presided over issues affecting their communities with the help of councilors. The chief would look into the problem from many angles, with the aim of finding a solution that produced peace and harmonious relations among his subjects.

This form of justice was seen as democratic by the people who were using it. If one was found guilty of an offense, he or she would be fined a number of livestock. In some communities, the livestock were taken by the chief. In others, the stock were slaughtered and all the people in the area would feast and rejoice. The offender was thus pardoned for his or her offenses.

With the defeat of the African people during the colonial era, the white rulers imposed a Western justice system. Whites sat as magistrates and judges on African cases, in spite of the fact that they had no knowledge of the social background. People were banished to prison if found guilty for the first time. As a form of social control they were removed from society and put in quarantine. Africans could neither understand nor approve of this type of foreign justice, since whites clearly had no respect for African culture. In fact, the only step whites took was to Africanize certain functions, such as interpretation. In a few cases, some blacks were used as magistrates, but only under the conditions imposed by Roman Dutch Law or English Law.

But as resistance to apartheid stiffened in the 1970s and 1980s, black people began to undermine white justice, partly on grounds that it was undemocratic and disrespectful of black culture. Political activists initiated what are popularly known as "people's courts" in the townships.

In Alexandra, each of our youth camps developed a people's court in 1986. People in the community were actively discouraged from reporting their problems to the apartheid police and courts. Instead, people reported their problems to the people's courts. The courts reduced crime in part through organizing communities into strongly structured entities that could police themselves independently of the illegitimate white regime.

The people's court system functioned similarly to the African justice system, because the emphasis on communities meant that instead of going to prison, people were educated about the causes of social problems. They were therefore politicized about the nature of apartheid oppression, the economic imbalances that accompanied apartheid, and the relationship of these to individual acts of crime in the black communities. The justice system was sophisticated in the sense that the emphasis was on education, rooted in democratic values and principles.

In Alexandra, one of the more interesting people's courts was on 7th Avenue. Initially it was run by the youth, but the elderly were later called in to preside. The courtroom itself was a tiny corrugated iron shack with benches to sit on and a table for the secretary to write minutes on. Both the accused and the complainant would sit among people respected in the community. The chairperson would open the discussion on the issue. The accused and the complainant would then give their sides of the story. The house would deliberate on the issue. One rule was that no one would be undermined or threatened. At the end, an amicable solution to the problem would typically be reached. Both parties would embrace each other.

Here is one example of a case: two sisters were fighting physically on grounds that one would not cook because she was lazy. The matter was brought into the attention of the people's court. What struck me was the manner with which the matter was solved: after both had given their versions, the house deliberated on what appeared to be a non-issue, because there was simply no food in the house to cook. The discussion then centered around unemployment, the unequal distribution of wealth, and the need to build organizations to solve these problems. The women embraced, because they both understood that capitalism is the problem that creates such tensions in society and within families.

People's courts had strong support. However, their integrity depended upon a community mandate, and (as described in Chapter 9) when the civic leadership was locked away, some people's courts began to degenerate.

The direction of civic politics

How do we explain the AAC's success during those momentous weeks and months? First, we must recall that it was crucial for the AAC to establish the proper relationship between the youth and the adults. Since young people and their parents were originally in conflict, and since Alexandra's heart and soul was the working class, there was only one way to engage in progressive politics. It was logical that the youth asked Moss to help organize an alternative to one civic that was anti-youth (ARA) and to another that did not really exist (ACA).

But more importantly, it was also logical to carefully plan the role that disciplined youth would have in organizing their community. Once the link was made, parents began to have the confidence to come to meetings. That was the single key breakthrough. And that breakthrough was based on the way we understood the dynamics of Alexandra, which was based on class analysis, but which had a mass line.

Class politics were crucial to our project, and partly for this reason we have been compared to the Paris Commune of 1871. In the exiled ANC journal *Sechaba* in September 1986, the great young Communist Party intellectual Mzala wrote that in our "liberated districts," the AAC and other civic organizations had achieved an "embryonic stage of 'people's government' ... inasmuch as People's Communes exist, inasmuch as they are a power in the townships and have replaced apartheid institutions of rule." I don't think that this is an exaggeration (it is interesting that two years later our conservative opponents in the ACA began to use the term "commune" to justify their taking part in the Alexandra Council election).

In his book *The Civil War in France*, Marx applauded the self-emancipation of the working class which was already becoming evident during the short-lived course of the Paris rebellion:

The working class did not expect miracles from the Commune. They have no ready-made utopias to introduce *par decret du peuple*. They know that in order to work out their own emancipation, and along with it that higher form to which present society is irresistibly tending by its own economical agencies, they will have to pass through long struggles, through a series of historic processes, transforming circumstances and men [*sic*]. They have no ideals to realize, but to set free the elements of the new society with which old collapsing bourgeois society itself is pregnant.

This was the spirit in which we approached our work. Aside from blunt repression, however, we faced one debilitating constraint: lack of resources. This was not necessarily a purely financial problem, for it included the capacities of our own personnel, many of whom could not read or write. Many comrades were not skilled at running meetings. Many were not able to become independent-thinking activists. There were just too few resources and too little time to address these problems. So while yard committee structures functioned quite well, comrades were sometimes not completely aware of their role, or of how to interpret important issues. Sometimes the comrades were left to address *symptoms* of problems, without a clear analysis of the *causes*.

Some of the problems were internal in nature, caused by a lack of understanding of civic processes. There were occasional allegations that favoritism was practiced by some yard committee activists, who did not know better (or in some cases who were mafioso in their intentions). That kind of activity conflicted with, rather than reflected, the way the AAC organized the mass base. When the leading AAC activists went around the community, we were sometimes told of these problems, and did our best to solve them.

But in some cases, people had a tendency to lose confidence in the yard committees, and instead respected the township-level AAC leadership. Had we the resources to maintain an ongoing political education program, which would have identified the contradictions in the society, such problems of favoritism could have been solved. Democracy is by no means easy, but the process of building township-popular democracy was well and truly underway at that stage.

It was because democracy was beginning to work in the form of organs of peoples power that the security police moved in, to, in their words, "nip the revolution in its bud." The combination of repression and lack of material resources in Alexandra in early 1986 made it difficult to develop the second- or third-layer leadership, and so the police were successful by taking away the top layer. The cream of the activists were either detained or had to go underground simply to survive. Some of the activists were killed, and others left the country. In sum, police harassment and the state onslaught on civic structures that followed the detentions were devastating to our movement. As a result, the emerging layers of leadership became relatively dormant, and the state could proceed with frightening the people into quiescence.

Some critics of the civics trumpet our internal divisions (class, ethnicity, gender, generation), and focus on the difficulty of having a unified community movement. In the history of civics, however, AAC represented a new, dynamic approach, because it was able to harness the energetic youth, who helped set up structures by which the AAC could function. In turn, the parents accepted these structures and began to participate directly in the struggle to make their lives better.

This dynamic relationship was possibly carried further in Alexandra than in any other situation in the history of South African civics. The dynamism also made it possible for the AAC to analyze the changing political landscape, and bring that information to the people at a grassroots level. In turn, the people began to ask for, and consider, alternative ways of living their lives. But before we explore some of those alternatives, let us first reflect on what I think are some of the lessons learned by others from the 1986 uprising.

5
Lessons of the Uprising

Aside from civic leaders and activists, there were four groups who learned lessons from the 1986 uprising in Alexandra. First were the academics, whose fashionably cynical analyses we must scrutinize very carefully. Second were the regime's forces, who not only snuffed out our insurrection, but tried to ensure through ever more sophisticated strategies that we would never agitate so effectively again. Third were big business representatives and their liberal associates, who saw the opportunity to make money and fill a void during the period of civic repression. Fourth were ordinary people, who never lost sight of the need for solidarity, even during the darkest months and years.

Myopic academics

The accomplishments of the Alexandra Action Committee in 1986 were not so impressive that good criticism and analysis, which we in the leadership always welcomed, should be withheld. This chapter begins by considering commentary from several academics who examined our principles and our organizing program. I take this opportunity to defend the AAC, for if our critics had evaluated the situation in a way that took seriously our political intentions and the practical constraints we faced, that would be one thing. However, many intellectuals have the habit of using rose-colored glasses to interpret a reality they were never part of.

This is an important problem, because academics then feed into a larger political debate about the possibilities for, and methods of, social reform. Debates about civic movement strategy and tactics continued into the 1990s, and generated further theories from conservative intellectuals and commentators who wanted to denude the civics of their militancy (see Chapters 8 and 13).

My concern is that, having misunderstood the struggle in Alexandra, many of the overall conclusions of these commentators about the state, communities, and political resistance might also be questionable. The reader must decide this for herself or himself based on a rigorous survey of the literature. But in this literature, our civic point of view is rarely put forward, and so developing a response to the critical intellectuals is one purpose of this chapter.

The debates have been fierce, even when they are just words on a page. "Ungovernability," for example, has a terrible reputation among some academics. "The concept embodied a destructive logic," comments Charles Carter, "which was counterproductive to the long-term consolidation of political organization—the invocation of an alternative idealised concept of 'people's power' notwithstanding." Others, such as John Kane-Berman, claim that the ungovernability strategy was simply bad analysis and worse political practice. Indeed, many commentators build their case on our activities in Alexandra. We will return to these specific claims shortly.

The most serious academic interpretation of the 1986 protest in Alexandra is that of Charles Carter, who wrote an Oxford University doctoral dissertation on the township's politics, as well as two articles in the *Journal of Southern African Studies* in 1991. (After leaving Oxford, Carter became an official of the Anglo American Corporation, which is rather telling.) In general, his analysis of "The Alexandra Rebellion of 1986" is flawed by the classic problems academics face in a foreign community.

Let us have a dialogue with the argument that unfolds in Carter's Oxford thesis. Here is Carter:

"The movement from communal outrage to overt rebellion was underpinned by the activities of a range of civic and youth groupings.... The complex overlay of organizational and ideological activity made for a politically effective identity amongst a grouping of young people and adults alike."

True.

"It was in the milieu of violent encounter between the police and the people that organized political activity occurred."

This is only partly true, since the roots of the AAC are to be found in the failure of other Alexandra civic groups, beginning in late 1985, in the months prior to the massive increase in state-initiated violence.

"While organizational activities around local grievances often informed local resistance, these organizational activities were at times also captive to the upsurge in communal defiance."

In fact, "communal defiance" was actually grounded in addressing "local grievances." Moreover, the organizing strategies of the AAC were neither in contradiction to, nor captive of, communal defiance.

"The ANC's strategic rhetoric of 'ungovernability' was not without its local critique. Alongside sentiments which endorsed a commitment to national liberation came appeals to a sense of community, 'brotherhood,' and working class solidarity."

True, but there is no inconsistency here, since in Alexandra, working class and community issues were firmly integrated into national liberation politics via the AAC, and not derailed by either ARA workerism or petty bourgeois nationalism.

"Thus the ideological constructs which held currency in the township in 1986 were as diverse as the range of youth and adult activists who articulated a political position."

True, but this did not detract from the central, universal thrust of the broader struggle. Our operational strategies were, after all, broad enough to incorporate people with many political perspectives, so long as they were committed to tackling local grievances and to defending the township against the apartheid state. As a result of this openness and flexibility, the overwhelming current of politics flowed toward the AAC, and the consensus quickly emerged throughout the community that there was no need for another broad civic organization in Alexandra.

The logical progression of Carter's argument is becoming clear: there was no coherent civic "ideology"; the success the AAC encountered in organizing is somehow tainted by the fact that this occurred during a time of unprecedented violence; defending against the violence prevented the civic from actually addressing local grievances, and therefore, the 1986 rebellion is best explained in terms of "communal outrage" which, like the famous Paris Commune rebellion of 1871, "engendered a feeling of hatred and revenge, the conviction that it really was a social war that had begun." (Although in a way there were indeed general parallels between Alex in 1986 and the Commune, as noted later, Carter's squeamish argument about communal outrage obscures the political nature of the AAC strategy.)

To his credit, Carter does concede that the AAC was "undoubtedly the prime mover"—and "effective"—in organizing the people of Alexandra at street level. Yet in general he misses the point by stressing what he calls "the nexus of confrontation and conflict/repression and retribution," especially in the violence provoked at funerals, in the formation and development of the AAC. (In fact, Carter places far too much weight on our mobilizing for funerals, which was the subject of many of the pamphlets and court testimony he studied). Carter claims that "these themes appear to colour, if not overshadow, the political activity taking place in the township at the time."

The AAC strategy, in contrast, *combined* an understanding of militant resistance to state repression with the increasing maturity of community politics in Alexandra. Our maturity with respect to our basic political principles and an organizing strategy to match, preceded the killing of Michael Diradeng and the Six Day War (even if we only formally launched the AAC during the war).

The main point Carter is making is that the power of the AAC *depended* on the "milieu" of violence. Other commentators also believe this to be the case. In my view, the reverse is true. The organizational roots of the AAC were growing before the violent outbreak, and in fact were ultimately uprooted by the violence—state violence and police repression later destroyed the AAC for several years.

Academic commentators on Alex were not particularly close to the ground as we organized, as we experienced ever harsher oppression, and as we responded by organizing ever more frantically. The political confusion that arises from academic analysis of the sort Carter offers is reflected in the debate over ungovernability. (In the case of John Kane-Berman, which I review in a sidebar, it may be less a case of confusion and more a matter of longstanding hostility.)

Ungovernability became a catchword for challenging the regime. In this sense the ANC call for ungovernability reflected the objective conditions on the ground. It was not an abstract call. For while ungovernability was aimed at hitting state organs, the next step beyond ungovernability was to build organs of people's power. When we talked about day-to-day issues ("local grievances") caused by apartheid and capitalism, we were firstly trying to make the township and country ungovernable, and secondly sowing seeds so that, given the opportunity, we would actually have something in place to actually solve the problems.

All of this was done both to support the liberation of South Africa and to further the material interests of workers and residents. There was no contradiction. When Carter implies there was a contradiction, he does so on the basis of the evidence later presented at the trial of Moss, myself, and three others for treason. It could be argued, however, that Carter's analysis and conclusions are faulty based on this evidence, which for obvious reasons does not reflect the whole truth. This is especially the case when the ideologies of liberation and of civic struggle are interpreted during a highly inflammatory period. Do not forget that even saying the phrase "anck" (for "ANC") could land one in jail. In this context, successful pursuit of ungovernability was a recipe for being put away on treason charges, if captured.

Academics must learn that activists are more effective in articulating such ideas outside the courtroom, in small gatherings and meetings in soot-coated shacks or hostel rooms, or even at rallies and marches, than in the bourgeois press, in academic journals, or inside the courtroom, where the prosecuting team is hanging on every word. Simply said, most activists want to avoid prison if at all possible (not, of course, to the detriment of the struggle). As a result, during the Mayekiso trial, the AAC's political orientation, and the strategy for gaining self-government and development for Alexandra, was not only downplayed but often denied. After all, a conviction for treason in our case could have meant death. As Richard Abel remarks in *Political by Other Means,* his excellent study of our trial, "Such repudiation of achievements, ideologies, and loyalties may be one of the most insidious attributes of treason trials."

Jeremy Seekings (who also trained at Oxford) also uses the Mayekiso treason trial evidence uncritically. Seekings writes in an important article on "Civic Organization in South African Townships" in *South African Review* 6, that "Even at the high point of civic activities in 'well-organized' townships such as Duncan Village and Alexandra, [civics'] prominence exceeded their direct importance. Civics were negotiating *for* greater formal participation in local state decision-making" (Seekings' emphasis).

This comes as a surprise to Alexandra civic insiders, who primarily wanted to *destroy*, not participate in, the Black Local Authority (our "direct importance" in this regard is witnessed by the fact that the BLA dissolved in April 1986, and again in May 1991, under civic pressure). I do not recall anyone in our AAC ranks, and indeed very few out of the thousands of civic activists across the country, who ever advocated taking a real stake ("formal participation") in the racist local government system. Had we wanted to do so, we would simply have turned into councilors.

Seekings's confusion is further apparent in the claim that "The phenomenon of 'people's power' was largely the result of the collapse of the local state," when exactly the opposite is true; the collapse of the BLAs was the result of radical civic activism, inspired by the theory of people's power.

Civics, Seekings continues, "often exhibited marked continuities from conservative-led antecedents." Support for the civics during the 1980s "reflected a curious combination of their conservatism and their radical-ism.... Civics attracted support through their tactical pragmatism and 'reformism' rather than their ideological or programmatic radicalism."

It should be clear that Seekings pushes his generalizations way too far (partly because of other faulty information, derived from Soweto, as I show in Chapter 13). For if this were true in Alexandra, then Mike Beea, not Moses Mayekiso, would have won hegemony. In fact, the strategies, tactics, and programs of the AAC broke with the undemocratic, right-wing populism of Beea's ACA (home of tactical pragmatism and reformism), just as they broke with the sterile workerism of the ARA.

In some other places (the settlements KTC and Crossroads in the Western Cape, for example), it is true that traditionalists and conservatives were deeply involved in civic leadership. But without an ideological basis, these conservatives were entrapped by state strategies, strategies that they could never effectively challenge or cut links to.

Successful conservative leaders had to ride the tide of militancy or risk being swept away. Shadrack Sinaba, the well-known former mayor of Daveyton on the East Rand, is a perfect example. But in most places, conservatives were replaced by more progressive civic activists when their conservative approach to civic activism became indistinguishable from the state's puppet council structures. Or as in our case in Alexandra, the conservative approach (Beea running for a seat on the Alex Council, for example) was simply bypassed and ignored.

The last two chapters established the fact that our movement to build organs of people's power was not "conservative" or "reformist," as Seekings would have it. But Karen Jochelson, in her *Journal of Southern African Studies* article, "Reform, Repression and Resistance in South Africa: A Case Study of Alexandra Township, 1979-1989," is just as insulting when she bends the stick the other way in arguing that we were revolutionary adventurists:

> I suggest that the demise of people's power was not due solely to a clampdown on popular organization by the state. People's power was informed by an insurrectionary strategy which gave rise to hasty organization and was based on a limited conception of state power.

First, it should be clear that our strategy was "insurrectionary" in that it was in harmony with the ANC call for ungovernability. Was the organizing behind the strategy "hasty"? No. Prior to the outbreak of violence there were attempts to organize for the long-term, and our meetings continually stressed the permanence of civic structures. To carry out the strategies adopted in early 1986, we had long sessions concerned with how to organize, and we rooted that strategy in concrete class analysis of the situation on the ground.

But Jochelson (also an Oxford doctoral student at the time the article was published) appears hostile to using class analysis as the basis for political strategy:

> The heat of February's battle, and widespread support evident at public meetings, led comrades to believe residents were "ready" for new forms of organization. Activists intended street committees to play an educative and political role. Discussion would root local grievances in a broad analysis of apartheid and capitalism, providing the foundation for informed political resistance.

Jochelson does not agree with this approach, nor the type of resistance that logically followed: "The transformation of popular opposition and emergence of people's power did not reflect a period of dual power as activists believed." She calls it "overly simplistic" to say that "reform policy has been eclipsed by repression in response to the strength of political opposition."

But was it overly simplistic? For one, Jochelson's article does not include any coverage of our devastating boycott strategy or any other outcomes of the momentous 13 April workshop (Carter at least treats this workshop carefully). But even more importantly, she downplays the fact that AAC structures were established to represent the aspirations of the people of Alexandra. In this respect, the AAC offered people the constructive, democratic empowerment to make decisions about how to make progress and control their own lives. This was not a process to be accomplished in a month's time, but instead a long-term effort to empower people to eventually do away with apartheid state organs.

In some ways, therefore, we had dual power, in that we overruled the state through our rent boycotts, alternative local justice system, and rejection of bantu education and its replacement with new classes. Dual power actually existed in these important respects, even if in formative stages. The Alexandra Council collapsed as a direct result of such pressure, and of the rise of new organs of people's power, especially in some aspects of maintaining order, like the people's courts.

Opponents of dual power theory say that this approach can never reach the central state. But in fact it did reach the central state, which set up structures aimed at destroying the local civic movements. If there had been many more Alexandras, the effect on the central state would have been completely debilitating. Indeed, other township revolts approached the intensity of Alexandra across South Africa in early 1986, and this led directly to P.W. Botha's declaration of a State of Emergency to try to destroy the militancy of the people. The police acknowledged that there were twenty-seven townships in the Eastern Cape under ANC/UDF control, and other uprisings were seen in the Johannesburg area in Duduza, KwaThema, Tsakane, Katlehong, Daveyton, and Kagiso.

At its mightiest, the power of the central state is always well-informed about what is happening at the local level, and there is evidence to suggest that President Botha and Minister of Defense Magnus Malan had an intimate knowledge of Alexandra, where their "oilspot" philosophy uprooted the seeds being sown by the new system of people's power. Of course, even this philosophy didn't hold in the long-term, which is one reason for the concessions of 2 February 1990.

Jochelson is disadvantaged in trying to understand all of this, partly because of some incorrect reasoning. For example, according to Jochelson, "AYCO and the AAC could draw huge crowds to meetings. Perhaps some people were coerced, or attended due to fear, as newspapers and the SABC insisted." In other words, the AAC was not actually popular, and relied on duress.

This is a misinterpretation of what was happening, of course. As an organizer in charge of the youth mobilization, I can attest to the absolute discipline exercised by the AAC and AYCO youth, who were continually taught the behavior needed to make the house-to-house strategy effective. There were occasional complaints about coercing people into supporting funerals, but those were not against AAC or AYCO activists but unorganized youth in the township. During the 13 April workshop, the AAC and AYCO made a firm call to these youth to have more discipline. And the boycott was marked by total discipline.

It is easier for Jochelson to argue, based again entirely upon misleading courtroom evidence, that "reckless militancy, widespread criminal activities, and harassment and coercion of adult residents transformed 'the youth' into a considerable threat." Later in the book (in Chapter 14), I address this haphazard labelling of "the youth."

Drawing directly from Jochelson's pessimistic, biased, and faulty article, other academics came to even more hostile conclusions. In 1988, Mike Morris and Vishnu Padayachee wrote an influential article on "State Reform Policy in South Africa" in the journal *Transformation*, where they took these insults to the extreme. In the space of three short pages they accuse the AAC (the only group referred to by name) and other democratic, mass-based township organizations of the following:

> Misplaced euphoria ... an inadequate theory of the state ... a strategic error about the characteristics of the political period ... failure to respond to the state's reform process in anything other than a totally dismissive manner ... [being] limited by their own historical patterns of viewing reality ... non-collaboration inherited from the flood of black consciousness activists [into the ANC] ... [inability] to see that there existed other options.

In a funny mix of old-time workerism and new-and-improved reformism, Morris and Padayachee argue, "Given the dominance of the ANC, the pervasiveness of its world view within the mass movement, and the respect accorded to it, it is not surprising that this occurred." And, they conclude, "The misreading of the period by the popular classes had its own tragic consequences.... We are already paying the huge costs, in human and organizational terms, of a mistaken slide into an insurrectionist strategy."

Let us coolly examine the reality. Within a short period of six months, the AAC's supposed "mistaken slide" helped Alexandra organize itself in a manner never accomplished before or since. The sacrifices of the comrades who took part, including the dozens who lost their lives, were made with the clear understanding that no reasonable alternative existed.

The pros and cons of each strategic development were carefully weighed. This period of *intifada* was the most sophisticated ever either in the national liberation struggle or of strategy deployed by any urban social movement in South African history. The regime, not only locally in Alexandra, but also nationally, was near collapse.

For Morris and Padayachee, however, the armed might of the Botha regime made this unprecedented popular protest inevitably futile. (If the peoples of Eastern Europe had felt as Morris and Padayachee did in 1989, they never would have dislodged their seemingly invincible ruling elites.) In large part because of our strategies and tactics, the regime did, in the end, have to recognize the ANC and SACP as organizations with which they would one day share power.

Morris and Padayachee mapped a much more reformist route to "transformation," namely "qualified participation (in local government), or locally negotiated agreements." But this reformist road, pursued first in 1990, was also densely littered with false hopes, broken expectations, and massive amounts of bloodshed. In "human and organizational terms," it is by no means clear that the negotiating strategies of the more recent period did not entail even higher costs, as I describe in later chapters. (I will add here that *Transformation* rejected publication of a version of this chapter in 1993; its editors, including Morris and Padayachee, were perhaps "limited by their own historical patterns of viewing reality," and so my article criticizing academic interpretations of the Alex uprising was published instead in *Southern African Review of Books*.)

It is not surprising to receive such commentary from academics. Anyone without the benefit of first-hand experience on the battlefield of township social change is susceptible to serious misinterpretation, especially if coming from a more conservative stance. Without understanding why a youth activist resorts to throwing a stone against a passing police or army vehicle, the armchair theorist takes the apartheid state's late 1980s "reform" attempts too seriously. The regime was serious about reforms only within the logic of repression, and in its attempt to move the social system from racial to class division and exploitation (the case of the East Bank of Alexandra is examined shortly to clarify state strategies during the late 1980s).

Finally, we come to the Trotskyist analysis, which always offers a certain hope, even if misplaced, for transformation. In his book *South Africa Between Reform and Revolution*, Alex Callinicos attacks civic organizations as if by instinct (since they are not factory-based *soviets*): "The street committees were community-based bodies, based on an alliance of various social layers in which middle-class UDF leaders and school-students, rather than workers, were likely to predominate." Here we see repeated the sterile ARA analysis. (Callinicos does, however, concede that Alexandra had delegate structures that extended deep into the township.)

The need for township activists to have their say is reflected in the problems that many academics have in understanding community struggles, since they depend on other academics' interpretations, on questionable court documents, and on biased newspaper accounts. And when this academic analysis was applied to social policy in the early 1990s (by conservative commentators like John Kane-Berman), the interpretation of ungovernability in mid-1980s Alexandra took on even greater ideological importance.

The legacy of ungovernability

In this article, excerpted from the Southern African Review of Books, *November-December 1993, I review more recent debates over our strategy and tactics.*

Not only is the violence in the townships of the early 1990s a direct consequence of the "ungovernability" approach of the ANC and its allies during the mid-1980s, it was a misguided anti-apartheid strategy in any case. That is one argument. The other is that township violence results from a combination of state terrorism and the decay of the social fabric that has accompanied economic crisis. Ungovernability was in fact the correct approach to social change, because it gave people who were excluded from the dominant society a meaningful voice for the first time, and one they may even use again to assure political and economic democracy in the future.

Which argument is correct? John Kane-Berman believes the former. I take exception. The central thesis of Kane-Berman's book *Political Violence in South Africa* is that "The people's war, directed in theory against the state, in fact helped to unleash massive violence within black communities. Black people, who were the victims of apartheid itself, became also the victims of the struggle against apartheid."

The reason for taking this up now is that the history of the mid-1980s in places like Alexandra offers a basis for understanding the present transition. The potentially revolutionary situation during this earlier period was based on a popular association of apartheid with capitalism, not simply with a lack of civil rights. It is our response to this condition that must be clearly understood if the first democratic government aims to achieve social stability.

There is another reason. For those of us committed to a vibrant post-apartheid civil society, the mid-1980s also taught us what we know about politics: how to organize, how to bring structural analysis to bear, how to contest both geographical and ideological turf, and how to build a national democratic movement featuring economic justice. We make no apologies for doing all of this in the context of ungovernability.

A new spirit was born in Alexandra in early 1986. People's memories of how, during that period, they dealt with their problems in a democratic manner, remain strong still today. Even during the late 1980s' harassment, feelings of solidarity were not extinguished. The social base of the AAC was not completely broken. There were numerous lessons about strategy and tactics learned by key civic activists, and a longer term vision of community-controlled development was brought forward to the next set of struggles in the early 1990s.

The AAC held that people had to be involved in making their own future. Community economic empowerment, through cooperatives and community enterprises, was also to have been a priority. The rise of the AAC gave us confidence that urban civic structures could take up and win these issues. We retain that confidence today in the AAC's successor, the Alexandra Civic Organization, no matter the confusion and difficulties that surround the transition period.

As civic movement strategists, there were other lessons. There is no question that the process could have gone more smoothly than it did, had we greater resources for communication, administration, and hence democratic accountability. But the basic political approach was, in retrospect, the right one.

Accordingly we take this tradition honorably into the next phase of struggle, where new barriers appear. Attempts by civic associations across South Africa to upgrade services, democratize development, and achieve non-racial local government and in the process agree to the government's request to end rent boycotts have been by-and-large unsuccessful thus far. When not rewarded with real changes in living standards, which remain deplorable in nearly all South African townships, community residents will simply not pay their rent and service charges.

Here it is critical to understand that community organizations used rent boycotts and consumer boycotts not only for political purposes, but also to offset declining income levels in townships during a time of rising rent and service charges. The strategy, in other words, is both one of ungovernability, and a cry for economic justice.

This deserves some amplification. If white areas had not been subsidized by black townships during apartheid (because of the location of commerce and industry in white areas, which benefitted from tax receipts originating from black wallets), the rent and services boycotts probably would not have become such a crucial element in our reconstruction of the apartheid city. In other words, it was not because of the "culture of non-payment" that the boycotts have continued, as Kane-Berman and many others argue. Instead, there was a material basis for withholding rents and service payments until residents discerned a tangible improvement in services, and until the creation of non-racial local governments with a common fiscal and tax base so that poor blacks didn't continue to subsidize rich whites.

It is no wonder, therefore, that in cases such as Soweto, where there was no noticeable change in living conditions during the early 1990s, the rent and service boycott continued long after several Soweto Civic attempts to call it off. Struggle strengthened not only the survival strategies of ordinary residents, but also our vision of a future society free of apartheid and socioeconomic despair. This principle is deeply ingrained, not as a "culture of non-payment," as it may appear on the surface, but through the grassroots constituents of a social movement demanding decent living conditions as a human right.

This remains true today. Like the Soweto Civic, the Alexandra Civic and nearly all other civics have had problems in the new environment, but we are regaining our influence over day-to-day affairs. The reason for our persistence, in contrast to many international urban movements which fade after a short period, is that the apartheid state failed to crush our political and economic program: the struggle to transform society through consciousness-raising, economic empowerment, participation, and control of community planning, strengthening of civil society, and democratization of government.

Within Alexandra, we sometimes experience conflicts with other organizations which oppose progressive social change, and even the ANC Alexandra branch has come into conflict with the civic. For Kane-Berman this is the stuff of "black-on-black violence" and is the logical outcome of the civic movement's occasionally vehement campaign that Black Local Authorities resign. Yes, in some instances the struggle has been extremely fierce, reflecting the deep-seated anger of the oppressed people. But Kane-Berman should know that the pressure we mounted against the BLAs was not directed against individuals, but against the system itself.

Is violence rooted in our political strategy, or in the conditions of political repression and economic despair? Those of us who have lived under constant persecution, state-sponsored violence, poverty, and deprivation, after all, had no formal democratic channel to voice our concerns. Violence is often the result, be it organized or unorganized. This is a basic fact of life, not unique to the South African struggle, but it is a fact that has passed Kane-Berman by. He has not experienced poverty, and so he argues in *Political Violence in South Africa,*

> One should beware of blaming the violence too strongly on socio-economic factors. Personal income per head in the Johannesburg area is more than double the national average, but this region alone has at times accounted for half the violence in the country. There are also localised causes, such as the battle for market share among taxi owners.

Kane-Berman never acknowledges the deeper economic crisis of South African capitalism, even the obvious facts that income has fallen rapidly in townships and that the majority of retrenchments have taken place in the Johannesburg area during the depression of the early 1990s. Now we know that all the great hype about the future of black economic empowerment through entrepreneurialism was a farce. Not long ago, in *South Africa's Silent Revolution,* Kane-Berman called the taxi industry "the most dramatic black success story so far," but today he must concede the fact that the celebrated taxis' battle for market share in an overtraded township easily becomes a gunbattle. His privileged perspective is of little use in understanding either state terrorism or economic deprivation.

In conclusion, it is a pity that Kane-Berman and other academics, including those who may see themselves as progressives, interpret our struggles in ways that are beneficial to the establishment. This happens in two ways. First, the establishment aims to show that civic leaders in particular and the democratic movement in general have unleashed a monster which we cannot control. In reality, however, ungovernability was a beneficial weapon in the struggle to weaken the state apparatus, with the result that the civics took leadership in the local version of the multiparty talks, namely the Local Government Negotiation Forum.

Second, the attack on the civics has a deeper meaning, because it is an attack on the relationship of our ideology to our practice of material struggle. "To the extent that ideologies are historically necessary they have a validity which is 'psychological'; they 'organize' human masses, they form the terrain on which men [*sic*] move, acquire consciousness of their position, struggle." So said Gramsci, in *Selections from the Prison Notebooks*. We defend this relationship through the classical Marxism of Gramsci:

> The analysis of these propositions tends, I think, to reinforce the conception of "historical bloc" in which precisely material forces are the content and ideologies are the form, though this distinction between form and content has purely indicative value, since the material forces would be inconceivable historically without form and the ideologies would be individual fancies without the material forces.

> In sum, the civic movement entered a theater of war, and we believe that while battles remain to be fought achieving the concrete implementation of our goals, the war itself, against apartheid, was won. It remains, ideologically, for the victors to collect the spoils: the recognition that ungovernability was central to our fight, in spite of unfounded efforts to negate our proud tradition.

Subtler state strategies

It was not just academics, but also the apartheid state, and particularly the police, who learned certain dubious lessons from the awakening of politics in Alexandra. These are more interesting because in a strange way, they were more accurate. The state and capital learned that they had to have certain conditions in order to get what they wanted, namely political stability and profits.

For example, police strategies quickly evolved in order to repress the mass-based organizations. The "Brazilian Option" was one part of this: community leaders and trade unionists were tortured and killed, while their followers were given a few handouts. The strategies aimed at "winning hearts and minds" (WHAM) while at the same time repressing community and worker struggle.

The police used these methods because they believed they were faced with a "total onslaught." In 1986, the *Weekly Mail* explained how the "oilspot" solution was to be applied in Alex: "Government strategists have likened Alexandra to a drop of oil dispersing over the surface of water; its shining new image is expected, in the same way, to spread to all the other riot-torn townships."

Indeed, Alexandra was the most important of thirty-four oilspot townships that were to receive attention by a new "Joint Management Centre" (sometimes called "mini-JMC") which evolved after the failure of repressive strategies tried during the 1986 uprising. Across South Africa, these JMCs combined the functions of security, welfare and finance, intelligence gathering and monitoring, reestablishment of black local authorities, communication of state policies, and other campaigns.

In Alex, the involvement of the South African Defence Force (SADF) in the JMC was led by Colonel Geoffrey Holland-Muter, who was later to appear in court in 1992 on corruption charges to the tune of R250,000. In early 1988, when Alex was relatively quiet, Holland-Muter told *Business Day* that the "elimination" of "revolutionary forces" was needed to achieve stability. In 1988, a total of forty members of the AAC were in detention. "In all honesty," township administrator Steve Burger concluded to a reporter, "it must be said the Emergency has definitely managed to create a climate of peace and security."

Other activities by the Alex JMC show how deeply the state needed to intervene in township life. When drivers from the state-subsidized PUTCO bus company went on strike, the JMC Security Committee acted against illegal taxis. In June 1989, worried about our release and the worsening incompetence of the Alexandra City Council, the JMC wanted to incorporate the municipal police into the South African Police "in case subversive elements got control of the Council and used the municipal police as a private army."

According to Andrew Boraine in his well-circulated paper, "Managing the Urban Crisis, 1986-1989," the JMCs tried to "'eliminate the agitators,' on the one hand, and establish ways in which local authorities and the security forces can 'communicate' with township residents on the other." Much of the JMC activity in Alexandra that occurred after the 1986 uprising and the jailing of leaders is still visible, from tarred roads to high-mast lighting. Boraine concludes that "The central aim of current state strategy is the creation and maintenance of a variety of social, geographical and political divisions."

In March 1987, a *Star* story on WHAM strategy in Alex quoted a senior security official: "The counter-revolutionary organization must train people and ensure good government. If you want to win you must have a philosophy, strategy and plan. It is all about welfare and security—and the masses in the middle."

A month later, Burger and security force Major-General van der Westhuizen announced that they were using the JMC as a vehicle for "countering strikes, consumer boycotts, sabotage and stayaways on the economic front, and alternative education, liberation theology and organizations for youth and women on the social front." The JMC was chaired by Police Colonel Kukard, who attempted feeble WHAM tactics such as a sportsday, for which the developers Murray and Roberts pitched in R8,000 worth of prizes.

Other JMC soft tactics included an attempt to counter our August 1989 AAC township clean-up campaign by holding two JMC/Council campaigns, one and two weeks earlier, to do the same. Holland-Muter contacted Sandton and Midrand for assistance, and private contractors were brought in. Alexandra's black puppet councilors asked the SADF not to put up posters advertising the clean up on the grounds that it would have been too embarrassing, and also asked that one of the days be changed. Although the JMC overruled the Council, according to minutes, the JMC did agree that "at the Council's request, the SADF will maintain a low profile so that the radical element in Alexandra won't be upset and so that the Council will get all the credit for the campaign. The SADF will, however, conduct its usual patrols for maintaining law and order."

In November 1989, when President de Klerk promised to terminate the JMCs, the Witwatersrand Co-ordination Centre was the body set up to inherit the JMC structures. The "Alexandra Advisory Committee" (with its ironic acronym, AAC) was the simple name change. Among its members were the police, the Transvaal Provincial Administration, the Bureau for Information, the Department of National Health and Population Development, the Department of Manpower, the Department of Education and Training, the Post Office, the Development Bank of Southern Africa, and even businesses like Kellog's. Burger, from the Alexandra City Council, chaired the meetings, accompanied by councilors and staff.

Having learned a few lessons from the uprising, Burger bragged to the press that he received community support when he took over in June 1986. "With my committee members, I took immediate steps to establish contacts with all existing organizations in the township. This helped to create a joint focus on the upliftment of the township and a new master plan for this purpose was created for the next six years." He told the *Weekly Mail* in 1987, apparently with a straight face, that "militant political groups attended some of the first meetings to discuss plans for upgrading Alex, but have stayed away recently." He meant us; we stayed away, of course, because we were in prison.

Burger attempted to implement a R140 million township upgrading plan drawn up in September 1986 by staff from Eskom, the West Rand Development Board, and a private company, Goulty Moller and Associates. To his credit, Burger's plan would not have resulted in ripping down and tearing apart much of Alexandra, as the original 1979 plan did. Burger knew that "there is still considerable bitterness on the part of the community," as he wrote in a 1990 letter to the Transvaal Provincial Administration. But he foolishly attributed this simply to "loss of property rights."

Therefore in his 1986 plan, Burger aimed for more rapid homeownership. His intent was that "cost recovery from selling the houses would finance further development. Employers, Building Societies and Financial Institutions would assist in the privatisation program. This would avoid continuous subsidisation by the state and would give the community a stake in the land." Although he had the endorsement of the Alexandra Traders Association and the Alexandra Chamber of Commerce, no Alexandra residents, and indeed no blacks, were featured in the preparation of the report.

In addition, Burger was instrumental in developing the East Bank of the Jukskei River, where he gathered a middle-class strata of police, teachers, lawyers, doctors, nurses, and civil servants who had access to state and building society loans for housing. The point there was to continue the divide-and-conquer strategy, this time along class lines. Burger also tried to win hearts and minds by issuing newsletters with cartoon characters called Comrade Rat and Alex, who were meant to demonstrate how Alexandra's citizens should live their lives.

But achieving his goals on the basis of cost recovery in such a poor township was an impossible feat. Burger was quoted in the *Sowetan* in 1987 as saying the Alex Council intended to build more than 7,000 homes. This was unimaginable, considering the past record. He was still dreaming when, in early 1989, he claimed to the *Financial Mail*, "By the end of 1990, Alexandra will boast the completion of full services to the township. The transformation is unbelievable. Old houses are being refurbished and sold off, while brand-new houses are being built. Civic pride is also evident, as residents use the garbage cans that have been provided."

Sowetan reporter Don Seokane investigated on 5 October 1990 and offered a different point of view of Burger's "transformation":

> Filthy, squalid and trash heap have always been words used to describe conditions at Alexandra. Even now, notwithstanding changes to the township, conditions are still the same. Bucket system toilets, crowded yards with at least seven people sharing a room and a poor refuse removal system are features. The streets are always littered with garbage, streams of dirty water and congested squatter areas which create an unhealthy environment. There are more than 10,000 shacks in the township and their sites are unserviced, without any toilet facilities. Street corners, particularly at shack settlements areas, are disaster areas with piles of garbage heaped across the road. This situation presents a major health hazard.

Aside from lack of community involvement, Burger's upgrading plan suffered two crucial technical flaws: first, it was only meant for a township populated by 92,000 people, less than half of Alex's population in 1986; and second, as a result of a faulty ideological assumption, the plan called for "swift movement to private ownership on the basis of permanent title, so that owners can assist local authorities in creating order, promoting cleanliness, limiting crime and preventing squatting."

The head of the Alexandra JMC agreed wholeheartedly with this aspect of the plan because, as he told the *Guardian* newspaper, "We believe that if a person owns his own house, he will not tolerate stone-throwing or petrol-bombing in the vicinity." Here we see that the capitalist dream of homeownership, no matter how myopic for poor people, is also beneficial to the repressive state because it increases the system's social control. But the capitalist dream is worth consideration of its own.

Capital's agenda

Big business also learned lessons from the problems in Alex in 1986, and also adopted a fairly transparent ideological agenda after the AAC was repressed. "The Sandton Chamber of Commerce is interested in creating a capitalist attitude in Alexandra and spreading the entrepreneurial spirit which does not exist there," said Warren Dale, the Chamber's president in 1987. "They must realise that personal advancement will come from hard work, not slogans. Our interest is in the development and maintenance of a capitalist framework."

We can appreciate this honesty. The leading capitalist politician, Zach de Beer, was even more specific when he gave a speech to a housing finance conference in 1988: "When people are housed, more especially when they are home-owners, they are not only less likely to be troublesome. They are also likely to feel they have a stake in the society and an interest in its stability."

So Alex became a pilot project for a simple strategy of petty-bourgeoisification. The East Bank was a breeding ground, and there developers Rabie, Murray and Roberts, and Tri-Time gained access to the bulk of the land for middle-class development. Two-thirds of the houses built on the East Bank were selling for more than R50,000, which cut out more than 90 percent of the population of Alexandra. A quarter of the East Bank houses cost more than R80,000. The housing director of Murray and Roberts explained to the press that "Up-market projects will fulfil a vital function of motivating township residents toward a better lifestyle."

By the end of 1986 there was R600,000 in residential building activity on the East Bank and in Old Alex. The next year the figure rose to R1 million, and in 1988, R20 million. Other developers, such as SM Goldstein, Gough Cooper Homes, and Schachat Cullum, were also making good profits, and had nothing to say about the fact that the township's leaders were in jail. But in 1986, 80 percent of the township lacked sewage or water services, and only 10 percent of the streets were lit. For more capital to penetrate Alex, a lot more state money would be needed.

That came in the form of a grant from the Regional Services Council and a loan from the Development Bank of Southern Africa. In a later chapter we will explore how the leftovers of apartheid, including the Development Bank's activities in Alex, affect the way people have had to establish community control of development. For us, though, there was an even more basic challenge: to maintain any organizational memory in the wake of state repression in 1986.

The memories of the people

Residents of Alexandra learned one crucial thing from the uprising, and that was to be prepared for a clampdown by building several strong layers of leadership, so that every individual is capable of becoming a leader. In spite of the shortage of resources we faced, the AAC was immersed in that process, but was interrupted by events no one could predict. Our leading layers were nearly all demobilized in one way or another as a result.

The 1986 repression provided lessons on how to survive a very difficult situation, in which the state aimed to destroy the organizations of poor and working-class people. For example, people had to "hunker down" and go underground. When they reemerged, they were far more careful about self-protection.

Rising rent collections by Alexandra authorities reflected the success of repression. From a low of R19,000 in June 1986 when the boycott strategy was most actively pursued, R47,000 was collected in July and R104,000 in December. (This was still a level only two-thirds what the Council could raise prior to the formation of the AAC; our rent boycott had a lasting impact.)

However, memories of resistance and of democratic organization that were generated by the first half of 1986 could never be crushed. What was most important about the yard committee leaders was their strength of resistance. As police searched yard after yard in 1987 in search of allies to testify against imprisoned community leaders, the good memories of the AAC persuaded many activists that they could not testify against us. Of course, some of the activists were broken by the police, and agreed to testify. But when they later saw us in the court, they changed their tune and told of how our role was a very good one. The prosecutor's frustration was great, and the judge was very impressed that state witnesses turned into defense witnesses with no prompting!

In mid-1989, when our treason trial was over and we returned to Alex, we saw how those memories had stayed alive. We were overjoyed by the response to our return. The yard committees were still there, even if open organization was not possible during our time in jail. Once we started organizing again in 1989, the lessons of 1986 all returned, and yard committees became active again.

There were also long-term lessons for community-controlled development that were brought forward to the next set of struggles. At the point the AAC leaders were detained, for example, we were beginning to negotiate with Burger about how to supply necessary services to the people and how to alleviate the terrible conditions in the township (these negotiations were a far cry from formal participation in state decision making, as Seekings might view it, but involved mainly logistical issues). We were trying to address the housing backlog, health, education, transport, and infrastructure. And Burger knew that as long as the AAC was strong, a top-down approach would no longer work.

The AAC programs for community development were delayed, but not canceled, by the June 1986 detentions, as discussed in later chapters. One reflection of the lessons learned about the development process is that the term "development" has no meaning if it does not refer to *community control*. "The way out of Africa's grinding spiral of poverty and environmental degradation," concludes Ben Wisner in his excellent book *Power and Need in Africa*, "does not lie in further integrating women and other rural disadvantaged groups into development." According to Wisner,

> The poor are already integrated into an unsustainable system. The strong Basic Needs Approach poses the alternative of production for need in a system which is locally controlled and locally organized. Alternative organizational initiatives of this sort do exist in Africa. Self-government in Alexandra Township in Johannesburg in the face of military occupation by the racist South African regime is a testimony to the social creativity of ordinary people.

And it was precisely that social creativity that sustained many of us in the South African civic movement for so long, notwithstanding the growing sophistication of the apartheid state and of capital, or the cynical view of academics that we succeeded in mobilizing our comrades merely because we were fighting police violence or because we offered a misguided insurrectionary vision. The relevance and legitimacy of our approach can be judged on the basis of our work in the 1990s, as well by our 1986 hegemony. But the debates in this chapter, as well as subsequent intellectual criticisms of the civics, are evidence that our militant road was continually monitored by armchair political mapmakers. The next question is, how did we remain on that road during the years we were in jail?

6
Behind Apartheid Bars
(1986-1989)

For nearly three years, from June 1986 to April 1989, I was under threat of death from the courts. Charges of high treason, sedition, and subversion were filed against me and four other AAC activists in early 1987. We found ourselves at the mercy of the apartheid state, with the likelihood of execution if it was proved that we had committed treason.

Caught!

The people of Alexandra were seething in May 1986. Toward the end of the month, we held a meeting of what we called the "organizing collective," trying to assess the situation and determine our strengths and weaknesses. We decided we needed a tour of the township to look at how organizationally solid we were. Four of us got into a car: comrades Richard Mdakane, Naude Moitse, Phangi Msezane, and myself. Richard was general secretary of the AAC, and the rest of us were AAC organizers. Naude was a hard-core student activist who ended up in exile, and Phangi was a recent recruit who was still getting his feet wet. (Phangi later broke down under police pressure in a State of Emergency detention in 1987 and never returned to the movement.)

As we moved through the township, a police vehicle (a Caspir) picked up our trail and began to follow. Trying to evade them, we went into a shop. According to our analysis of the police, our greatest danger was their "shoot-to-kill" attitude. Our rule was: when followed by a suspicious vehicle, slow down when you are in an area where there are witnesses, and give them a chance to drive by. Better yet, pull over and stand openly but with plenty of people nearby. We had too many experiences of ambushes, kidnappings, and shootings, where the police later claimed that activists were trying to escape. When out of public view, bodies of dead activists had AK-47s and limpet mines planted on them.

That day, the police caught up with us as we were going into the shop, searched our car, and then searched us. They alleged we had guns, but their search gained them nothing, so they left. We proceeded along the journey, but once again were followed, this time by more army vehicles. We were heading toward the outskirts of the township, but pulled the car over near a crowd. A military truck stopped next to us, and a large group of soldiers surrounded us. The army searched us, again found nothing, but then called the security police.

We were detained that day, 22 May 1986, under Section 50 of the Internal Security Act, and spent the next fourteen days in prison under detention-without-trial. Released on 5 June, I had only a week of freedom. On my release I decided not to sleep at my house for fear of being detained again. On the evening of 12 June, I decided to visit my brother Thami at the Mayekiso house on 7th Avenue. Only Thami was at home at the time.

At midnight I decided I would sleep at home that night, a crucial mistake. Within an hour, the police had the house surrounded. A tiny window was available for me to escape. I had left my clothes near the bed, but Thami was forced to let the police come in, and I did not have time to do anything but dive out that window.

The window led directly to a shack used by two other people. I jumped under the blankets between them. But inside the house, the police saw that the bed had been slept in. There were my clothes, and the window leading to the shack was ajar. One cop looked through the window, and figured out that I was in the shack next door. We were all laying on the floor under the blankets, defenseless, so when the police came in they had no problem grabbing me and leading me away.

My suspicion is that an informer had been trailing me, and told the police when I went to the house. Moss was overseas at the time, and his children were safe in the Transkei. (Moss was arrested right off the plane when he came home.) The national political situation was at the boiling point again, and a State of Emergency had been declared at 11:30 that very night. I think I was the first victim. It was a tough time to be imprisoned in South Africa.

The personal challenge

I was initially put in the Sandton police station, and then transferred after a few months to Johannesburg New Prison in Diepkloof, Soweto, which was popularly known as Sun City because of its external beauty. What is it like to be a prisoner? This was now the third time for me, so I was beginning to get used to it. Now, however, I was to spend almost three years inside.

In Sandton, I was placed in solitary confinement from 12 June 1986 until I went to Diepkloof in August. Sandton is worth describing in detail. You get only a bible to read, written in Afrikaans. You have no access to newspapers or even junk novels. The only soap is meant for cleaning horses, so I picked up quite a bad rash. There were no toiletries, no wash cloths, changes of clothes, combs—nothing.

From the first detention, I grew long dreadlocks that reached to my eyebrows, so when I was transferred to Diepkloof, not even a brush would return my hair to normal. As a result I was nicknamed "Rasta," and "Peter Tosh" in prison. The common-law Rasta prisoners, some on drug charges, would always address me in a funny dialect which I did not understand a word of, except something like "Ahoy Badroy," which is roughly "Hi Brother," in solidarity with others seen to be slaves. "No, I'm not a Rasta," I laughingly responded.

At my first court appearance in April 1987, my sister Nobantu wept because she knew my unkempt appearance reflected how hard things were. I finally organized a haircut after the cell committee made an appeal to the authorities to get scissors. That haircut was the longest and most difficult I've ever had! The police had to take new photographs of me, since they had only the dreadlocked Mayekiso on film.

During the early part of the detention I was denied visits to doctors and dentists, and only saw a state district surgeon who did not give me proper attention. He was really a policeman in doctor's garb. There was no one to treat the extreme headaches I began to get in that environment. The frustration and the feeling of loneliness in prison is intense. When the police move up and down the passage, the noises of jangling keys make you even more nervous.

The food was junk, a hard porridge of corn flour stirred once or twice and served with black tea. There was a bit of soybeans as well. Common-law white criminals got much better food. Some political detainees organized a hunger strike. At one point there were twenty-four of us, and the state doctor did nothing to help us.

That was the first time I went on hunger strike. We only consumed a bit of hot water with some sugar. After a week of this they conceded to our demands, and brought in eggs, bread, and soft porridge for breakfast, and some rice and meat for lunch and supper. But that incident led to my transferral to Diepkloof.

The boredom and loneliness were overwhelming in Sandton. Interrogations followed. I was not permitted to see any relatives or friends. Introspection led me, and other activists, to ask if we would ever work so hard in the struggle again. Many people are not strong enough to withstand this pressure, and turn. The police use them effectively to spy against their own comrades. We were sometimes suspicious of some of the comrades who came out early, for they acted very nervous. When we found these guys, we had to isolate them.

The interrogations often happened in the middle of the night, and always at Sandton. Even when I was based at Diepkloof, they would handcuff me tightly with arms behind my back and take me there in a Ford Sierra. The same treatment for movement was used even when I was going to the hospital.

During interrogations the death threats were regular, and the power of the cops seemed complete. They used the famous good cop, bad cop strategy. The senior officer would talk in a very appealing manner, warning of the bad guys working there. He would bring nice food, and try to make you feel at home. Then he would leave, and the bad cop would come in and manhandle you. I was told to stand up for an hour during one of the interrogations. Sometimes I was told to sit under a table when asked questions, but I would refuse.

We always had to consider carefully, of course, when it was feasible to resist interrogation. It was easier for me than for most, given the strong international solidarity campaign. For those who lacked the help of publicity, such tactics would have provoked harsh repercussions, including "slipping on a bar of soap" out of an eighth-floor window (the police explanation for several deaths-in-detention). And even when I resisted, the torture had a lasting effect. It was after when I returned to the cell and my comrades that I recovered, slowly, from the physical and psychological pressure.

Prison routines

In Sun City I was with other political prisoners sharing a single communal cell that held thirty-eight people. It was then that I met a large number of comrades from townships across the Johannesburg region. In general, we shared the same problems, but some of those detained were children as young as eight years old, and others were ordinary comrades, not from the leadership.

What was most remarkable, I think, was their transformation during their prison stay from untrained street activists into mature political thinkers, a process in which I was to play a role. We had to comfort many of the comrades who experienced the trauma of prison. We were foster parents to the young children, some of whom didn't even really realize they were in prison. Sometimes they would cry for their parents, but then would turn into normal happy children.

We had a roster for cleaning our communal cell, keeping our beds neat, and coming up with a code of conduct. Each cell elected a committee, composed of four comrades. My cell was named Luanda. We formed a catering committee, sports committee, and cultural committee. Knowing that our detention was for the long term, our aim was to transform the living conditions in prison so that we would all feel somewhat at home there.

We also had schedules where study groups in each cell would pick up topics and have regular discussions. Sometimes there were political disputes between those of differing progressive ideologies (mainly ANC and PAC), but it was generally good, constructive debate. The media committee would gather information about what was happening on a daily basis. We smuggled in books, including two volumes of Marx's *Capital*, plus some of Lenin's *Collected Works* and newspapers, and analyzed the news. We had to hide that material in the cell, and eventually negotiated that the police would not search us.

All of this was done on the basis of a rigorous timetable. The timetable began with wake-up at five-thirty in the morning. We proceeded to make beds, have a discussion, go to wash in the showers, sweep and polish the floor, open the windows to air our cell, and go to the kitchen and food kiosk. We bought food as a collective, and shared the preparation, eating, and clean up. Those who had no visitors, food packages, or outside support participated equally, which helped us develop our socialist consciousness (Sipho Kubeka popularized this using the term *umadlandawonye*, roughly meaning collective sensibility). Breakfast was normally porridge, milk, and two slices of bread. The prison food, which was not nourishing, was supplemented with better food bought from the kiosk with money collected from the comrades. Groceries were kept in lockers and the catering committees would dish out food. All the dishes were then collected and washed. As usual we emphasized the sharing of responsibilities.

We were permitted outside to exercise for forty-five minutes each morning, and we used the time for our own general meetings of all political prisoners. Initially, the authorities did not want us all to go together to the prison playing fields, but we won that right. Coming back, we had our lunch—fish, meat, pork, bread, and cooked corn—and then we were locked up in the cells from three in the afternoon for the rest of the day.

At three each afternoon, we had a discussion in our cell about the situation outside, built around analyzing the news. We usually sent a comrade to the prison clinic, or, if he was very ill, to a hospital outside the prison, where a few sympathetic doctors would give us newspapers to be smuggled back into the cell. And we would communicate to our families to use the hospital as means of getting further information about the situation outside.

Each day one comrade would chair and open the discussion. We would then come up with a suggested program of action to change the political landscape outside. After this we would have supper. Again, the comrades were divided into sub-groups, which would share their supper equally. We would then go back to the discussions, or have a meeting on how our prison strategies were progressing.

We would often encourage talented comrades to compose plays and songs, which we practiced in the evenings and performed on special days, sometimes during exercise times. Songs composed in prison were then sent outside. A poet like Jackie Seroke, now a Pan African Congress (PAC) leader, would read his work. There was also occasional recreation, as the prison made available games like Monopoly and chess. There were a few approved books around, about Cold War spies. I recall that in these books the CIA was featured as a heroic force. We read them lightheartedly and added our own more critical analysis, of course.

All our days would rotate in that manner. We would commemorate important days like 16 June, May Day, 16 December (Umkhonto Day), Mandela's birthday, 26 June (Freedom Charter Day), and 12 January (ANC founding). Once we even celebrated Karl Marx's birthday. Certain comrades were assigned to work out programs and presentations to educate and to sing freedom songs. It was a lively time.

Prison struggles

But I am misleading if it seems like we had an easy time in prison. There were many negative effects. For example, the authorities would introduce some people into our cells who had never been activists. Some were criminals, and others were simple people who would break under the pressure, missing home, girlfriends, friends, and the niceties of life outside. Some even refused to participate in the collective prison struggles.

Everyone was encouraged to feel at home by participating. The promotion of the collective approach may have been rigid, but I think it was good. Sun City became known as "The University." Some of the ordinary prisoners who came in for a short period—fourteen days or so—received our special attention. They were quickly refined into comrades who would respect politics, and even into hard-core activists who would work in the movement outside in our absence.

Nevertheless, some of the prisoners tried to stage coups against well-established cell structures. One example occurred in my cell, where a group began smoking dagga, which we discouraged in the prison. Dagga was often used by the regime to set up comrades for drug busts. In fact, the whole comrade community banned it, once our own analysis of the potential dangers was clear, and this caused a minor rebellion in our cell.

One group of prisoners with us was not political. They respected us in some matters, but occasionally refused to obey collective orders. Some evenings they went to the toilets to smoke, and were then called in to disciplinary hearings. But at one point this grouping became very strong. After a whole night smoking in the loo, they returned, changed the name of the cell from Luanda to Jamaica, and plastered to the door an insignia someone had drawn: a handsome Rastaman relaxing with a joint under a tree.

That particular coup was a great threat, since it represented a psychological breakdown of sorts. We felt we had to impose discipline at this point, which consisted of both lectures and rough threats. We eventually persuaded the Rastafarian group through reason to change their ways.

But other more sinister attempts were made to break our unity. Some guys in the cell confessed that they had been sent by the security police to eavesdrop on certain comrades. We had to interrogate them to learn from them, and then turn them into real comrades who were able to understand the situation.

And there were also fierce struggles against the bureaucracy of the prison. One official procedure was to strip incoming prisoners, a humiliating, dehumanizing experience for the comrades. We won that struggle, as part of a package of demands we made at one point.

Other struggles occurred around issues of food, dirty blankets, and the lack of soap and other cleaning materials. We even agreed to clean the kitchens, to safeguard our health. We went as far as taking over dishing out food, because certain non-political prisoners did not seem to be in solidarity with us.

We did, however, influence many prisoners to become political activists. Even some black guards were recruited to our point of view. They would then communicate information to lawyers, and bring in new information and news. This was especially helpful when we had to make important decisions, such as going on hunger strike.

The white guards and other prison officials wanted us to respect them. For example, we were meant to fall in line outside our cells in the early hours each morning, and again in the early evening. We refused to go outside again, and took no notice of the guards. If they wanted to count us, they would have to do it when we were inside the cells. This was a great insult, and some guards tried to beat us up. We fought back, and on one occasion I was put into a tiny, freezing isolation cell for a week; the same happened to Richard Mdakane. Other comrades immediately went on a solidarity hunger strike until we were released from isolation.

Life in the prison was hard for some, and there were suicide attempts. Some of those who tried to kill themselves were good activists, but the pressure of long periods behind bars was immense. Suicide was sometimes attempted with the white polish used to clean the cells, which was stolen and injected into the veins. Others would take huge doses of tablets all at once. Once a comrade learned that his mother had died, and in a very upset state of mind he went to the top of the second bunk and tried to electrocute himself on the electricity line to the light bulb. No one actually died, though. Prison was extremely frustrating. Some even regretted participating in the struggle, and were never activists again after that.

Building the movement from inside
We soon realized the need to build our political resources beyond the barrier of our own cell. There were three to four cells on each floor, and so a section

committee representing around twelve cells on each side of the prison emerged. There were six floors, the bottom two of which were for criminal prisoners. We opened the windows when we needed to have general meetings of all prisoners. The police knew we had the network within the prison, and were not happy about it.

Whenever someone new came, we had a meeting to welcome them. Among those who did time in our cells were Murphy Morobe, Valli Moosa, Amos Masondo, Zwelakhe Sisulu, Vusi Khanyile, and many other big names of the 1980s struggle. (White prisoners such as Raymond Suttner were in other cells, segregated in a different section of the prison.) We emphasized the need to have the best comrades scattered throughout the cells, so as to create a more balanced spread of political leadership.

In prison, there was always time to think back. Introspection led us to question whether this or that act was the right thing. The whole experience was aimed at this, so our response was to ensure political unity. Even when we were in isolation cells, we could empty the toilet of water and then talk among ourselves. We sat on the seat as if we were relieving ourselves, and then leaned down to talk. We called this the telephone. It was especially important to communicate after interrogation sessions, and this gave us the capacity to act uniformly.

Part of our movement-building work was to smuggle out letters to our lawyers, family, and the international community. We actually used the uniformed police to smuggle the letters out. Back at the Sandton jail, for example, some of those serving as police were blacks from Alexandra who had been driven out during the days of isolation. Surprisingly, some of those guys were in fact cooperative with me, perhaps because they wanted to normalize their relations with the residents. They were living in deplorable conditions in tent shacks a few kilometers from Alex, and would come to me when there were no white policemen around, and try to prove their innocence or the circumstances that forced them to join.

It was a time to try to organize them. I asked them to buy paper and envelopes, and to give my letters in a sealed envelope to a particular address. It worked. The letters were delivered unopened, and responses would also come back through them. Along with donations by doctors, this was another route by which we acquired newspapers, which we then smuggled throughout the prison.

In contrast, white policemen at both Sandton and Diepkloof remained thoroughly racist. They did not even want to talk to us, because their indoctrination about "communist" detainees intent on destroying the country was very powerful. Some of the black police had the same reactionary attitudes, but others were understanding because they themselves had no rights. (Even a junior white constable considered himself superior to a senior black police officer.) The idea of getting black police to consider a union then grew, and these discussions spread so as to lay the basis for the eventual founding of the POPCRU union.

The security police had the most powers of all, and were feared by the uniformed police. If the black police were discovered to be communicating with us, it was the security police who would expel or detain them. Some of the white security cops were notorious for their cruelty in treating political detainees. This is well known.

Charged for treason

The trials and tribulations of prison life continued through early 1987, and our resistance became more sophisticated. But once the charges were filed for the Alexandra activism, I was transferred from the "F" Section of Diepkloof to the "D" Section. Instead of just State of Emergency detainees, we now kept company with ANC and PAC guerrillas who were also charged as political prisoners. Ten units of the ANC army Umkhonto we Sizwe and one PAC/Azanian Peoples Liberation Army unit served time in D Section. D became a holding section, because after sentencing political prisoners were moved to another prison.

My other comrades from Alexandra were now close at hand. Richard Mdakane and I had first met in the struggle in early 1986, and quickly became close through our work. We had both been arrested on 22 May, locked up at Sandton, and released at the same time. So we were familiar with the ropes.

But when I was arrested in June, Richard and I were separated. We met, almost by accident, in Diepkloof, where we ended up in the same cell. Meanwhile, Moss and Obed Bapela were kept in the police prison at John Vorster Square for the first six months (the second half of 1986), and were then moved to Diepkloof.

We were never beaten up, partly because of the high level of publicity, and partly because the charges were so severe we would likely get a death sentence if convicted, so the regime felt it was applying sufficient psychological pressure. Physically we were safe, but psychologically the solitary confinement was a harsh experience.

I was finally charged, on 15 April 1987, with the crimes of treason, subversion, and sedition. This followed by about three months the charging of the other four treason trialists: Moss, Richard, Obed, and Paul Tshabalala. Around this time, eight other AYCO comrades were charged for the same crimes. In the early stages of their case, however, treason charges were dropped and the prosecution focused instead on relatively mild people's court and anti-crime campaign activities. The Alexandra Eight were found guilty of sedition and sentenced to prison by Judge Grosskopf in September 1988, even though they expressed remorse and conceded that what they had done in making Alex ungovernable was wrong.

In our case, the Johannesburg magistrate decided that the charges were so grave that he must refer them to the Supreme Court. The five of us were targeted because of our high positions in the AAC. Moss was chairperson, Paul was deputy chair, Obed was publicity secretary, Richard was general secretary, and I was organizer.

The police wanted to capture the entire executive board of the AAC, but they missed Mapule Morare, the treasurer. She was a very active, strong comrade who was in hiding. An intense police search failed to locate her. Another comrade they missed was Naude Moitse, who was detained in May, released, and then managed to skip outside the country to join the ANC military.

When the charges were levelled, we knew the implications: the death sentence, or the possibility of a long-term imprisonment. We were conscious of the consequences. Yet the whole idea of being sentenced by an apartheid court for struggles against an abhorrent system was a tragic farce. As administrators of an inhuman system, they had no right to try us.

The lead defense attorneys were Norman Manoim and Amanda Armstrong from the firm Cheadle, Thomson and Haysom. The senior advocate was David Soggott, and the junior counsel was Nicky de Vos. The four of them made an extremely strong team.

From jail, we were involved from the outset in putting together the strategy. It was the most democratic kind of legal experience, for we felt part of the whole process. It was an extraordinary piece of teamwork.

The preparations included almost daily consultations. It took a long time to build the trust between us all, and we went through some fights over strategy. At times we prisoners felt that we would have to sacrifice our principles in order to win acquittal. But in the end we worked through those issues and found a harmonious approach.

On trial

Our trial began on 19 October 1987, in the Supreme Court, in a courtroom located in central Johannesburg. We were alleged to have planned to overthrow the state by violent means. We were alleged to have been part and parcel of the ANC/SACP onslaught. We were alleged to have planned to make Alexandra ungovernable through people's courts and the yard committee system, which subjected the residents to our whims.

The truth of the matter, of course, was that we organized so as to make people independent, so they could arrive at clear decisions that served their own interests. In essence, that was all we were doing. And we were happy to try to show that this was the case in court.

When the trial started, Justice van der Walt had to decide whether he wanted assessors (advocates or other prominent legal people) to come to the trial to back up his decisions. If the trial warranted a death sentence, two would be needed, so the judge would not be alone. On the opening day, van der Walt said he had read the opening indictment, and then decided that there was no need for assessors. That was very good news from the beginning, for it was an indication that we would not receive the death sentence.

Right from the outset we knew that international support would be crucial. The International Jurist Committee of Ten was set up to monitor our case at the behest of the United Auto Workers (UAW) in the United States. The UAW was the sister union of our Metal and Allied Workers' Union (MAWU). After the trial started, MAWU merged with other unions in the motor sector to form the National Union of Metalworkers of South Africa (NUMSA). Moss was named the first NUMSA general secretary while still in prison.

UAW president Owen Bieber and his associate Don Stillman tried to visit us in prison but were denied access. The UAW rallied other unions across the world, including the Trades Union Council in Britain. However, things were not so smooth in London. It was saddening to hear that there was an actual campaign against our case underway in Britain by misguided exiled comrades from within the South African Congress of Trade Unions. SACTU London representative Zola Zembe and some like-minded comrades persuaded the Anti-Apartheid Movement in Britain, which was among the world's strongest human rights organizations, not to take our case seriously, using the argument that the Mayekiso treason trial promoted personality cults. There were also insinuations that Moss was a "workerist," and yet the rest of us came from the Congress of South African Students and other groups from the Congress tradition, which always held the Freedom Charter banner very high.

Despite this, most informed trade unionists across the world provided excellent solidarity. And there was also a "City Group" of activists in London, a collection of leftists and others outside the mainstream of the Anti-Apartheid Movement, who also campaigned seriously. In our view, we were not sectarian about our supporters, and did not do a litmus test of people's ideologies, as long as they were sympathetic to the fight against apartheid. Our ideology as activists within South Africa was very important to us, but for our international comrades the common denominator we demanded was simply a thoroughgoing opposition to apartheid.

To show that our solidarity was non-sectarian, we also welcomed the presence in the trial of ambassadors from Reagan's United States administration (Edward Perkins) and Thatcher's Britain (Robin Renwick). And we knew that the primary reason they came day after day was the power of their citizens to keep the anti-apartheid struggle on the local agenda, and to demand continual press and official updates on our situation.

It was an amazing experience to feel the rumble of the working-class movement in so many places across the world. It was precisely that campaign which made an impact on van der Walt. Van der Walt was seen as a *verligte* judge (an enlightened Afrikaner), and I suspect he was also able to understand the need to neutralize that international pressure against South African apartheid.

Testimony begins

The trial began on 19 October and lasted into December. It was the time to stand up before the judge, take the oath, face the allegations that could lead to our deaths, and tell our side of the story. The defense team interviewed many of the residents responsible for building AAC structures, including youth. They tried to interview everyone, and invited many people to testify.

The police searched high and low for people to turn sellout and strengthen their case. Not a single AAC executive member was seduced, however. The hunt for witnesses continued, and the state found a few residents who had attended people's courts, which was the heart of the case against us.

For example, Willie Khumalo, who was a council employee and later became town clerk of Alex, came forward as state's witness. But Khumalo had been an active AAC yard representative in early 1986, and in fact testified in our favor. His testimony failed to implicate us in anything anti-social, but it does show how powerful the security forces were in getting people to switch allegiance.

The state opened the trial with a parade of witnesses. They began with white and Indian businesspeople from Wynberg, Marlboro, Bramley, and Kew. We knew some of the guys, because they were specific targets of the consumer boycott. They testified that youths came and forced them to close, intimidated customers, and inflicted heavy financial losses. Some black businesspeople also came to testify, from establishments like Mielie's, Freddy's, and Goldie's Hair Salon.

The quality of state's witnesses was low, and most of them failed to implicate us directly. There was only one extremely nasty incident. One guy, clearly intimidated by the police, alleged that Paul Tshabalala told him he should be necklaced. The defense quickly demonstrated that this witness could not be trusted. That was the only person who was dangerously off the mark.

Nearly all the testimony from other state witnesses reflected the chaos and disorder in the community, implicitly indicting apartheid as the cause. Some state witnesses even described how harmonious things were at the high point of AAC organizing in early 1986. They talked in an angry mood about the police in the township. These were not incriminating statements against the AAC.

In Alex today, I occasionally see some of the policemen that testified against me. Indeed, some of them subsequently arrested me again. They must have a long-term grudge that, hard as the apartheid state tried, it was impossible to break our activist spirit. Yet even the police could not testify to particular crimes by the AAC leadership. They just made general statements about the killings, necklacings, and so forth, but had no information about who was present. Their point was that whatever was happening was inspired by us. It was a conspiracy theory that had room for every kind of anti-social activity. The state even brought in Brigadier Herman Stadler, who testified about how ungovernability fit the ANC/SACP revolutionary program.

The prosecution's case was junk. The state became foolish in its desperation to prove the charges. In our defense we also had expert witnesses, such as Professors Colin Bundy and Belinda Bozolli. Steve Burger, the

Alexandra administrator, provided testimony favorable to the defense. Ricky Valente of Sandton was also a creditable defense witness. Father Cairnes from the Catholic Church in Alexandra, a social worker named Refilwe Mashigo, and other professionals also endorsed us. Mashigo explained our yard committee organizing: "When you are apathetic, when you feel that life won't ever change, you need someone to shake you and if that person comes with clear ideas and you see the steps and you are aware that maybe if I am involved I can also bring a change in it and if it has worked somewhere let me try it."

Our case was well planned from the beginning. We realized that any mistake on the stand could be fatal, literally. I took a personal interest, because when I was at school I had ambitions to become a lawyer. After failing my exams, however, I couldn't go further. I was infatuated with the law. Mandela, Tambo, and Hani were all lawyers. We understood the great need for more progressive lawyers to represent the very poor.

But I do not feel that way any more, because there are so many good lawyers supporting activists, and in any case the constraints are so great to being a radical stuck within the system. The constraints mean you have to manipulate—not reject—the racist, sexist, or capitalist laws. If the radical's principle is to overthrow an unjust system of government, which is clearly an illegal act, then radical lawyers must be very well attuned to those constraints in order, at best, only to weaken that system from the inside. The radical's strategy here would merely be to get as many activists as possible out of trouble with the legal system, so that they could do more to overthrow it from the outside. Instead of going further into law, I opted for a career in city and regional planning, where there are fewer African specialists and which, as a civic activist, I believe is more urgently needed to build a just future for South Africa.

By the time I testified in the treason trial, I was the last defendant. So many witnesses had gone before me, including the four other accused. The defense questioned me initially, followed by cross-examination by the state. I was ready, having been well-schooled during the trial, listening and learning all the time. Our preparations with the lawyers were rigorous. Like an actor who learned the role, I knew what to expect.

In the Supreme Court the judge intervenes from time to time. I was cross-examined by junior counsel van Staden. He did a good job in turning over stones, but I was able to respond effectively. Questions from the state that were irritating and ignorant were meant to provoke me into becoming a martyr for the cause, and it took great discipline to avoid angry responses.

Out of prison

Thanks to the international pressure, we were all released on bail before the trial was actually finished, on 12 December 1988. We had to pay a total of R30,000, and we faced severe restrictions. In effect we were taken out of a small apartheid dungeon and put back into the bigger prison, South Africa. We could not be in the company of more than ten people. We could not address the press. We could not organize. We were prevented from going home to the Transkei. Indeed, we could not go beyond the magisterial area of Johannesburg, and we could not go on even a visit to Alexandra. We reported daily between 8 a.m. and 1 p.m. to the Hillbrow Police Station, not far from the center of Johannesburg.

We lived in high-rise buildings on Hillbrow's busy Pretoria Street, Moss in the Highpoint apartment complex and the rest of us at Nedbank Plaza. The cosmopolitan, big-city neighborhood of Hillbrow was not yet officially desegregated, but there were many so-called Indians, colored people, and Africans living there illegally. The judge's intent in ordering us to report to Hillbrow was so that the police could visit us from time to time.

Imagine. You have been in quarantine for three years, then released to a slightly less restrictive quarantine where you must police yourself. Once very early in the morning, the cops came to check up on me, banging loudly on the door and swearing in Afrikaans. I was so distrustful of their intentions that I climbed out the second floor window to get away, carefully scaling my way down the gutter pipe, only returning to confront the unwelcome visitors when I had the building's security personnel with me. They swore some more but then left me alone.

In addition to this type of harassment, my personal feeling, for the first time ever, was that of a social reject. After so long behind bars, it took me quite a while before I felt like part of society. We were still, after all, subject to potential conviction on charges of high treason, and this made even close comrades wary of being seen with us.

We tried to build up our lives again, slowly but surely. In March 1989, Richard and I began studies at Khanya College. At that point the judge allowed us to go into classrooms with more than ten people. I studied sociology and African history. That was a great experience for both of us, especially after the long isolation.

Grateful as we were to be out of jail and able to study, we believed we had to break the conditions of release. In early 1989 on four occasions late at night, I went to Alexandra to visit highly trusted comrades. We needed to get a full debriefing about township events, discussing and analyzing the way forward for our movement. Since we were not sure if we would be spending a long period in prison, given the seriousness of the charges, we had to take the risk of seeing our comrades again.

Then, on 23 April 1989, we went back to court for the final time. A new era was about to dawn, in which Alexandra Township would again find itself at the cutting edge of struggle and social change, this time in the interregnum—the painful, ever uncertain transition—between apartheid and liberation.

PART 3
ALEXANDRA IN THE INTERREGNUM

7
Back to the Streets and the Struggle (1989-1990)

The trial and our imprisonment finally ended. But we found that over time the situation in South Africa had become more fluid, and the township organizing challenges more complex. Nevertheless, the security forces and the local apartheid councilors remained the obvious targets. We found that our militancy had not waned during the prison years, nor had our willingness to take even life-threatening risks. And the regime's repressive arm continued to flex, long after the liberation movement parties were unbanned in 1990.

The verdict

Located on busy Pritchard Street, the Supreme Court, opulent inside with marble and glowing hardwood, is normally intimidating. My experience in many visits there had been that the court's deathly silence was only momentarily interrupted by the proceedings in our trial and by other court business. The power of the law was suffocating, or at least that was how it had seemed to someone facing a possible death sentence. The place was like preparation for the mortuary.

But on the day of our judgment, 23 April 1989, the court was transformed. The verdict was awaited by comrades in their thousands, and the courtroom overflowed. People refused to stand for the judge, and instead shouted at him. It was only when the accused entered the courtroom that the people all stood. We did not know what to expect.

Judge van der Walt took fifteen minutes to deliver his verdict. Among his comments were, "In the spectrum of politics of our citizens—from black to white and from far left to far right, with their grievances and aspirations, in most cases legitimate—most of these citizens are just striving for a better South Africa."

As van der Walt spoke, the mood gradually changed. Our supporters gradually realized that the verdict was going to be in our favor. From anger and disparagement of the judge, the sentiment turned to interest, engagement. People listened with growing respect. Judge van der Walt instantly acquired a new nickname: "Comrade Judge." The verdict was acquittal.

People streamed outside and began toyi-toyi-ing and singing freedom songs. The Central Methodist Church, across the street from the Supreme Court, quickly filled to capacity. The entire Khanya student body was there. NUMSA shop stewards and members from as far as Natal had come, and workers from all over Johannesburg turned out. There were representatives from the UAW in the United States and the Trades Union Council in England.

And not to be forgotten, the riot police also showed up, intimidating people and provoking small skirmishes. The international press put a spotlight on the whole event. After the party atmosphere on the street, the press conference at NUMSA's head office emphasized our resolve to resume organizing civic structures in Alexandra where we had left off in 1986. As leaders returning from apartheid jails, we were now ready to call upon the community to begin reactivating the civic structures. And we conceded that although there was great relief among us, it was also a time of anger.

Our anger was based on having spent three years in prison for nothing. On the one hand, this had been the most important treason trial since the Rivonia Treason Trial in which Nelson Mandela was convicted. It had kept South Africa in the sights of the international legal and human rights community for many months. On the other hand, police and vigilante harassment had certainly made their mark on us. Even the celebrations and gatherings to welcome us back to Alex in late April were banned by the police.

It was clear that the courts had failed to uphold the work of the security apparatus in this instance, but this fact would never prevent the state's death squads and vigilantes from trying to assassinate us. We assessed the dangers of returning to activism, deciding that while we would dedicate ourselves during the daylight hours, it was too risky to actually move back to Alexandra to stay at night. Our fears were proven to be valid, as Moss continued to find his name on hit lists exposed by the press. Moss was provided bodyguards once he took up his general secretary position in NUMSA. I felt it safer to stay in Hillbrow for another year, until mid-1990, and then went back to live in Alex (until in early 1991, and then I returned to Hillbrow when Alex again became more dangerous).

Nevertheless, all the other shackles of staying penned up in Hillbrow and central Johannesburg, and reporting daily to the police, were now removed. It was a license to return to work. Kombi taxis full of residents from Alex came to fetch us immediately after the trial. Back in the township finally without fear of immediate police persecution, I was elated. For the first time in nearly three years, we were free to continue our struggle.

Same problems, under changing conditions

The strains of going to Alex regularly and being a full-time Khanya student began to take their toll, but I felt I could not leave the township work. Conditions in Alex remained desperate in 1989, and in the vacuum left by the AAC leadership, nothing much had arisen to challenge the authorities.

For example, a 1988 comeback by the Alex Civic Association, Mike Beea's group, had ended as a joke. The ACA disintegrated completely when Beea attempted to conditionally endorse the Black Local Authority elections in October 1988. His attempt to participate in the elections led even the ACA vice-chair, Mack Lekota, to call Beea an "opportunist." Beea responded that Lekota had not bothered to attend meetings for five months, and Lekota rebutted by saying neither had Beea come to meetings following his release from a year's detention. The two finally buried the hatchet in order to hold a mass meeting to canvass community support for an election campaign. But only fifty-eight people attended, including nine candidates for the Alex Council. When some of the candidates praised Alex administrator Steve Burger, they had gone overboard and were immediately heckled by the crowd. Then Beea was forced to turn against the candidates, saying, "They have created a monster that is going to destroy them." The ACA was formally disbanded and restructured by a Joint Working Committee of UDF groups.

Press conference after our release from detention, April 1989. From left to right: Paul Tshabalala, Sipho Kubeka, me, and Richard Mdakane. *Photo courtesy of the* Star, *Johannesburg.*

In the wake of this kind of confusion, the re-launch of the AAC was going to take time. The street-level structures would first have to be back in smooth operation. Aside from the 1986 veterans, who had retained their old positions in the interim period, the AAC leadership had co-opted other activists to move into vacancies. Our goal was to launch a new, democratic civic by December 1989.

Rebuilding the civic movement in Alex required us to come to grips with the issues again. Problems such as transport and housing were still extreme, even if the form they took had changed and conditions had become more complex.

For example, the PUTCO bus company was having major problems on its Alexandra route, ranging from driver trade union activity to customer hostility and competition from the kombi taxis. Even worse, though, taxi wars were getting very hot. Rivalries had been intense for a couple of years, but by early 1989 the turf battles over routes and taxi ranks were claiming the lives of drivers, passengers, and bystanders.

Before our detention, the civic had worked well with the taxi owners and drivers, who were quite progressive when it came to civic and political struggles, assisting in getting our comrades in and out of the township to meetings and conferences, and helping with financial donations (indeed, historically, apartheid transport policies were often aimed at punishing black taxi entrepreneurs when they played a progressive role). But when we emerged from prison, we found that the taxi association had split into two. It was rumored that the neo-apartheid Joint Management Centre, which now oversaw township security, was behind the split, but there were also structural problems, especially the tendency of unregulated free markets to lead to ruinous competition. Engineering a split when conditions were so desperate would not have been too difficult. The way this appeared to ordinary people was chilling, with assassins wearing balaclavas and dustcoats, plastic bags covering their guns so as not to lose empty cartridges. It was a new level of mafioso sophistication, beyond the normal violence of tsotsis and cops.

Attempts by the Alexandra Council to put the two factions back together in March 1989 failed. Minister of Law and Order Adriaan Vlok did not respond to urgent requests by taxi operators to end intimidation at the taxi ranks.

The Council had been resurrected in 1988, when voters boycotted the polls and a motley crew of unopposed puppet councilors was installed. They were still very unpopular. Agnes Pooe, an elderly former nursing sister who became mayor, complained in a confidential discussion early in March 1989, that she "was perturbed by the fact that the Council was elected on 26 October 1988 and had been in office for four months without making any substantial contribution in the interest of the community." According to Council minutes, "She considered four long months had expired without any noticeable achievement." At least that point we agreed on.

Finally, with the threat of AAC reorganization, the Council moved into action. One of their first activities was to remove hundreds of shack dwellers by force in the weeks immediately following our release in April 1989. Official estimates were that 10,300 families were living in shacks, and the Council had 7,000 families on its housing waiting list.

One day in May, as winter began, sixty-five shacks were razed on Eighth Avenue, including that of Buzizwe Mbatha and his sixteen-month-old daughter. Mbatha told the press: "We were both in the house when household stuff started flying. A stainless steel pot hit the baby on the head. I was very furious. Later the shack was burnt down. This is the humiliation we have to live with in the urban areas. I wouldn't have come here if I was not desperate for work. I cannot go back home because my family will starve. I have tried to get a decent, legal place to stay but all was in vain."

This experience was typical. In fact, the Alex Council had quite a record of winter evictions. In May 1988, town clerk Piet Genis had requested that the unwilling manager of the Springbok Patrols security firm evict 200 families from a private Springboks hostel that the Council was trying to buy. A few months later, Genis tried to move 1,500 people to the Vaal triangle before running into protests, saying, "The Council is aware that most of the squatters work around Johannesburg, but we could only get them land in Evaton." The Alex Council even hired Del Kevan, a notorious Progressive Federal Party politician (once party chair in the Randburg Council), who also worked for Soweto Council as housing director. A "hardliner" who insisted on evicting residents during rent boycotts, she was blamed for the deaths of twenty-seven Soweto residents in 1987 when municipal police used violence to carry out her orders. Her Randburg house was later bombed and she quit the Soweto job to work in Alexandra.

The Alexandra Action Committee realized that the housing issue would have to be the basis for a major campaign. During our three-year absence, the township had expanded by one hundred hectares onto the East Bank of the Jukskei River and a new residential development had been established, but this was kept off-limits to squatters. Our leadership released a statement immediately: "The constant violence by the Alexandra Council against the people is abhorrent and not acceptable. The people of Alexandra are entitled to decent treatment and proper accommodation."

On the ground, the shack dwellers' spirits were not broken. One resident, Simon Hlope, told the newspapers, "We are sleeping in the open and share facilities with those whose shacks are still standing in the vast squatting camp. They want to move us to make way for the building of houses which we cannot afford. But we will not be lured by empty promises of Zozo huts or Orange Farm." Orange Farm is an apartheid site-and-service city sixty kilometers southwest of Alexandra, designed to grow to the size of Soweto by pulling people from illegal settlements across the Johannesburg area. There are, as in many such dumping grounds in South Africa, very few jobs nearby, and transport to Johannesburg is expensive.

Many residents of shacks refused to move to Orange Farm, and this was one of the acts that suggested a renewal of grassroots confidence now that

AAC leaders had been released and the organization was being revitalized. Even those who did move told us that they had been forced to go after signing papers that they did not understand. Meanwhile, construction of housing for the middle class on the East Bank was continuing, and a golf course was being planned for the buffer area between the East Bank and the white residential area of Lombardy East.

The East Bank therefore continued to be the focus of the state's divide-and-rule strategy. As Moss remarked, "When I was acquitted, the people of East Bank were warned, 'Mayekiso is out. You are now in trouble, because he will attack you with his comrades.' They locked their doors. These people were fearful, and it takes time to reassure them."

The Council embarked on a second housing strategy through its "Committee on Privatisation, Housing and Trading," led by Councilor Prince Mokoena, who would play a major role in Alex politics over the next few years. Mokoena and Burger—now termed the Council "advisors" but still acting as administrators—attempted to sell some of Alexandra's formal houses to the residents. But each house contained four or five families, and backyard rooms and shacks hosted another dozen or more families. So the formal transfer of these properties to a single owner was extremely divisive. As the AAC commented to the press, "The Alex people believe this is a plot by the authorities to counter the rent boycott and to create conflict among the residents. People are now being pushed by the new standowners to pay rent."

At this point, the AAC estimated that 1,000 shacks were being constructed each month in Alexandra by incoming residents. We launched an "Affordable Housing for All" campaign in June, and met Mama Pooe and her councilors, but to no effect. When we asked why valuable land on the East Bank was going to be used as a golf course, the written official reply was, "'All work and no play makes Johnny a dull boy' so goes the adage. It would be bad planning to develop a residential area without providing the necessary recreational facilities.... Surely, residents of Alexandra deserve such facilities. Don't you think so?" The Council neglected to tell us about a 1988 letter from the Johannesburg City Council, which insisted that, if its land was to be sold to Alexandra for housing, then the golf course buffer zone must be developed as a first priority.

Given such attitudes, it dawned on us how much work still had to be done to develop the issues and come up with concrete alternatives, and also to build our popular base so that the Council would pale into insignificance.

Back to organizing

The experience of being a student was only a partial one, given all the developments in Alex. But many students demanded that I become the general secretary of the Students' Representative Council at Khanya College, and after the acquittal the demands grew stronger. Under pressure I took up the post, and served for five months, trying to develop democracy and a critical, dynamic political analysis within the student movement. Students came from many different backgrounds, and there were plenty of ideological contests.

For example, I was challenged by one clique led by the publicity officer of the Students' Representative Council, who was purportedly Khanya's leading authority on Marxism. He and one of his allies from the old Alexandra Youth Congress constantly accused Moss, Richard Mdakane, and me of being "ultra-left" workerists. This forced us to revisit socialist theory, and to develop our position that self-organization of the working class could occur not only in factories but in our communities. Our civic politics position usually won the debates. The Khanya students, after all, came from poor and working-class communities themselves.

Yet because of the ivory-tower nature of many Khanya debates, student politics were sometimes frustrating, and my heart was still in the community. In Alexandra in mid-1989 we helped build the Mass Defiance campaign—now called the Mass Democratic Movement, or simply MDM (essentially a revival of the UDF plus COSATU). With our Affordable Housing for All campaign, we were quickly confronted by appalling living conditions across the township. As a result, rejuvenation of organizational structures proceeded well. The security forces still active in Alexandra and other townships were not happy about all of this, but did not have a clear idea of how to respond.

For example, we had a clean-up campaign in August which gained great support. The police harassed anything that had a political smell, but a clean-up campaign was relatively innocent. The State of Emergency was still in effect, but in spite of a heavy police presence, people came out in far greater numbers than they had a couple of weeks earlier for a staged, half-hearted police-led clean up. Ours was joined by a famous participant, Winnie Mandela, and the press reported that her involvement represented political rehabilitation, after the MDM leadership distanced themselves (and the MDM) from her in the wake of the tragic death of Stompie Moeketsi and other controversies.

The MDM's condemnation of Winnie was not popular on the ground, among the small but powerful layer of activists who represented the main contact with the masses. MDM leaders had not bothered to canvass either activists or the people in mass meetings, and in Alexandra Winnie continued to be seen by many as a heroine. Her clean-up invitation by the AAC executive board, following canvassing in our ranks, was an indication that the MDM resolution was not widely supported. Murphy Morobe, the UDF publicity secretary who was Winnie's most vocal MDM critic, was also invited to the clean up, but did not come.

The clean-up campaign was a great success. It was supported by the whole student body of Khanya, following an all-campus vote. An army of soldiers followed behind the cleaning teams with cameras, intimidating the crowd. We picked up trash, and sung freedom songs to draw people back to our fold. The police correctly analyzed this as a political tactic, and they didn't want it to succeed. But it was the rebirth of civic politics in Alexandra, and after three years behind bars, nothing would prevent us from building grassroots organization.

Another arrest

The police clamped down on our organizing in September 1989, so once again we went into hiding. The police came to our decaying flats on Pretoria Street in Hillbrow (Nedbank Plaza), where all the treason trialists except Moss were staying. Paul and Obed were caught, but Richard and I went underground, living in different suburbs of Johannesburg, avoiding school for a week, wearing disguises, trying to avoid the cops. We got used to the lifestyle of outlaws in late 1989. Obed was even the target of a firebombing attack when he was staying with our lawyer Norman Manoim and *Weekly Mail* co-editor Irwin Manoim in nearby Yeoville. We faced exams under this sort of pressure in November, but they went okay.

At the end of November, the police finally caught us. We had tried three times to have mass marches in Alexandra to protest the councilors, but the magistrate and police banned each one. (Council minutes recorded that the councilors "were afraid of the consequences of the protest march, which could lead to a bloodbath.") On the third rejection, on Saturday, 30 November, the growing civic movement decided to defy the banning. A large crowd came to the stadium for the march, at around 9 a.m., but the police intervened and sent people home.

Nevertheless, we regrouped at the Eighth Avenue Anglican Church, and organized an impromptu meeting where we decided to march up to the shops at Pan Africa Centre, on the border of Alex and Wynberg. At 10 a.m. we arrived, and attracted by the growing crowd, the police now gathered and quickly cordoned off the route to the Council. We had aimed to be at the Council offices by noon. By 11 a.m. nearly a thousand residents had already massed at Pan Africa.

At that point I stood up to give a speech, and decried the terrible living conditions, once again pushing the demands for the councilors to resign. The toyi-toyi, freedom songs, and protest chants were getting louder. By now the press had flocked in, yet senior officials from John Vorster Police Station took no notice of the cameras and ordered the cops to respond with a show of force. After my speech, the cops were instructed to place me under arrest. Interrupting an interview with the press, the police grabbed me.

The crowd surged and tried to pull me back. A scuffle broke out, and rubber bullets, birdshot, and tear gas were fired. Everyone sat down, refusing to move. Paul Tshabalala, Richard, and the trade unionist Sipho Kubheka (general secretary of Paper, Printing and Allied Workers Union) were also arrested. A serious fight began, and the police finally pushed the residents out of the area.

Hardball prison tactics

Later that day, in custody once again at Sandton Police Station, we began a hunger strike (my third). Along with Paul, I also decided to try a water strike to dramatize the problems we faced in our desire to conduct simple anti-apartheid protests.

The first day I was starving, and desperate for water. By the third day I couldn't feel anything. Weakness set in. I couldn't stand upright, or walk even a short distance. Walking from my cell to the interrogation office, a short distance away, I had to balance myself against the wall to stop from falling.

On the fifth day we were rushed to Johannesburg Hospital. Paul was admitted but I was taken back to the prison. Then they drove Richard, Sipho, and me to Bloemfontein with our hands handcuffed behind our backs, not caring if, as in the case of Steve Biko, the back of their Ford Sierra would become our deathbed.

We were still not taken to the hospital in Bloemfontein, but instead checked into another prison at around 9 p.m. For three hours we sat there, and my condition was deteriorating. I still had no real urge to take food or water, but instead just collapsed onto the floor. We were finally taken to a state doctor after midnight. I was then admitted to Pelonome Hospital, because the Bloemfontein authorities thought I might die in their prison.

Doctors then forced intravenous fluids and glucose into me through tubes, and I found myself under round-the-clock guard. After a few days my situation had improved. The police there insisted that I must have solid food, and taunted me that they would not consider releasing me until I ate. That made me more determined to continue my fast, and I rejected even the intravenous fluids. I went back to the hunger and water strike. The doctors came to plead, as did the superintendent of the hospital.

My only statement was that I had been illegally arrested, and I demanded my release. I wrote to Minister of Law and Order Adriaan Vlok and told him I awaited his response. Vlok sent word that if I started taking fluids, he would release me. Richard and Sipho and I met on a Friday, and were interrupted by doctors telling us they had a definite commitment that we were to be released. I then began drinking orange juice, because the doctors said I was not fit enough to begin eating solids. I drank for the entire weekend, and was released on 20 December about seven or eight kilograms lighter than before. The Alexandra security police came down to Bloemfontein to give us a lift back.

The doctors warned us of the consequences of this tactic, including permanent physical damage. The press was reporting that I would die within days. We had often heard about the Irish Republican Army hunger strikers in Belfast, especially Bobby Sands, who died after two months without food. I had fluids for a brief period, but had stayed off solid food for three weeks. My first solid meal was the day I was released, 20 December. I threw up the rice and mashed potatoes, and it took a week before I was ready for solids.

It is funny to consider this in retrospect, but the prospect of death through a hunger strike suicide was not really that alarming. As an activist I was always on the edge of running into the enemy, the security forces, which could be lethal. The hunger and water strike was a desperate, hardball tactic, but important to our cause. It was meant to add a sense of urgency to our protest, and to increase the pressure on the prison authorities. After so many months and years behind bars, and after so many arrests without being charged, I was growing fed up. That led me to this drastic approach, one I would resort to once again a year later.

In fact, the hunger strike is the only powerful weapon that prisoners have. It is like a sword, with a sharp edge that your enemy feels, but a sharper one that comes back to haunt you. Later I consulted with Professor Kalk at

Johannesburg Hospital, and was told that perhaps my thin body was an asset for this sort of tactic. That is not something I understand very well; nor do I have any desire to try the tactic again.

The early days of the Alexandra Civic Organization

My protest generated publicity, and with the regime appearing intransigent and unreasonable, that was to the good. I arrived back in Alexandra in time for Christmas, and prepared for the traditional trip home to the Transkei. Some of my loved ones had opposed my hunger strike, while others had supported it entirely. Both arguments had their strong points. But all of this paled in comparison to the news that while I was imprisoned, the Alexandra Civic Organization (ACO) had been formally launched on 5 December.

The youth wanted me to join the leadership of the South African Youth Congress, working on their issues. But the ACO delegates insisted that I serve as Organizing Officer, in charge of mobilizing residents, carrying out campaigns, and relating organizational positions to and from the grass-roots, a position I did not leave until mid-1992 when I moved to the United States for my studies. The ACO agenda was full and demanding, but Christmas offered a brief cooling-off period before work resumed in 1990. Many comrades joined our family in Askeaton. We were home for two weeks, and met comrades from the local area. Hearing reports from other places, I began to realize that I had been denied a working knowledge of most of South Africa. I needed to know the country, not merely as a politician, but also socially. We must act locally, but thinking and acting regionally and nationally (and indeed globally) is crucial, too.

We returned to Alexandra at the beginning of January, and began building the new civic. Until June, we accepted the offer of an office from Ian Bernhardt and the nonprofit Alexandra Development Fund (ADF) in Bramley View, which gave us a free telephone, fax, and photocopiers. For a long time we had operated without an office. Bernhardt's R1 million ADF was supported and overseen by big businesses that had workers in Alexandra or needed to appear to be socially responsible.

Politically, there were problems with taking the offer, partly because of the business ties and because the ADF had experienced criticisms for its middle-class housing development in Alex. But we felt we would not be co-opted and that our approach to development would not be affected.

Rally at Alexandra stadium prior to the march, 3 February 1990. *Photo: Anna Zieminski, Afrapix/Impact Visuals.*

Later, at the Council offices, 3 February. In front row, from left to right: Moss, Winnie, a councillor, Agnes Pooe, and Mokoena. We are presenting our list of demands. *Photo: Anna Zieminski, author's collection.*

Bernhardt, formerly a Communist who had contributed enormously to the cultural struggle by founding Dorkay House in Johannesburg, and his wife and partner Jo Dunstan, had integrity. Until he passed away, Bernhardt continued to help us liaise with business interests. We believed the ADF earnestly intended to build decent houses, even if they were unaffordable to most and soon experienced serious cracks and other faults.

During the month of January, we set up an office routine, and also organized a successful mass meeting on education issues. Then in early February, just after F.W. de Klerk's unbanning of political parties, we held a march from the sports stadium to the Council offices that attracted an estimated 80,000 residents. This was our third attempt, and whether or not de Klerk had raised our hopes was beside the point. A great many of our comrades marched on the Council out of pure frustration, even hatred at the way things were going.

In organizing this massive event, the ACO was helped by youth, students', women's, and labor organizations. The main demands were affordable housing for all and non-racial local government democracy. The main speakers were Moss, Popo Molefe (later ANC chair in Alex and the first premier of the Northwest Province), and Winnie Mandela.

Two weeks later we held a commemoration of the 1986 "Six Day War" and attracted 20,000 people. Jay Naidoo said that the day was at hand when factories would be controlled by workers and the wealth of the country redistributed to the masses. An Alexandra Youth Congress speaker attacked the imperialism of Bush and Thatcher. Early 1990 was the opening of a new chapter in Alex, and conclusively proved the support that we retained from four years earlier. But all of this was impossible for the Council to accept.

Fighting local apartheid

To discuss the Alexandra City Council in 1989 and 1990 with a straight face is difficult, because it was truly a comedy of errors. The Council was a collection of incompetent, toothless individuals operating in a bureaucratic structure that twisted them every which way, never permitting them to realize their better ambitions. They only became extremely dangerous in late 1990.

Some councilors—Rev. T.K. Motshele, A.A. Matome, and the late B.M. Mkhonza—were former AAC activists. They told us that their families had suffered too much police harassment when they were on our side of the struggle, and so now their intention was to work

to end apartheid from within. When I went to meetings between the ACO and the Council, Rev. Motshele would always pronounce, nervously but loudly, that he had saved me from police arrest once in 1986 by hiding me under other passengers in his car.

Then there was Prince Mokoena, a brash and vocal councilor always attired in handsome African ethnic clothing, who came to Alex from KwaThema on the East Rand. L.C. Koza was a former councilor under Sam Buti who had resisted quitting until the very end of Buti's reign in 1986 and then resurfaced for the 1988 elections. Koza and T.J. Vilakazi were initially the two Inkatha-aligned councilors. Then there was Dennis Tao, a leading social figure in Alex. The mastermind continued to be the "advisor," Steve Burger. Former AAC yard leader Willie Khumalo was deputy town clerk, and in 1989 was promoted to acting town clerk. If this ragtag group had one shared characteristic, it was opportunism.

So many little incidents were revealing. An example of a Council priority was the allocation of funds for Khumalo and Mkhonza to attend a September 1989 "Civil Defense Association of SA" conference in Cape Town to discuss "civil defense as component of a total survival strategy" and "the population explosion and its influence on civil defense planning." Another reflection of Council attitudes was Pooe's comment in March 1990 that "ACO was using the [open-air] gatherings to attack the Council and that this had to be checked and not be allowed," according to Council minutes. She was not only authoritarian to us though, for three weeks earlier Councilor Motshele complained of humiliation over "the Lady Mayor's action of always stopping him, he could not contribute in discussions."

Actually, there were some rather important conflicts and alliances in the Council which the ACO attempted to take advantage of. In early 1989 serious altercations occurred between councilors, and particularly between Mokoena and Willie Khumalo. Mokoena told the Council that after midnight on 1 January he had been paid a visit by a balaclava-clad, pistol-wielding man, and that a police source subsequently confirmed a report by an informant that Mokoena was the subject of a murder plot. According to Mokoena, this was linked to a threat from someone he was trying to have removed from a Council flat, who "revealed that Mr Khumalo had approached him to assist with the murder of Councilor Mokoena and that Mr Khumalo was working on a 'mechanism' to make the plot a reality." But Burger, assigned to investigate this incident, concluded in February that Khumalo was not involved in any such plot, and that he was owed an apology by Mokoena. However, Khumalo was found to have violated Council standards on secrecy and was slightly reprimanded.

Council minutes record Mokoena's response to Pooe's endorsement of the investigation: he "jumped up and strongly
opposed the Mayor. He stated he had paid R300 in September
[presumably a candidate's fee] and this had not been paid to
have a woman dressed in black [i.e., so his wife would become
a widow]. He then referred to the first effort [at assassination],
which was perceived here and had failed. The gunman was
however still around—'here,' he indicated as the Boardroom and
'still around,' he indicated as around the Council Boardroom."
Mokoena was then tossed out of Council meetings for a month
and a half and replaced as head of the Privatisation, Housing
and Trading Committee, through which he was handling the flat
occupancy deals.

In June 1989, Mokoena was under attack again, this time as
chairman of the Council Management Committee. The other councilors signed a no-confidence letter accusing him of allocating flats
based "on favouritism not merit," making decisions concerning
the taxi feud, and "As much as we know that Councilors are not
supposed to drive Council vehicles. But the Chairman did. Conse-
quently the disappearance of two such vehicles." Mokoena
handed in his keys and accepted the motion of no confidence in
the interests of "unity within Council."

But Prince Mokoena would return again and again, like a bad
dream, eventually gaining the Mayor's seat in mid-1990. Early in
1990, he had realized that the newly launched ACO would be the
major popular force in the township. This was easy to deduce,
coming on the heels of our mass march to the Council at which
resignations were demanded. Here Mokoena began to transform
his hostility to his fellow councilors into support for us. Ten days
after our march, he told Council, "Councilors must not dodge the
fact that they were not accepted by the community from the onset
but were only allowed to come in when it was said that the Advisor
would remain in Alexandra; thus Alexandra Council was the only
Council which had an Advisor." True, the community knew that
Burger still pulled the strings, but Mokoena was foolish to try to
justify the councilors' own role, which continued to be legitimizing
the Council, and with it, local apartheid.

Because Pooe had gone on television news after the march to
condemn the ACO and our followers as "outsiders," Mokoena
complained that this reaction was not mandated by Council. But
other councilors attacked Mokoena, alleging he "fed words into
Mr. [Moss] Mayekiso's mouth," including the demand that councilors resign within thirty days.

So from ACO's side, we now believed we had persuaded
Mokoena to come over to our side. Mokoena turned over infor-

mation about the Council's activities, and declared his loyalty to the ANC. We talked to other councilors privately, and tried to convince them that it was in their interests to join us. The community didn't hate them as individuals, but hated the system. ACO gained influence over some of them, and received information on the Council in return, including minutes of the Joint Management Committee.

We soon came to the conclusion, however, that Mokoena did not want to resign. Ironically, Pooe resigned first. In April, her house was attacked on several occasions, and the police set up regular patrols and even installed semi-bulletproof glass. Yet the attacks continued (six in all), and Pooe was apparently shocked into resigning in July when attackers managed to throw a fire-bomb through a doorway.

In August, Moss announced that Pooe had joined the ACO and intended to join the ANC: "She is urging other councilors to take the same bold move by leaving the unpopular, unaccountable bankrupt council and joining the people's progressive organization to fight for the improvement of living conditions and democracy. The ACO is further demanding that the government authorities not replace Mrs Pooe with another mayor but disband the City Council."

Privately, Pooe told us that she thought the firebombing was the work of some other councilors engaged in a power struggle. In some Council minutes from May, the city engineer, Geoff Halbig, confirmed "that there appears to be a split between the eight remaining councilors with four wanting progress, and the other four wanting to subvert the process." After a gap of a few months in which there was an acting mayor, Mokoena took over as mayor. We were now campaigning more actively for his resignation, and were not alone. Sandton Councilor Willem Heffer, for example, wrote a letter of resignation from the Coordinating Committee between the Sandton and Alexandra City Councils on 13 August 1990:

> My worst fears have proven well-founded. The committee has now met six times and our officials have spent a good deal of time preparing for and attending these meetings. Nothing has been achieved and there is no prospect of progress. There can be no reasonable doubt that under the present system of Black local government, the representatives of Alexandra are either incapable of or disinterested in dealing with the awesome problems of their township. I do not believe that we can reach the inhabitants of the place through these so-called councilors. Propping them up is in my opinion counterproductive and we should instead be concentrating on their departure.

8
Civics and
"Working-Class Civil Society"
(1989-1991)

With the unbanning of the ANC, the South African Communist Party, and the Pan Africanist Congress on 2 February 1990, civic associations were no longer the only broad, multi-issue anti-apartheid organizations. What should the civics do now? A myriad of opinions surfaced. But the notion that we in Alexandra had been developing since the mid-1980s—of mass-democratic, independent, non-party-political instruments belonging to poor and working-class people, carrying out advocacy campaigns, playing a watchdog role, and helping to proactively guide township development (all hinted at in the phrase "working-class civil society")—soon became dominant across the civic movement. It was also a role that, after heated debate, the ANC itself gradually came to accept.

Civics in the new situation

Even before 1990, there had been very strong indications of a rapid change in the balance of power at the national level. The release from jail of comrades Govin Mbeki and Walter Sisulu in 1989 suggested a reshaping of the political situation. P.W. Botha had come to the end of his road in mid-1989, and was overtaken by a man we had always considered one of the more conservative Nats, F.W. de Klerk. But de Klerk had taken a new personal direction, which was probably due to the economic problems faced by large-scale Afrikaner capital, but which he explained as a consequence of the collapse of East European Stalinism. More importantly, de Klerk seemed to have power among his own civil service and military to get away with the then unthinkable: unbanning the liberation organizations.

Looking back, it was clear that Botha himself, the great crocodile who epitomized the cold, hard "securocrat," had tested the waters of reform. This was done in part through secretive meetings with Nelson Mandela, but also through "reforms" which represented meager changes to apartheid, yet which we could actually feel on the ground. These included granting trade union rights, discarding the Pass Laws, adopting the philosophy of "orderly urbanization," withdrawing the neo-apartheid Riekert Commission proposals to stabilize the urban proletariat, establishing Regional Services Councils to make some township infrastructural investments, and so on. But the unbanning of the ANC and Communist Party were unfathomable during Botha's time.

So it was a great day, on 2 February 1990, when de Klerk's speech to Parliament indicated to us that for whatever reasons, the regime was now reeling. We asked each other, what do we do in this new situation?

In Harare the previous year, the ANC had drawn up a blueprint for negotiations. The Harare Declaration set the national context for negotiations during the early 1990s. At the local level, a parallel process began to take off. The apartheid state was suddenly prepared to negotiate with militant civic organizations rather than just wipe them out (which in any case the state was incapable of doing). De Klerk dissolved the Joint Management Centres (or at least claimed he did). He even promised R2 billion in aid to communities through a new institution, the Independent Development Trust (IDT). And for the first time, the IDT boss, Jan Steyn (formerly the boss at the Urban Foundation), was careful to consult with some progressive people on the ground in the initial stages of spending his money.

Yet we knew that all the concessions that were now underway were not a result of new-found benevolence, and that they would not go very deep in their initial stages. Local apartheid was still very much in place, as witnessed by the local puppet councilors who had made a comeback. Moreover, we soon found that the new situation created serious divisions among progressive forces. Even though there had been major ideological struggles underneath the surface, progressives had been something of a homogenous political group, united against apartheid. We were now faced with very different ideas about how to move forward.

There was little debate, of course, over the need to enter into negotiations. No matter how insincere the other side was, negotiations would be worth attempting. But first, we had to take stock. What kind of organizations were the civics at this stage, and what did our heritage of struggle represent? Going back to the late 1970s, community-based organizations had emerged in several key areas to improve the lives of ordinary poor and working-class South Africans, mainly under the name "civic associations." In the political sphere, the main theme was democratization of communities. The introduction in 1983 of the Black Local Authority system for very limited self-rule by black councilors made the situation more difficult. Even though the progressive forces met this neo-apartheid strategy with firm resistance and an electoral boycott, there were many opportunists who tried to move into the apartheid state from a civic base. Alexandra, we have seen, had more than its share. Residents were not fooled for long, however, and returned to mass-based organization and protest beginning again in 1984.

In the mid-1980s, the United Democratic Front was able to blend and weld the community struggles into a solid force capable of shaking the foundations of racist rule. But States of Emergency and the progressive forces' need to consolidate the national political struggle meant that no space emerged for the building of a national civic movement, the way COSATU represented a national instrument of trade unionists.

Yet we knew that the civics were active in most of the townships, and in many rural villages and hostels. The values, the mode of organizing, the strategies, the tactics, and the issues had been fairly uniform. The basic unit of organization is the street committee, which brings together families resident in that street, normally under a chairperson, secretary, and treasurer. These leadership structures are flexible and at times may include defense committee delegates and educators. Above the street committee are the block committees, composed of the representatives of the street committees. Block committee representatives make up the area committee, which is the basis for a civic's central committee, and also elects the civic executive.

Various township civic organizations come together to form the provincial structures. Regions operate through a regional council, using a delegate structure with representation from each local community, as well an elected regional executive that looks after the day-to-day running of the organizations. The regions form the national structure, which also operates on the same principles of a delegate council and an executive body.

This was the institutional form that characterized most civics in 1990. Many were now just beginning to claim the additional political space that the unbannings of February 1990 provided. As civic structures were becoming stronger, the prospects for civic politics appeared very encouraging.

At this point, fundamental questions emerged, such as whether the UDF should continue to exist in its broad, anti-apartheid form. Civics began to debate whether they should become local ANC branches, or stay independent of party politics. The idea of civics retaining an independent basis within civil society began gaining ground.

The civics and "civil society"

By the early 1990s, nearly all the progressive forces of South Africa were committed to the maintenance of a strong, vibrant civil society, even after liberation. By "civil society," most people mean *organizations that operate between the level of the state and the level of the individual and household.* The great Italian Marxist Antonio Gramsci used the phrase to mean "the ensemble of organisms commonly called 'private'."

While it has often been said that our understanding of the need for a strong civil society comes from the failed Eastern European countries—in particular, our analysis of the failures of their strong centralization of political party power and weak structures representing people's ordinary interests—this is not correct. A firm home-grown movement for an independent civic structure was not inconsistent with the Congress movements' principles, which have stressed since at least the mid-1950s that the *people* shall govern, the *people* shall share the wealth, etc. As early as 1986, we were debating the possibility of civics as permanent forces in the townships. But only after 2 February was there space to explore these issues fully.

The organs of civil society must be considered in the context of the base from which they emerged. Understanding this in both concrete and abstract terms requires class analysis. On the one hand, it is clear in South Africa that the most developed organs of civil society serve the bourgeoisie: their chambers of business, their northern suburb ratepayers' associations, their parent-teachers' associations, their sports clubs, heritage foundations, cultural associations, and so forth.

For working-class people, on the other hand, the organs of civil society include civic associations, trade unions, the women's groups, youth groups, churches, burial societies, and other organizations, formal and informal, that represent the interests of poor and working people.

Politically, the emergence of the civil society concept in the progressive rhetoric, beginning in early 1990, was very important. Three positions gained support:

A weekly meeting of hostel-dwellers, 1990. Men typically stand at the back of the room, deferring to women, who are given seating priority. *Author's photo.*

• Within the South African Communist Party, some comrades (led by Blade Nzimande and Mpume Sikhosana of Natal) attacked the idea of civil society as bourgeois, highlighting its capacity for dividing progressive forces from the liberation movement, which would threaten the drive toward socialism.

• Some liberals (especially Steven Friedman) attacked the idea of civil society as conservative, highlighting its threat to the ability of the state to provide "representativeness, accountability and public contest to the vital areas of social life."

• Some progressives (Mark Swilling, for example) defended civil society as the basis for what seemed to be a class-free sphere of liberty, even an "associational socialism."

From the perspective of the township civic associations, it was possible to advocate a fourth position: in favor of organizational instruments of *working-class civil society* (such as civics, unions, and many women's and youth organizations), which would serve a "watchdog" role and provide the raw material and energy from which to construct socialist building blocks.

It is important to say, first, that from classical debates on civil society I have found no uniform definition or conception of the term. According to Hegel and the young Marx, civil society embraced the economic base and aspects of the superstructure. In this usage, the essential distinction was between the state on the one hand, and all other dimensions of social life (being civil society) on the other. By contrast, Gramsci tends explicitly to locate civil society in the superstructure (though his bald assertion that "in reality civil society and state are one and the same" encouraged Nzimande and Sikhosana to argue that civil society is a tool of the bourgeoisie).

My conclusion, however, is that because civil society interrelates dialectically with class divisions at the level of economic production, and with the state (still essentially controlled by the capitalist class), it is itself a terrain of class contest and struggle. A given civil society needs to be located within its particular conjuncture. In South Africa, the civil society of the bourgeoisie has been dominant. But this dominance is being challenged by the movement of South African workers and community residents—coordinated by their organs and instruments of working-class civil society—which struggle collectively for basic economic rights (housing, health care, education, etc).

The civics and political society

What was mainly at stake in the civil society debates, and where I departed from Nzimande, Sikhosana, and Friedman, was whether or not partisan political programs and state functions would determine our activities as working-class activists and intellectuals within civil society. Would we in the civic movement bow to the need that a democratically elected government would have, in South Africa's difficult conditions, for national unity? Would we let our extra-parliamentary class politics fall away, once liberation was achieved?

Friedman, a relentless critic of the civics who says that the liberal democratic state must be "as inclusive as possible," responded affirmatively to these questions. "To insist, as one civic strategist does, that civics cannot stand for local government office because this would 'bureaucratize' them is to collapse, as Lenin did, the state's political and administrative roles into one." In the interests of a mythical state-centered harmony, Friedman seemed to want the civics' working-class advocacy voice to be quickly and conclusively muffled. (This was taken to extremes later, in 1994, when he publicly opposed the inclusion of civics in the Government of National Unity's National Economic Development and Labor Council.)

From a very different perspective but with much the same conclusion, Nzimande and Sikhosana argued that as organs of people's power, civics must essentially transform into ANC branches, and be absorbed in the political struggle for democracy *only*:

> To suggest that the building of democracy is a task for civil society and its organs is plain naivety of the nature of political struggle. In fact it is such a conceptualization that has led to the problematic practice that is beginning to emerge within the national liberation movement and the mass democratic movement, for example, that issues about services and development in townships are for civics, and "political issues" are for political organizations and parties.

At their most provocative, Nzimande and Sikhosana claimed (in the ANC magazine *Mayibuye* in June 1991) that we who believe that "civics should take up issues of rent, electricity, roads, etc … fall squarely within the strategy to separate the ANC from its mass base." This austere line of attack fostered unnecessary divisions between civics and the ANC (especially in Alexandra, but also in the Natal Midlands, the Eastern Transvaal, and some other areas).

As the debate continued, the future role for civics, and civil society, remained somewhat unclear. The democratic forces within the ANC would put their feet firmly on the ground of the state, without doubt. But how long would they be able to stand, if other pressures—the Nats, the Democratic Party (that misnamed political instrument of white liberals and some big capitalists), domestic business and international finance capital (especially the World Bank and the International Monetary Fund), Inkatha, the white far right, and others opposed to the working class—pushed and pulled our working class—leaders, politicians, and bureaucrats away from ANC traditions?

Examples from Africa and elsewhere told us that simply because nationalist organizations like the ANC are apparently progressive today does not mean they will remain so. The fact that there are, within the ANC, numerous class forces is a reason in itself for strengthening independent organs of working-class civil society. Class struggle will continue long into the post-apartheid era. As early as 1990, the ANC was committed to a so-called mixed economy, a code phrase for business as usual. Indeed, if that meant supporting private property rights, then there would necessarily be conflict with the working class.

On the other hand, if the ANC government in principle became strongly supportive of working-class interests, it would, in turn, need a strong working-class civil society to safeguard a progressive approach. The civics and unions would need to continually challenge capital's interests, to move as quickly as possible from a mixed economy to a socialist economy. If these conflicts heated up, what might then occur with the state and civil society? All these issues were the subject of enormous debates in 1990.

We considered one scenario: Zimbabwe. After Mugabe came to power on a supposedly "Marxist-Leninist" ticket, what happened? Within weeks, trade unions were systematically smashed. More squatters were displaced in the cities than under even the racist Smith regime, and fewer houses built for the working class. The nationalists, even with their superficial socialist ideology, quickly proved capable of inheriting an oppressive state and using it against the working class. The problem in Zimbabwe was that it then took a decade for comrades to begin to reorganize working-class organs of civil society to the point where they could contest issues with the Mugabe regime. While Mugabe may still call himself a socialist, the reality of holding state power in a third world context is that he follows the economic dictates of the international financial institutions. And this leads logically to political repression.

In what used to be the East Bloc in Europe, civil society remained in a situation that Gramsci called "primordial and gelatinous," even after liberation from the Czar in 1917. Indeed, any independent organs of the working class were periodically and conclusively smashed by undemocratic Communist Party rulers. There was no opportunity for a strong and vibrant civil society capable of being a watchdog over the rise of the bureaucracy.

In post-apartheid South Africa, instruments of working-class civil society should, we believed, give direction to the state. If the movement within the ANC toward meeting basic needs began to falter, it would be logical to expect that working-class organs would continue to press for programs that met those needs. This is the famous "watchdog" function of working-class civil society. To return to the concrete results of this theory means to understand how, even in its formative months, the South African National Civic Organization was adopting a close but critical relationship with the ANC.

SANCO emerges

The story of national civic organizing begins with the disbanding of the United Democratic Front, which appeared inevitable by mid-1990. Many organizations that called the UDF their political home had to rethink their future after the unbanning of the ANC and SACP. The UDF had outlived its historical mission, yet many of its components didn't fit into the ANC's unitary

structure and system of individual membership. The loose coalitional character of the UDF would never fit within the ANC, and the wide range of UDF
groups (which included non-party-political human rights organizations like
Black Sash) could not simply become swallowed up as branches of the ANC.

There were some exceptions, of course, such as some of the women's
and youth groups which became ANC substructures. But for members of
trade unions, churches, and civics, this was not feasible if we took seriously
our desire to draw as many individuals from the grassroots as possible into
our struggles, and to develop strong organs of working-class civil society.
Debates ensued about our role as civic associations. It was soon clear that
we would have to build first regional and then national coalitions that would
keep the civic movement character alive. We began with the Civic Associations of the Southern Transvaal (CAST), which was founded by dozens of
civic groups from around Johannesburg in August 1990. It was extremely
successful, and we had many demonstrations of civic unity. There were also
major strategic and tactical differences of opinion within CAST, of course,
and at one point this led to the resignation of the spokesperson, Cas
Coovadia, who made controversial comments about the Johannesburg
Metropolitan Chamber that were not organizational policy.

Several regional civic organizations were baptized in the fire of intense mass
action in 1990 and 1991. For example, one Saturday morning in November
1990 CAST called a large march through central Johannesburg to protest the
authorities' switching-off of essential municipal services in several townships.
The march provoked immediate police repression, including a street battle
(never before witnessed in the downtown area), and, late in the day, the
shooting deaths of two comrades (and, as a negotiator, I felt the sharp end of
the police dogs' teeth during that day's fracas). Following the launch of CAST,
a variety of interim regional coalitions of civics developed, in the Eastern and
Northern Transvaal, Western Cape and Northern Cape, Transkei, the Border
and the Eastern Cape, the Southern and Northern Orange Free State, and
Southern and Northern Natal. These regional organizations banded together
to form the National Interim Civics Committee (NICC) in early 1991. They all
had formal launches of regional congresses during 1991 and early 1992.

Two UDF staff members, Pat Lephunya and Zora Ebrahim, were seconded
from the national UDF office, which in early 1991 was folding up to assist with
the NICC launch, and became the national coordinators. The UDF also controlled
the funding we required for a year's worth of publicity work and planning

meetings in locations across the country. It was less than a democratic beginning, given the top-down appointments by the UDF, and the process was considered unsatisfactory by those who attended the first NICC meeting in Johannesburg. As a result, a new chairperson was elected, Thembile Bece, from the Eastern Cape region. I had been elected to the NICC steering committee from CAST, along with Sithembiso Dlamini from the Vaal. Sithembiso was then elected general secretary of NICC, but coordination was still handled by Pat and Zora. This caused tensions between the regions and the outgoing national UDF structure, but as NICC took control of its own future, Pat dropped out and Zora's role was minimized.

We eventually brought civics from thirteen regions of the country into the process. Southern Transvaal and Eastern Cape were always the power-houses, the best organized and most militant. Regional debates influenced decisions over when and where to hold the formal launch, the structure of the organization (unitary or federal), and where it would be headquartered.

Eastern Cape comrades also had their own choice for president, Thozamile Botha. Thozamile was a comrade who had cut his teeth in the first major trade union and civic struggles of the Eastern Cape (as an auto worker leader and as founder of the Port Elizabeth Black Civic Organisation) and who had had to flee into exile, where he pursued his studies and joined the ANC. Because of his extremely strong legacy, when he returned in 1990 he was seen as the logical standard-bearer of the national civic movement. But we in CAST had our own candidate, Moss Mayekiso (then CAST president), who was considered among the most prominent of civic and union leaders. Thozi, in contrast, was seen as an active office-bearer within the ANC, holding the portfolio of local government. This was, then, a moment to assess our emerging policy of independence from political parties.

Because the launch of the national body was in Port Elizabeth in March 1992, and because Moss was detained from attending due to an upsurge of Inkatha violence in Alexandra that week, there was a general expectation that Thozi would win the presidency. But when several hundred comrades from the regions voted, the overwhelming choice between the two well-re-spected comrades was Moss. In addition, Dan Sandi from the Eastern Cape was elected general secretary, Lechesa Tsenoli from Durban was chosen as deputy president, and a full contingent of executives from across the geographical spectrum was elected. Unfortunately, we had only one woman executive member, Trudy Thomas of the Border region, who was chosen because she was extremely active and well-respected in the townships even as a white person (this was a reflection of our commitment to non-racialism, and our future goal of expanding the civic movement to white neighborhoods which were then represented by ratepayer organizations that had little in common with us).

In the constitution adopted at the launch, the structure chosen was unitary (as discussed in Chapter 13), in spite of the Southern Transvaal's arguments for a tight federal structure. The head office was chosen to be Bloemfontein in the Orange Free State because it was geographically closer to the center of the country and because it was felt that too much power in our progressive movement in general was centralized in Johannesburg (this was later recognized as a serious mistake, and within a year we had relocated our head office to Johannesburg).

The name of our new body was the South African National Civic Organization, SANCO. Our Southern Transvaal region lost another fight over the name, which we thought should have been *Civics,* in the plural, to reflect our diversity. But our launch did prove our non-partisan character, as we invited presentations from across the political spectrum of the liberation movements (the PAC and the Azanian People's Organization, or AZAPO, did not attend, to our disappointment). It was an important lesson in the formation of an organization so full of tensions, fractions, and different ideologies. Despite these differences, there was an overriding collective commitment to move to the next stage of national struggle.

And there was also some thinking, now, about how civics could move society beyond simply national liberation and into socialism.

Civics, working-class civil society, and socialism

Serious intellectual struggle began when the most important political issue came under consideration in the civil society debates: socialism. How could we best use the notion of civil society to promote the transition to socialism? What are the roles of mass-based working-class instruments such as civics and unions, as well as other non-sectarian organizations in which socialists are active? To answer these questions, given the objective conditions in South Africa, it is useful to first address the red herring concepts of "democratic socialism" and "associational socialism," which were deployed within the SACP and the civic movement, respectively, to describe our political trajectory.

The vast majority of delegates to the SACP's December 1990 conference argued that "socialism" is inherently democratic, and does not need any prefix or adjective. This is no Stalinist position, and to label it as such (as many outside commentators did) limits debates, and dissuades people from thinking carefully about the concept of socialism. The term "democratic socialism" is not particularly helpful, for it implies that there has been socialism elsewhere, *whose problem was that it was not a democratic socialism*. In fact, socialism has not yet been successfully implemented. If socialism is indeed inherently democratic, then we must confront what was called socialism in the old East Bloc. And looking at that evidence, we must conclude that it simply was not socialism. It was an experiment along those lines, which failed very early in the day, at around the time of Lenin's death. (This is certainly not a Stalinist position.)

Next is the idea of "associational socialism" advanced by Mark Swilling. The problem here is Swilling's studied avoidance of class categories (in the tradition of trendy international "post-Marxists" like Norberto Bobbio, Paul Hirst, Ernesto Laclau, and Chantal Moufe). Eloquent on the need for strong "voluntary" and "associational" organizations, Swilling never argued that these were anything more than groupings of what he termed "ordinary, everyday citizens." But township civics are enormously different from the voluntary residents' and ratepayers' associations of the northern suburbs, and Swilling's woolly-headed thinking left the civic movement open to the attacks by Nzimande and Sikhosana that civil society was just a bourgeois distraction.

As the conflicts that emerged between the Alexandra Civic Organization and the ratepayers' associations of Sandton and Randburg demonstrated, the interests of the working class and the bourgeoisie are in complete opposition in the sphere of community development. It therefore made no sense to lump what we do in democratic, accountable civic associations with what undemocratic, unaccountable northern suburb ratepayers' associations do. (It is true, however, that Swilling's mistake here was mainly a semantic one, in inventing fancy new words. He was correct on the main point, which is that strengthening the civics must be a top priority for socialists.)

Where Swilling was also often at fault was in describing the movement to socialism in terms of reforming capitalism. This is a view of socialism as simply a set of activities that take place in a pluralistic society to make capital nicer. There is no analysis of the underlying tendencies of capitalism, a flaw which prevents Swilling from embracing socialism in all its richness. As a result, Swilling's "socialist principles" are little more than simple liberal reforms, fine in their own right, but by no means socialist in content. They do not aim to change the *relations of production*, but merely to accommodate a shift in power toward the progressive forces. The difference between this and the politics of working-class civil society is immense.

In contrast, Nzimande and Sikhosana took issue with my argument that civil society should be considered from the standpoint of class analysis and socialist politics. They argued, in contrast, that "civil society is primarily, under capitalist society, in the service of the bourgeoisie." To me the phrase "working-class civil society" is a simple way to describe that *part* of the wider civil society which must gain hegemony.

This did not convince Nzimande and Sikhosana, because, they insisted, "'civil society' emerged out of the bourgeois revolutions as a precondition for the consolidation of capital accumulation," and hence civil society must *always* serve accumulation. But the absurdity of this position becomes apparent, I rebutted, if you simply substitute "the proletariat" for "civil society" in their sentence. If we use the logic of Nzimande and Sikhosana, then because the proletariat is a class which capitalism founded to serve the process of accumulation, *we should simply ignore it as a concept to be utilized in the struggle for socialism.*

Nzimande and Sikhosana forget the very basic point of all dialectical materialists, which is that capitalism always throws up contradictions as it unfolds through history, and our task as socialists is to be creative about using whatever contradictions (including the emergence of trade unions, which are essentially reformist organizations) are present to build an ever-stronger working class.

I was now coming to the conclusion that under the prevailing balance of forces, which did not offer any real scope for socialist insurrection, the civic movement, trade unions, and other potentially socialist forces could instead get a toehold through non-profit, collective developmental principles and community-controlled institutions. The move toward socialism is a move toward meeting the needs of poor and working-class people in our society, but in a particular way. More precisely, those needs cannot be met by the normal functioning of the free market.

The more we tried to reduce the power of the market by demanding "affordable housing for all in Alexandra" and the like, the more we confronted the need to set up an alternative to township capitalism. South African capitalism just was not delivering the goods, because by its exploitative nature it *could not* successfully deliver the goods to the majority.

Instead, the move to socialism requires us to build a working-class movement around the basic needs that all human beings have a right to expect. Under a democratic political economy, the state has the obligation to find resources to meet everyone's basic needs, and deliver them to the communities. But then there arises the danger of excessive state bureaucracy. To avoid that, the progressive movement began to call for a "strong but slim state," that on the one hand is capable of capturing resources from the capitalist sector and on the other is slim enough to funnel those resources to community-based development institutions.

Those development institutions, in turn, will only succeed if they *decommodify* the basic-needs commodities. They can do this by making it feasible for poor people to live on what is otherwise expensive land through a Land Trust, or to save their money with a People's Bank that lends on socialist principles of affordability (as just two examples).

What does working-class civil society mean here in relation to the state? It means empowered, class-conscious communities whose good relations with a progressive democratic state will permit a redistribution of wealth that also leads to new social relations. The examples used above are drawn from our community struggles, but there are strong parallels to progressive union struggles for worker control of the means of production. Worker-owned cooperatives, for example, should be given protection from capitalist competition through preference buying and through the nurturing of a set of related cooperatives to supply goods and services, as in Spain's Mondragon region.

Community-based development institutions, and experiments in worker management and ownership, are the building blocks of a new mode of production, similar in their function to the petty bourgeois enterprises of the eighteenth century, which arose in the decay of feudalism to challenge and transform social relations. In the conditions of France under Marie ("Let them eat cake") Antoinette, the seeds of capitalism grew quickly. Our hope was that in the conditions of 1990s Alexandra, in a decaying apartheid-capitalist society, the seeds of socialism would also grow, nurtured both by organs of working-class civil society and by the first democratic South African state. To do that required us to learn the ropes of development, and to avoid the potholes that we always seemed to find on the development path trod by apartheid capitalism.

9
From Protest to Development?
(1989-1991)

The civic movement agreed that it would not disappear into ANC branches. But even if our political niche was secure, there was another danger: "From protest to development" quickly became the refrain of those who wanted to deradicalize the civic movement. Would top-down development via state agencies and large private sector foundations, removed from its political context, be successful? Would our proud traditions of struggle over issues such as housing and community justice be forgotten? Would civics manage to carefully negotiate the difficult terrain, avoiding a blunt rejection of the resources our constituents needed, but also avoiding a slide into capitalist development deals that didn't make any sense?

"Development"

The apartheid government and business interests had tried to "develop" Alexandra according to their own interests for many decades. Many local initiatives had also been launched. But all failed to make a dent in the overwhelming poverty and decay in the township. So, we concluded, a fairly revolutionary approach to development would be necessary. This chapter and the next describe how civic thinking and action progressed from fire-fighting against forced removals to proactive development planning in the early 1990s.

At the time ACO was launched, in December 1989, Alexandra's living conditions were worsening steadily. Insufficient funds had been allocated by the central government to a local government that in any case was presided over by apartheid stooges and run by an administrator intent on maintaining the political status quo. What with the end of the Pass Laws, more and more people were moving to Alex, some of them quite desperate because of the rural crisis, displacement from commercial farms, violence in Natal, and the like. In Alex they found filth, disease, crime, a massive housing shortage, deteriorating services, and rising unemployment.

Remember from Chapter 5, in early 1989 Council administrator Steve Burger had bragged to the *Financial Mail*: "By the end of 1990, Alexandra will boast the completion of full services to the township.... Civic pride is also evident, as residents use the garbage cans that have been provided." Here is how the *FM* viewed Alex in January 1991: "Alexandra township—that sinkhole of liberal hopes—is once again floundering under the weight of garbage. Despite a R200 million upgrading project, sewers spill their effluent into the streets, new stormwater drains don't work, and the roads remain possibly the most rutted of any township in the country." As for Burger's claim about the garbage cans, the *FM* reported: "Garbage bags are not distributed in the township and anything not placed in specific bins—which the civic says are too few—is not collected. For the rest, a construction company comes into the township regularly and pushes all leftover garbage into huge, fly-buzzing piles on street corners."

In short, the money committed by the apartheid state was poorly spent and in any case a drop in the ocean of need. The 1980 redevelopment plan cost R25 million to implement, and delivered just 257 houses and some new services to a very small area. The National Housing Commission paid the bill, and was asked to pay another R42 million in 1986 for the first phase of the new urban renewal program designed by Eskom. The second phase began in 1988 and cost R46 million, with loan financing from the Development Bank of Southern Africa (DBSA). The Central Witwatersrand Regional Services Council promised a grant of R25 million for the third phase, and in 1990 also took over payments to the DBSA. Then there were a myriad of other development ventures, including several tens of millions of rands spent on new private housing in the East Bank and Old Alex.

The money barely scratched the surface. By 1992, according to the *Sowetan*, Alex's population had risen to 360,000, with at least fifty times more people per hectare than neighboring Sandton, and four times as many dwellings per hectare as in Soweto. There were nearly eleven people per house in the 10,500 formal housing units. And then there were another

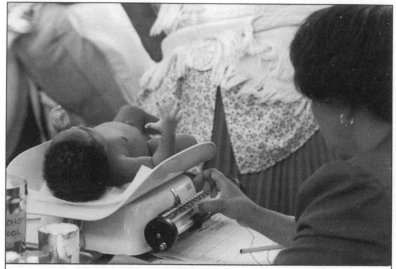

Postnatal care at the Alexandra Health Clinic, an independent community clinic funded primarily by individual donor organizations. *Author's photo.*

11,080 free-standing shacks in four areas of Alex, as well as thousands more backyard shacks and 9,420 hostel beds. By mid-1992, only 16 percent of our residents had access to electricity, and in 1988 only 1 percent had their own personal water supply.

Community facilities for so many people were nearly nonexistent. For example, there were just 2,000 places at preschools and crèches in Alex, but 32,000 preschool-age children. There were fewer than 20,000 places at four secondary schools and thirteen primary schools for more than 108,000 children of school-going age. There were just two community halls, one inadequate library, and two clinics only one of which was operated professionally—for the entire township. The eighty-five soccer teams in Alex had to compete for just four fields.

Alex was home to more than 80,000 unemployed people, and of those who had jobs, only 25 percent earned more than R1,000 per month (compared to 37 percent of workers in Soweto). About half of those with jobs were domestic workers, cleaners, or semi-skilled or unskilled workers earning less than R600 per month. Skilled workers accounted for one-third of those with jobs, and white collar workers and the self-employed were each less than 10 percent of the workforce. For those without a job, 21 percent admitted to surveyors that they resorted to crime as a means of survival.

A comprehensive development program was obviously in order. How to begin? What preliminary work would have to be done? What alliances would be necessary?

Since there had never been any scope for progressive, community-controlled development in Alex before, these were new questions in 1990. We were still thinking in an isolated way, tackling one issue at a time. When asked to list the five worst problems in Alex, 95 percent of survey respondents indicated housing, 70 percent said bad roads, 66 percent said lack of refuse removal, 65 percent said lack of electricity, and 55 percent said lack of street lighting. Our instinct was to address each of these individually, because each issue had particular complications that took us time to work through.

Nevertheless, we occasionally dreamed of what would be possible if we had access to resources. As early as July 1990, ACO filed a formal proposal to the provincial authorities for a comprehensive plan to develop the land of the Far East Bank in a much more appropriate way. But there were many steps along the way, the most important of which was in the arena of housing.

From people's courts to the Alex Justice Centre

When people's courts were functioning well, the community gained education and organizational capacity. The apartheid regime felt threatened, and many activists and community members were detained and arrested to face charges including treason, sedition, and subversion. People's courts were restoring respect and instilling morals and cultural values in the dehumanized black communities. But beginning in the mid-1980s, people's courts were dealt a severe blow as a result of the police harassment.

During our detention, some of the people's courts had degenerated into kangaroo courts where instant penalties were meted out without the judges having access to any facts. No political education was taking place. Fees were charged to complainants and fines were instituted. Bribery was the order of the day and people were sentenced randomly. If found guilty, *sjambokking* (whipping) was applied, causing extreme pain and embarrassment. Some judges were younger than twenty-one years, and had little respect for human dignity. Some people's courts were even hijacked by the tsotsi-thug element in the community and no longer served the interests of the community. Some of the courts changed from being places of community building and harmony into institutions of vengeance and hate.

After the acquittal and release of the civic leadership from prison in 1989, as civic structures were reorganized and people regained confidence, we started discussions on how to reestablish people's courts. Many felt the courts remained an important component of the general struggle for people's organs of power.

The ACO Central Committee mandated research on revitalizing the people's courts. With memories of kangaroo courts still vivid in the minds of many community members, ACO was asked to control the process. The Central Committee endorsed this request.

The next step was to find ways and means of operating within the parameters of the existing racist legal system. A meeting was set up in February 1991 with the Minister of Justice to inform him of the ACO decision and to start operating without raising the ire of the racist regime. He agreed that a working committee be set up to discuss the nitty-gritty of the structure. The ACO engaged progressive lawyers. Before long, the Alexandra Justice Centre was born.

For the first time, our personnel were trained in paralegal law, a giant step forward. The Justice Centre established a formal office from which to operate, and hired a registrar to head the project. Six local mediators from Alexandra assisted. The sessions were held *in camera* and the operation is now considered a successful model, so far unique in South Africa, but sure to be reproduced elsewhere.

Problems with housing privatization

From the time that ACO was launched, we enjoyed good communications with our grassroots forces, even as we tried to relay extremely complicated strategies over negotiations with the authorities on various issues. But from that standpoint an organization is never fully ripe. As an organizer, my job was always to monitor our strength, and to tighten here and there.

I faced essentially the same organizing tasks as before. Our yard, block, street, and zonal committees rapidly came back together in most parts of the township. Quite a few had been operating autonomously and continued to prosper on their own steam. But at the level of ACO as a township-wide structure, we now had to fit our traditions of militant organizing to the changing political conditions of South Africa, in order to best capture the mood of the time and take advantage of all opportunities. We had to be careful targeting the precise issues that would maintain our support.

Development was very tricky, because there were many opportunities for missteps, for co-option, for doing deals that didn't make sense. The terrain was very sensitive, and we sometimes stumbled. But there were also many deals that did make sense and that improved the lives of our constituents. And even in those cases where we stumbled, the organization developed and grew more mature in the process. We had excellent back-up support from the Johannesburg service organization Planact, where Andrew Boraine and his colleagues helped us come to grips with the detailed technical challenges. (Sometimes I disagreed forcefully with Planact's approach, such as the promotion of the Central Wits Metro Chamber, as I explain in Chapter 12, but I later spent ten fruitful months in 1994 working from Planact's offices.)

But whatever the issue, our basic principles—especially that of maximum unity in the community—helped us devise creative strategies. For example, Steve Burger, Prince Mokoena, and the Council were trying to privatize the housing stock, selling to individuals or their descendants who were said to be the original owners in some ancient records. That meant that backyard shackdwellers and tenants of rooms within the house, some of whom had lived there for decades, were often forced to pay higher rents to the new property owners or face eviction.

As soon as we were released from prison, this problem became very obvious. The initial strategy was an appeal for unity against the Council, on the grounds that the privatization of housing was "an attempt to break the rent boycott" which had started in 1986 and was still effective. In addition, housing privatization was aimed at getting "property owners to now do the government's dirty work," as Moss had told a unity meeting in November 1989. The Council had also called for the doubling of rental rates.

Our approach included hiring a top lawyer, Geoff Budlender of the Legal Resources Centre, to develop a method for preventing exploitation of tenants when houses were sold or transferred. Specifically, we succeeded in establishing a principle of consensus in the yard prior to Council sale of the property, so that any single household could veto the sale. And we continued to educate people about privatization in very political terms, which allowed us to build a large base of households that understood the housing question clearly.

However, this gave those few who owned property more of an incentive to support councilors opposed to our arrangement. Some of them even formed the Alexandra Land and Property Owners' Association (ALPOA) as a lobby group. They were concerned because every single case of property transfer that we heard about was blocked by lack of consensus in the yard. Our next strategy was to demand—and win—a complete freeze on the privatization of housing.

ALPOA complained in mid-1991 to *City Press* that "there are no property owners in this township" because of ACO. In fact, there were just 150 housing units transferred, out of a total of nearly 1,000 which could be sold to registered former owners or their descendants under the Council scheme.

ALPOA secretary Veli Mahopa was defensive: "We are not parasites, we are providing a good service to the people who need a roof over their heads." I was then quoted as explaining that angry tenants were generating the pressure against the property owners: "They are rejecting government-imposed property ownership. This government took advantage of the fact that all prominent community leaders were in jail at the time and imposed this system. This caused tension among the people, who resisted the sale of their property to selected property owners."

The effect of all this was to slow the transfer of wealth and income from poor and working people who were backyard shack dwellers—and who refused to pay rent to the Alex Council—to what might have become a new class of landlords. In the process, we also prevented the Alex Council from raising money which they could not earn by being a legitimate government of and by and for the people.

Of course, the Council could never understand this. In a letter to his bosses in the Transvaal Provincial Administration (TPA) in March 1990, Burger said that squatters "have become political pawns being used by the radicals to whip the Council, "who is unable to provide proper housing or services. The uncontrolled squatting also creates a shocking image of the South African situation."

ACO had a Shack-dwellers Coordinating Committee representing mainly freestanding shack residents, who led the fight against the Council's program of relocation to Orange Farm and later to another dusty shack settlement midway between Johannesburg and Pretoria, Ivory Park. Along with backyard shack dwellers, they were among ACO's most loyal supporters. As Harry Mashabela commented in his 1990 book *Mekhukhu*, "In the main, the major problem facing these [shack] communities is the fact that the wider community, including political activist organizations and trade unions, appears to ignore them— with the exception of the ACO in Alexandra." Burger's patronizing claim that they were our pawns was obviously false.

So in May 1990 Burger came up with another reason to displace squatters, in another letter to the TPA: "The major problem with the squatters is that a stage has now been reached that it has become impossible in certain areas to continue with the Urban Renewal Project, as the contractors are unable to gain access to the stands [plots to be redeveloped] as a result of the denseness of the squatter shacks. Should the Urban Renewal Project be stopped, Alexandra will develop into a total squatter town."

Burger was frustrated because the Council lacked sufficient credibility and power to redevelop Alexandra in his middle-class image. The East Bank was a key part of Burger's strategy, but even here the capitalist delivery system began to break down due to cracked housing, shoddy construction, and other reflections of the low-quality, fast-buck, private-sector approach to development.

Burger was not alone. In a meeting in late May it was revealed that the Johannesburg City Council would sell the Far East Bank "provided upmarket housing is built." This was something of a compromise given that Johannesburg had earlier insisted on a golf course buffer. But it was still unacceptable to us, since we demanded instead an increase in publicly funded, affordable housing.

Our specific objections to privatized housing were over exploitation, speculation, downward-raiding, shack farming, and landlordism. These need some explanation. Exploitation was already an obvious problem in Alexandra when the Council transferred housing to a single occupant of a large yard, who then tripled or quadrupled the rents of all the families living there. Speculation was also a problem in many townships during the late 1980s. During the brief frenzy of housing construction from 1986 to 1990, big developers bought land—often on the far side of a township—and held it vacant until it was profitable to develop. Many developers went bankrupt because of this gamble, and even the nonprofit Urban Foundation lost millions.

Another form of speculation happened when individual owners within a township bought land or serviced stands at a low price and then speculated by waiting until the land could be sold for a higher price. Related to this was downward-raiding, which occurs when a serviced site or even a small house provided free through a subsidy is later sold (below its value, usually) by the poor household living there to a middle-class household. Sometimes this happens because service payments (for water or electricity or other services) are too high and sometimes just out of a desperate need for money. As a result, the subsidy that the poor household initially received partly turns into cash, and is partly captured by a middle-class household that may not need it. The cash might be nice for the poor household, temporarily, but that household is now homeless and the low-income housing crisis worsens. Finally, shack farming and landlordism occur when a class of landowners develops solely to take advantage of the desperate shortage of housing. This easily leads to exploitation, coercion, and mafioso patronage politics.

In addition, women were especially disadvantaged, because many official provisions explicitly discriminate against women (because they give urban residential rights to a deceased man's brothers or sons instead of his widow), as do African customs about control of land. And a woman has a more difficult time getting credit than a man with the same income.

Elements of all these market and patriarchal factors can be found in Alex, thanks to privatized housing. We felt our township was in great danger from the unregulated market, in particular because Alex is quite well located compared to most townships. This led us to propose a "decommodified" form of housing.

Housing as a right, not a commodity

The housing question is an interesting one because, as Friedrich Engels put it so well in 1872:

> The so-called housing shortage, which plays such a great role in the press nowadays, does not consist in the fact that the working class generally lives in bad, overcrowded dwellings. This shortage is not something peculiar to the present; it is not even one of the sufferings peculiar to the modern proletariat in contradistinction to all earlier oppressed classes. On the contrary, all oppressed classes in all periods suffered rather uniformly from it. In order to put an end to this housing shortage there is only one means: to abolish altogether the exploitation and oppression of the working class.

Our alternatives to capitalist housing were developed during workshops in July 1990 and were included in a proposal for the Far East Bank development that the ACO submitted to the Transvaal Provincial Administration in response to a TPA tender offer. First, we suggested that land in Alex be held in a Community Land Trust that would allow for collective ownership, thereby preventing speculation, downward-raiding, shack farming, and landlordism. Second, we suggested that financial resources be channelled through a Community Development Loan Fund which would make housing finance available at an affordable interest rate. Third, we suggested that a Community Development Corporation be established which would be responsible for implementation, job creation, and so on.

Our main principle was that housing is a human right. We found ourselves nearly immediately contesting this with the IDT, a R2 billion semi-governmental agency that F.W. de Klerk founded in February 1990. By late 1990, the IDT announced it would give out R800 million for projects such as the Far East Bank (we eventually were granted R28 million by the IDT). But there was a catch: IDT Managing Director Jan Steyn was then considering a shack and freestanding toilet on a plot (site-and-service) to be "a beacon of hope," and he established this as the basis of the state's housing policy. Instead, it was a monument to mediocrity, a "toilet policy," as we called it.

South Africa could do better than this. On land that is surrounded by the wealthiest suburbs in South Africa, and for people who were suffering such enormous hardship, our traditional Freedom Charter demand (which ACO amplified) for affordable housing for all had to be made and met. We insisted that a home have four walls and a roof made of permanent materials, sufficient space for privacy and dignity, internal services, and decent community infrastructure.

In our struggle to establish our right to live in a minimally decent house, we even agreed, for once, with Sandton's Democratic Party councilor Frederick Ehlers, who wrote (in a letter to the *Star* at the end of 1991) that the IDT's Alexandra development "will be Soweto-style, except—you bring your own houses. We should by now be past frittering away our resources on this old South Africa stuff.... The result: a few unaffordable services, and a huge socio-economic wasteland worse than any Harlem or Gorbals because social and security services are uneconomic."

Our struggle for decent housing was not successful, because those who controlled resources and policy in the IDT, which activists began calling "I

Do Toilets," decided that black South Africans deserved only the R7,500 site-and-service grant, instead of the cost of a minimal house, which would be at least R25,000. We will discuss this in more detail in the next chapter.

One interesting backlash against the IDT policy, reported by *Business Day* in August 1992, was a threatened bond boycott by some residents of the East Bank. This was not an anti-bank bond boycott, but on the contrary was in opposition to ACO's efforts to secure low-cost housing funds through the IDT in the neighboring Far East Bank. Some residents called it a bond boycott against Moss Mayekiso!

Although misguided, the East Bank residents' response reflected class tensions that were perfectly natural. Later, a number of East Bank residents began working with the ACO to resolve their other financing problems (Patrick Bond's 1990 article in *Urban Forum* spells these out). We were quite proactive in trying to get the Perm and other banks in Alex to make concessions on cracked housing, high interest rates, arrears, and so forth.

Making contacts, making deals

In many areas of development, especially banking, housing, local government reform, and electricity, we came under pressure to moderate our demands and to consider deals with some fairly shady operators. As Moss explained when interviewed by *Work in Progress* after our 1989 acquittal, "If we want to undercut the power of the state we might be forced to make tactical alliances with other classes and other people closely linked to some state structures. But in doing so we must not compromise our principles. If we go into these alliances ignorant, we could betray the class struggle and socialism. Therefore we must clearly state our interest, the interest of the working class—that is, socialism."

Faced with the continuing power of the state and capital, ACO's goals were to have the right to consultation, to participate in development, and ultimately to ensure that communities controlled their own development. This began to be expressed as "From Protest to Development," a rather conservative slogan continually parroted by many apartheid bureaucrats who expected to suddenly have an easy time with their top-down approach.

But we were indeed drawn into deal making, perhaps too far. In January 1991 we unveiled our strategy, "Operation Khanyisa," and Moss told *New Nation*:

Phase one of our plan involves consultations with the community and big businesses, various government departments and ministers, and various political organizations. Phase two would be our drive to raise the necessary funds which would enable the people in Alexandra to own 50 percent of all ventures that would be embarked upon. Finally, phase three would be the actual implementation of the plan of action.

We began Khanyisa by agreeing to the Alexandra Accord and the establishment of the Joint Negotiating Forum (later called Northern Joint Negotiating Forum) with officials of surrounding areas. Then we attempted a high-profile joint venture with the PUTCO bus company, which was still non-operational as a result of a strike. In addition, we urged business leaders to donate funds and in-kind gifts to the people of Alexandra. During a business tour of Alex in April, we were joined by Dave Dalling and other Sandton and Midrand politicians, and got good support from Johnson Wax and a few other companies.

A few days later, Britain's Foreign Secretary Douglas Hurd came for a visit and gave a grant of R470,000 to the Alexandra Health Clinic. This was an interesting visit, because it very visibly raised the old tensions over who was representing Alex and hence over access to resources.

Paul Tshabalala and I showed Hurd around Alex, which made Prince Mokoena furious. Perhaps this was because Hurd, a Tory, was far closer to Mokoena's brand of "moderate" politics than he was to ACO's perspective, shaped as it was by egalitarian socialist ideals. "I feel bitter that a man of his stature stooped so low as to ignore me and my Council in this fashion," grumbled Mokoena. "His Western etiquette dictates that whenever a man of his calibre visits another man's territory he should contact him first."

So, threatened Mokoena, "Because of his rude manners, I will make sure that his promised grant does not reach the health center. It is a political clinic and people who work there do not have the interests of residents at heart." Moss had a rebuttal ready: "The man has never lifted a finger to upgrade medical facilities and the living standard in Alex." Mokoena was not alone, as ALPOA's Eric Mangele also accused ACO of wanting to enrich itself through Hurd, a groundless allegation.

Another major visit was by New York Mayor David Dinkins in November 1991. It is true that we sometimes appealed for organizational capacity-building support from our visitors. But this was not just for the ACO, but for

New York Mayor David Dinkins in Alex during his November 1991 tour of South Africa. With him are Sizakele Nkosi (third from right), then an executive member of the ANC Women's League, Alexandra, now councillor in Johannesburg's metropolitan government, and various other activists from the Women's League, the Youth Congress, and community organizations. *Author's photo.*

the whole of Alex. We also asked Dinkins to try to prevent New York banks from prematurely ending financial sanctions against Pretoria.

These visits were always interesting, even if they did not really empower our people or generate substantial resources. Instead, they gave us the impression that our civic perspective was being considered seriously among powerful people, even if some of them came because they wanted to mellow our perspective. Like some of the local government negotiating sessions, the deal making and visits pulled us away from our base, and diverted our time and energy.

Hucksters of the development industry continued to try hard to convince us that we were moving from "protest" to "development," as if serious development does not require active protest now and again (some examples of their reasoning appeared in articles which I review in Chapter 13). Arguments along these lines looked hollow under conditions wherein we simply could not get a good deal for Operation Khanyisa no matter how hard we tried. These conditions are discussed next.

10
Campaigns for
Community-Controlled Development
(1990-1993)

In this chapter I consider some of the early 1990s development campaigns that never came to fruition the way we would have liked. Barriers to our Affordable Housing for All campaign were discussed in the last chapter, and are reviewed below. The transport crisis is still with us. The environment remains degraded. The banks continue to exploit borrowers and non-borrowers alike. And although there is increasing electrification of our townships, it has been done through "pre-paid meters" which individualize consumption and thereby reduce community power. In addition, our visions of community-controlled development on the Far East Bank were foiled by the bureaucracy. Nevertheless, in each of the campaigns there were victories as well as many lessons for the civic movement and for democratic governments at national, provincial, and local levels to take forward in their development work. We also learned to identify our competitors and our opposition among other township organizations. For these reasons, not because we will achieve all of the goals outlined here in the short term, even the unsuccessful struggles we waged for community-controlled development during the early 1990s are worth reviewing.

Campaigning for people's transport

In April 1990, the PUTCO bus company shut down its Alexandra routes following a very tough strike by the Transport and General Workers' Union (TGWU). The strike lasted three months, but as settlement neared, PUTCO surprised the workers by announcing a huge rationalization of the Alex service due to the rise of the kombi taxi industry. Two-thirds of the routes and most of the jobs would be eliminated.

The basic problem was clear: as the state attempted to promote the taxi system for ideological purposes—"Free Enterprise Is Working" was the billboard slogan—subsidies were removed for trips less than twenty kilometers. PUTCO and the average commuter's pocketbook were the main victims of the new policy.

Dating from the famous 1940s bus strike, residents were highly politicized about transport, and ACO supported the TGWU strike even though it forced commuters onto the more expensive taxis. Now, with the strike settled, Alex was deprived of fifty buses on what had been one of PUTCO's most profitable routes (thanks to the generous government subsidies).

As a result, our poorest residents were spending more than 30 percent of their income on transport, according to one survey. In fact, a Department of Transport study found that in 1989, the average monthly income of bus commuters was just R471 per month, and that the shrinking subsidies were essential to make mass transit viable. To illustrate, commuters paid R1,70 for each taxi ride into Johannesburg, or R64 per month. In most cases, this was more money than was spent on housing.

Our constituents had other complaints about transport: fare increases without consultation, long queues at taxi ranks (especially during peak hours), a limited choice of transport and routes, limited taxi locations within Alex, taxis in unroadworthy condition, and so on. Our work on the issue began in late 1989 when we asked a service organization, Co-operative Planning and Education (COPE), to assist us in thinking about a transport cooperative.

In January 1991, at our Central Committee meeting of 350 street and area representatives, ACO endorsed the idea of a joint venture to restore bus service through an "Alexandra People's Bus Company." Along with our advisors in COPE, we met with PUTCO, the transport minister, lawyers, bankers, donors, accountants, the two taxi associations, and the union.

We suggested that the Company be 50 percent owned and controlled by the proposed Community Development Trust, by taxi owners and drivers, and by other community interests (with the other 50 percent owned by PUTCO). ACO would have representation on the board, along with workers represented by TGWU and PUTCO. PUTCO's response was to demand the position of permanent chair of the board, thus giving PUTCO effective

A taxi on its way to the East Bank passes by a development of flats for middle to upper-income families on Roosevelt Street. *Photo: Helen Shiller.*

control, which our financial advisors from the University of the Witwatersrand said was "totally unacceptable." We then suggested a rotating chair.

As we began to negotiate in earnest, we believed that the deal could be completed by 1 March 1991, and in February Moss announced that the community, including taxi associations, would raise R500,000 to buy into the joint venture with PUTCO. But then unprecedented violence flared.

Reeling from the Inkatha attacks, we overestimated our capacity, believing we could still go ahead with the feasibility study and fundraise from donors. In addition, the taxi associations soon realized that the bus company would eat into their own market share and they became more and more hostile. Then a small amount of what we considered "ultra-left" resistance emerged from a Trotskyist group working inside the ANC and TGWU. Called the Marxist Workers' Tendency, the group claimed that we were becoming a capitalist-oriented civic. The Tendency had neither a significant base nor a consistent political following, however. Its members were mainly white intellectuals with no clue about our system of township organizing; our local economic development projects remained outside their experience and vision.

These distractions we could have dealt with. More difficult was PUTCO's refusal to consider hiring ex-employees who had been laid off during the Alex strike, and their insistence on using twenty-nine workers formerly in Alex whom the TGWU regarded as scabs. We also had problems with the fare proposals coming from PUTCO: R2 per trip into town, which was 25 percent more than the taxis had been charging, and 33 percent more than PUTCO's earlier fares.

Then, to our dismay, on 24 April PUTCO declared a form of bankruptcy. Vic Coetzee, assistant to the PUTCO chief executive, told us that it was due to a decline in ridership from 353 million passengers in 1984 to 120 million in 1990, and the crisis caused by the taxi industry competition. He concluded, even more surprisingly, that "nationalization is the only solution to public transport."

At that stage we were ready to agree on the need for nationalization. But we also learned that PUTCO had in effect privatized billions of rands in transport subsidies and was now preparing to nationalize only the losses. Here is what a private source, *David Cobbett's Newsletter*, which tells capitalists the inside dirt on other capitalists, said about PUTCO at the time:

> In 1970 PUTCO was no great shakes as a company. Its total market capitalization was R500,000 and it was technically bust, having a negative shareholders' interest. It did, however, buy a lot of buses from Leyland, its controlling shareholder.

> In the mid-1970s Leyland withdrew from South Africa, the Carleo family came on the scene and things started to happen. Profits and losses fluctuated wildly, but there were more losses than profits. By the end of 1990, aggregate net losses under the Carleo's control amounted to R9m. In all that period shareholders paid not a penny of new money into the business. A disaster story, one might think.

> Not a bit of it! In the last five years, shareholders have received R100m in cash dividends and R50m in property shares, and they still hold assets with a book value of R85m: a grand total of R235m.

> How was it done? The financial wizardry need not concern us; the short answer is that the money came from subsidies paid by a government desperate to provide commuter services to citizens banished from the cities by its apartheid policy.

But now the music has stopped, thanks to the demise of apartheid, the phasing out of subsidies, and the advent of black taxis. The Carleos, now overseas, have not surprisingly decided to sell PUTCO. Good luck to them; they saw an opportunity and skillfully exploited it. But it will be a scandal if public funds are used to buy run-down buses that taxpayers have already paid for many times.

It was a good lesson to learn before any money had been invested. Without the subsidies, and with an exploitative company nearing bankruptcy sharing the driver's seat, the Alexandra People's Bus Company might not have succeeded. Like many development projects proposed by civics in the early 1990s, good ideas were not enough. Capitalists and apartheid bureaucrats now influenced by free market ideology were still in control of the resources.

Fighting environmental degradation

By the early 1990s, we were also becoming more conscious of environmental issues. Some of these were directly related to health care in Alex (the subject of an excellent Wits University thesis by Zwelakhe Tshandu). Many studies showed that crowding and disease were closely interrelated. And of course we were faced with many other environmental and health problems: air pollution, decimation of our trees, lack of pest and animal controls, lack of sewage and street maintenance, poor stormwater drainage, land degradation, inadequate recreational facilities, and so on.

There had always been a certain amount of township activism on the ecological front. People's parks are a good example. Solving refuse and sewage problems when those services were cut off is another example. And in 1985, an Alexandra Environmental Awareness Council worked with youth to clean up township rubbish, and also to resist the widespread dumping of waste in Alex by outside businesses. However, these efforts were interrupted by the subsequent violence and the detentions.

In addition to our 1989 clean-up campaign, ACO organized two more days in 1990 and then arranged for 250 rubbish bins to be installed. We were happy to see a general increase in community concern about the environment during the early 1990s.

This was evident even among toddlers at the progressive Montessori nursery school, who engaged in a beautiful march to town clerk Willie Khumalo's office in April 1991. Council had failed for four months to unblock clogged sewage drains, which made the whole area stink and attract flies, and the sit-in by two hundred children was successful: Khumalo acquisitioned new piping and Council workers installed it immediately.

But the problems kids face in the Alex environment are neverending. There are always unethical companies dumping toxic waste in the township, for example. As one resident told the *Sowetan*, at one stage six trucks per day were unloading hazardous materials in Alex dumps. "I have seen hungry children flocking to the dumps to scavenge for anything they can lay their hands on."

In February 1992 a chemical company left drums of the paint-removing substance Xylene at an Alexandra dump illegally, and fifteen children (as young as three years) and four elderly women were severely burnt when the stuff spilled. The Group for Environmental Monitoring joined us in demanding a code of conduct for companies in order to prevent toxic dumping, especially in the vicinity of residential areas. Richard Mdakane wrote to the Joint Negotiating Forum: "Residents of Alex are considering establishing roadblocks and patrols to take direct action against illegal dumping."

Although there were no further publicized incidents of toxic waste being dumped, we became extremely cautious. Indeed, the entire civic movement subsequently began to mobilize around the urban environment, in cooperation with the Environmental Justice Networking Forum in Pietermaritzburg. This is one struggle where we have had minor success, but where a whole range of urban environmental problems remains to be tackled.

The bond boycott weapon

One struggle that mainly related to the upper echelon of the working class was over fair treatment from the banks. Numerous demands emerged during the years banks were actively lending in black townships (essentially just 1986-1990). During that time, the banks put around R7 billion into housing loans (called bonds) for black customers. But because the smallest bond available was R35,000, only the wealthiest 10 percent of our residents could get access to bank housing finance.

Constituents of ACO and our regional body formed in 1990, the Civic Associations of the Southern Transvaal (CAST), began to make a variety of complaints about the housing bonds. For example, many of the loans were initially granted at a 12.5 percent interest rate in the mid-1980s, but soared by more than 8 percent over the course of just eighteen months (1988-1989), and stayed very high in the early 1990s.

Of all the township houses built by private developers across South Africa during the late 1980s, an estimate 90 percent soon had cracks or other serious structural defects, according to Lawyers for Human Rights. The promised upgrading of areas with housing developments, to include new schools, shops, churches, and the like often never happened. Some expensive new township houses remained without electricity hook-ups for years because the developers never sorted out the paperwork.

There was, in many cases, corruption in the sale of stands, in gaining approval from the illegitimate Councils, in bank valuations, and in the whole construction process. I have worked with Meadowlands residents who experienced all these problems. The banks had accepted false income statements from the corrupt developers and had even granted residents second bonds when the developer asked for them without the residents' knowledge.

In these cases, the developer often fled, so the only recourse in the community was to boycott the banker in order to put pressure on the developer. Banks had the power to do this, since the developers still needed to get new construction financing and bonds from the bankers. With just four or five major banks to go to, it should have been easy to compile a list of fraudulent developers, but the insensitive bankers never bothered.

The South African Housing Trust, an apartheid-era private homeownership agency, was at one point hit with fifteen bond boycotts—affecting half of its loans—due simply to bad construction by its contractors, for which it was forced to take the blame. In some cases, the Trust did admit its mistakes and settle the boycotts on the civics' terms.

Then in 1989 South Africa went into the long recession which led to hundreds of thousands of lost jobs and many tens of thousands of lost homes. Some estimates of the percentage of black families in arrears were as high as 33 percent.

But when the banks went to the authorities to foreclose on a house, the authorities found that they did not have enough power to go in and evict the defaulter. This was because our street committees considered a bond default in much the same way they considered a rent boycott default: if the problem was with the system, justice demanded that individuals not be kicked out of their homes simply because they lost their jobs or found the interest bill was too expensive. As a result, banks simply could not get access to their collateral.

To make matters worse, the resale price of houses in many townships fell rapidly when the Group Areas Act was lifted in 1991, allowing middle-class black people to buy houses in white areas, and when violence began to spread. But people still had to pay expensive bonds at the original price. This meant that they had no incentive to sell their homes, since they would still owe additional money—often more than R10,000—to the banks after the sale. This problem of "negative equity" meant that there were very few sales of houses going on in the townships.

So banks had simply stopped lending in the townships, and even in inner-city areas, when all of these problems built up by 1990. Their practice of "redlining"—geographical discrimination—meant that even a wealthy person could not get a bond in Hillbrow or a black township, because the bankers claimed the value of the house (the bank's security) would decline. This practice became a self-fulfilling prophesy which led to much lower sales prices since, when bank credit was not available, selling a house required a cash buyer.

The bankers also claimed that they would not lend anymore in black areas because of widespread bond boycotts. Many simplistic newspaper editorials and right-wing commentaries focused on this point. It was a red herring, because only a very few civics were running effective bond boycotts, in places like Khayalitsha, Botshabelo, and Etwatwa. Nearly all of these were against the state's South African Housing Trust.

But it was entirely logical for CAST leaders to threaten a bond boycott in 1991 to get the banks to come to the negotiating table. And in 1992, when SANCO was founded and Moss was elected president, the bond boycott tactic caused a national outcry.

The reason for this outcry is worth exploring briefly. SANCO did indeed *threaten* a national bond boycott, but never put in place the machinery to implement the boycott. The strategy of a boycott threat, followed by subsequent negotiations with the banks, was the outcome of extensive civic movement discussion in July 1992, after the multiparty talks (called the CODESA talks) broke down and after several dozen residents of Boipatong township in the Vaal were murdered by Inkatha.

This was a time of intensified mass action, with COSATU mobilizing for a nationwide general strike and the ANC and SACP organizing a huge march to Pretoria. But when Nelson Mandela returned from the Barcelona Olympic Games in July 1992, he read a very critical statement against the bond boycott tactic prepared for him by his staff.

This strategic conflict with the ANC made the democratic forces appear weak and divided. Nevertheless, the bank campaign demonstrated some very strong features of the civic movement. Moss actually renewed the bond boycott threat in August, even in the wake of Mandela's condemnation. This was the reason (according to Moses Mayekiso's year-end 1992 speech, "State of the Civic Movement"):

> At the SANCO General Council meeting in early July, in the wake of the Boipatong massacre, we resolved that big business has the capacity to influence the state, and that big business should come under intensified popular pressure to do so. Since September 1985, when the leaders of Anglo American and other corporations first publicly visited the ANC in Lusaka, the democratic movement has had to focus more attention on the potential conflict between the state and big business. Our aim was to test whether that bloc could be broken, either through negotiations or through mass action pressure.
>
> The civic movement searched for ways to develop greater power against big business, and we eventually decided to target the major banks through the threat of mass action, including a bond boycott on township loans. The banks have over R10 billion in loans of various kinds out to government, and that gives them certain powers over government.
>
> For example, there were several billion rand in bank loans to Ciskei, Bophuthatswana, KwaZulu, and other homelands in the form of "short-term overdrafts." This is a type of loan that gave the banks very high profits in the form of interest payments, and added enormously to the South African government deficit. The vast amounts of these particular loans reflected how badly the homeland and central government budgets were handled. But they also gave the banks some clout, because the loans had to be extended periodically. We hoped our forces would be able to pressurize the banks into, at the minimum, forcing Gqozo, Mangope, and Buthelezi to permit democratic rights of protest. The banks could threaten to call in the overdraft loans, and this would put added pressure on the regime.
>
> This approach was proven correct in 1994, just two weeks before the election, when it appeared that Inkatha would go ahead with its boycott and intensify the violence in Natal and Johannesburg. Pressured by the ANC, the Transitional Executive Council's finance committee finally got around to looking into Gatsha Buthelezi's bank accounts. The committee found more than R1

billion stored away in the First National Bank and other banks, which Buthelezi was counting on using for his threatened Unilateral Declaration of Independence. The finance committee then publicly announced it would target those funds and make sure Gatsha did not get his hands on them. Within two days, to everyone's surprise, Gatsha backed down and agreed to participate in the election. Of course, this tactic contributed to the TEC's military strategy against Inkatha, which was to shut down their training bases in order to prevent them from mobilizing their impis during the election.

But to go back to August 1992, one outcome of the bond boycott threat was that the Perm lost a great deal of support from its shareholders, and the stock price of Nedbank, its parent company, fell rapidly. This encouraged the Perm to cut a separate deal with SANCO in September in order to end the threat against Perm bonds (the other banks continued to hold a much harder line on issues such as loans to the homeland).

Perm officials quickly announced that the bank had made no loans to apartheid structures like the homelands. By doing a deal with the Perm, SANCO not only won that point, but also showed that it could be reasonable. A set of Perm development trust funds were set up for various regions, and although the relationships were relatively weak, they did lead to some progress in addressing local-level problems.

But the other banks remained intransigent. Finally, in February 1993, SANCO negotiated a deal which would have made it much easier for our people to deal with arrears, defaults, and foreclosures in exchange for permitting the banks to carry through foreclosures if all else failed. Two problems soon arose. First, a couple of banks were soon using the agreement as a foreclosure notice, without going through all the steps to help out borrowers who were in arrears. Second, the banks had agreed to help fund a cadreship of independent, community-based "ombudspersons" who could explain the deal and help implement it. They had even helped draw up budgets, and we were identifying where these ombuds offices would be needed. Suddenly, in August 1993, they turned their back on this commitment. They refused to give any reason for this.

I remember one meeting at that point, when a member of the Association of Mortgage Lenders told me and the other SANCO negotiators, in front of his colleagues and with a straight face, that the executive committee of mortgage bankers had decided not to give the ombuds offices any of the capacity-building support that was needed to take the agreement forward.

I looked at him for a minute, and then asked if I could see the minutes of the meeting. His face turned red. "There are no minutes," he admitted.

In view of this bad-faith behavior, the SANCO executive board then decided to retract our support for the agreement. But after about a year in which we had only hostility from the banks, and in which they continued to put barriers in the way of an overall housing policy in the National Housing Forum, we thought that by exposing them to other perspectives we could open their minds. Possibly, we reasoned, with a combination of our pressure tactics and their own growing knowledge, they would become sufficiently enlightened to deal with us on our own terms. I organized a tour of the United States in July 1994 for several of our regional leaders (their visit was paid for by four New York banks) and for several Johannesburg bankers.

We had two reasons. One was our desire to see a Community Reinvestment Act passed which, like the United States law, would give communities a say in enforcing a ban on redlining. The second was the wide experience that our best comrades in U.S. civic associations (like ACORN, National People's Action, and Industrial Areas Foundation) had in structuring financial packages with big U.S. banks.

But we were disappointed again, because shortly after the 1994 elections, the Department of National Housing, initially led by the late Joe Slovo, opened up negotiations with the banks, but without SANCO. Slovo's negotiators eventually came up with a loan guarantee program which was exceedingly generous to the banks, and very disempowering to community groups. It was also irrelevant to the lower 70 percent of the black population, because it did not push the banks to loan to the poor, nor did it reduce the very high interest rates on housing bonds (still higher than 16 percent). I could not blame comrade Slovo for this lack of consultation with SANCO; his director-general—who at one time had worked at Planact with the civics—appeared to take the view that shunning SANCO on this matter would serve the government's interests.

The one major breakthrough for SANCO was that at the time policy directions were being taken, we had become some of the democratic movement's leading experts on banking. The civics had raised many issues and forced the banks to address them in public, including redlining, international capital flight, lack of services in our communities, excessive profits, and the like. We were asked to give extensive input into the ANC's Reconstruction and Development Program (RDP).

SANCO met with the banks again in January 1994 to tell them that the new ANC banking policy would contain provisions forcing them to change their policies on lending to black communities, since they had failed to do so voluntarily. The banks were furious, and immediately put up a big hue and cry, with Standard Bank's Nico Czypionka saying that the proposed policies "make my hair stand on end." But the RDP provisions on banking remained unchanged. Whether there will be follow-up in coming years, however, remains to be seen.

Eskom's aversion to community-controlled electricity

Eskom was a central player in Alexandra, even though the supply of electricity to consumers was a recent development and far from complete.

The company, technically a parastatal institution which should be subject to democratic control, played a powerful role in the development of Alexandra, including design of the Alexandra Urban Renewal Plan in September 1986 and support in its implementation (alongside the Alexandra Council, DBSA, South African Police, South African Defence Force, and other members of the JMC). That plan depended upon the absence of strong community organizations, whose leaders were in jail. It came about through a manipulative process, void of community consultation, much less participation. It was designed to ensure military stability and security, not community welfare. It involved principles of privatization, which were used to displace and deflect popular resistance. It divided urban communities, especially on income and geographical lines. It offered no hope for the urban poor, who were not able to afford urban services under the terms of the Eskom plan. It operated on the principle that there would be no cross subsidization with the wealthy white areas nearby, and no integration with the surrounding economy. It accepted all the worst aspects of the existing system, from the Group Areas Act to orderly urbanization to resettlement of shack dwellers. It was top-down, based on inadequate information gathered in a short period of time, was neither comprehensive nor holistic, complemented apartheid urban policy, had no regional context, and propped up undemocratic—and indeed criminal—elements in our society, in particular the Alexandra Council.

Eskom may never again play a leading role in town planning, especially in townships. But in electricity provision, Eskom is the biggest in sub-Saharan Africa and one of the ten biggest utilities

companies of any kind in the whole world. However, even in its area of expertise, township residents were struck by Eskom's extreme contradictions. Although Eskom makes enormous profits, and although at least three quarters of black households still need electricity, Eskom spent the early 1990s laying off more than 20,000 of its employees (heavily biased toward laying off black workers) and cutting about 15 percent of its electricity output.

Why? It seems that Eskom expanded too far in the late 1970s and 1980s on the basis of bad planning. Eskom thought that the high growth of the apartheid era would continue forever, and did not account for the economic slump that engulfed the P.W. Botha and de Klerk regimes. Eskom was simply chasing profits, even at the expense of the terrible environmental destruction caused in the process. But as profits in the economy as a whole fell, those expansion plans went sour.

Rather than chasing profits, there were better principles for producing and supplying electricity, some of which were emerging directly from the civic movement. The Soweto People's Delegation, in negotiations with Eskom which went as far back as 1989, argued that electricity must be supplied to all in a non-racial way; that the community must control and make decisions on the supply of electricity; that electricity is a right for all; and that the electricity system must work as well in the township as it does in Johannesburg.

Soweto's civic leaders made some progress in their negotiations, and the same demands arose from Alexandra. But Eskom toughened up, and in 1990 tried to pull the electricity issue off the table in local multi-party negotiations (in what became the Northern Joint Negotiating Forum). And in the wake of the breakthrough Alexandra Accord in February 1991, which is described in Chapter 12, Eskom tried to avoid the implication that ACO would have a say in the long-overdue electrification of Alexandra. The ACO did not contest that point at that time, which because of the violence was still a traumatic period for the people of Alexandra. But such lack of cooperation was not quickly forgiven or forgotten.

To make matters worse, even though Eskom argued for a market-oriented economy geared to choice, the company offered the consumer in Alexandra no choice at all in terms of electricity consumption. For white areas, there was the option of getting conventional metering, as opposed to the new pre-paid coupon (S-1 tariff) which became the only type of electricity supply on offer in Alex. The S-1 tariff was a new concept and should have been workshopped with the community. If it had been, the community would have been much more committed to working with Eskom to iron out the issues.

Instead, Eskom unilaterally installed the new system, and consumers were very unhappy. Eskom's high charge for connecting the pre-paid meter was made worse by the fact that the cost per unit of electricity was also much higher (17-18c, instead of 12-13c under normal arrangements). In addition, Eskom continues to earn interest on our money because, under the new tariff system, as consumers we pay first and then consume later.

Finally, Eskom was impervious to our desire for community-building through consumption of services such as electricity. The civic sought a means by which community support could be offered when someone's house went dark because the coupons had run out. Instead, Eskom saw the whole market in terms of profit-making and individualizing electricity consumption. With this approach, there was little chance to solve Alexandra's electricity problems, especially the matter of affordability. Thus, rather than trying to define and support a community response, Eskom hired a private contractor (Masterlik) for Alexandra. If the ACO had been asked about this, it is possible that an alternative could have been considered. In Soweto, for example, the Soweto Civic Association proposed an electricity cooperative. This may not have been the best approach, but should have been explored, along with other alternatives that might better meet people's needs.

Our criticisms of Eskom never prevented us from meeting and discussing issues with the company, but the balance of power and bad bureaucratic attitudes kept Eskom from ever truly serving the people of Alexandra.

The struggle for the Far East Bank

Whether locking horns with PUTCO, polluters, the banks, Eskom, or other agencies, we never gave up our vision of a more humane route to development. Our July 1990 proposal to develop the Far East Bank (FEB) remains a very powerful statement of community-controlled development. But it has not yet been implemented. As the FEB became a site of struggle, quite a few conservative interest groups in and around Alex worked to prevent a holistic strategy from emerging.

It began, not surprisingly, with the Alexandra Council. In August 1989 the Council put out a Request for Proposals to companies or agencies interested in developing the Far East Bank land. But at the time, the land was owned by the Transvaal Provincial Administration (the TPA had bought the land for R14 million from Johannesburg). When, in February 1990, ACO complained about this and threatened to go to court to prevent the land from falling into the Alex Council's control, the TPA then decided that it would put out the request for proposals instead. ACO submitted a proposal in July, in which we suggested a process for developing the FEB in a manner true to our principles of community control.

That proposal was given consideration later in the year, when we made a major presentation to the TPA, in competition with another dozen or so private sector developers. Privately, we told the TPA that if the FEB was not devoted to low-income housing, they could forget about the Alexandra Accord. Implicitly, we threatened to pull out of the agreement ending the rent boycott.

Two months later, in February 1991, the TPA called our bluff and gave the FEB land to the Alex Council, but we were not bluffing. As we were on the verge of pulling out of the Alexandra Accord, the TPA retracted their decision within forty-eight hours and instead allocated the land to the Sandton Council in a way that ensured ACO would have a good deal of control over developmental decision making.

By this time, we had won the argument that low-income people should be given priority access to the FEB. But the TPA still agreed with Johannesburg that a golf course should serve as a buffer strip. And they insisted that a major highway cut right through the heart of the FEB land. A year later, we finally forced the TPA to drop the golf course and reduce the width of the road (no longer a major highway) to thirty-five meters, which allowed more space for additional stands. Altogether, we expected to get more than 3,800 new houses on the FEB land.

Unfortunately, the TPA also allowed an engineering consulting firm hired by the Alex Council, Goulty Moller and Associates, to set the planning parameters. When, in May 1991, a subsidy application was made by the Sandton Council to the Independent Development Trust (the only agency with sufficient funding available for such a large project), Moller's plans were used. These were little more than apartheid-era plans, and ACO strongly objected. We limited those plans to 1,434 stands in Phase 1, cut out the other work by Goulty Moller, and upgraded the Phase 1 services to include electricity (the IDT subsidy did not normally include even an electricity line to a site).

At this stage, ACO was conducting regular workshops. Our committees agreed not to pursue the Community Development Trust through this process, because the FEB was clearly being driven by the TPA, which retained ultimate power over Alex. We focused our attention instead upon acquiring other subsidies and loans so the FEB would contain real houses, not just IDT toilets.

Yet even though it took nearly a year for the sites to be serviced, we failed during that period to acquire sufficient funds for even modest housing (costing R25,000 per unit). To even get a toilet, residents of the new stands were now charged R250 each (on top of the R7,500 IDT subsidy). State housing policy was still dominated by a big business housing minister, Louis Shill, who had no interest in seeing subsidies raised to a decent level. Shill and the IDT also refused to help us with collective ownership through a Land Trust, since they were ideologically committed to a nuclear family ownership model. This will cause a major "downward raiding" problem in the future.

Meanwhile, Goulty Moller would not accept the fact that their services were only to be used for 1,434 stands, and made threats to pursue legal action. More and more delays occurred as the IDT put bureaucratic barriers in the way, even threatening to withdraw funding for other phases. It was not until mid-1993 that services were finally in place.

But then more than 4,500 families applied for the stands. There were still no formal commitments on schools, shops, churches, recreation, and other facilities. The allocation procedure caused a great deal of havoc with other organizations in Alex, so we continued to insist that the process be fair, public, and transparent. We suggested the appointment of neutral observers to oversee the process, and we initially called for a public lottery to apportion the stands.

The IDT's own criteria for how to allocate the subsidized stands caused new problems. For example, they insisted that a beneficiary had to be a South African citizen, over age twenty-one, the "head" of a household, and have less than R1,000 income per month. (Our desire to see a low-cost housing development did not mean that we did not want regular working-class families with a higher household income, so the R1,000 barrier did not make sense and was hard to verify in any case.)

Once we did our workshops on stand allocation and received more community input, we added some other criteria to create a point system. We gave extra points to long-time residents of Alex, to those with more children, to those whose present shelter was shack, rental, or in a dangerous location, and to those whose income was below R600 per month. And we suggested that at least a third of the sites go to female-headed households, which was the average for Alex as a whole.

We were also beginning to think in terms of integrated planning, instead of just product-oriented development. We gave the Joint Negotiating Forum a proposal which emphasized both our understanding of the complexity of planning and our insistence on community participation. Most importantly, we put this in the context of the northern Johannesburg area economic region, so that Alexandra would not continue to suffer ghettoization.

This led us to the argument for an "Alexandra-centered region" to incorporate nearby industrial areas in economic planning, instead of having an FEB "central business district," as the apartheid planners wanted. We expanded our "local economic development" ideas with the help of two leading progressive inner-city practitioners brought in from Chicago and San Francisco. We demanded an environmental audit, more recreational facilities, and better integration of transport routes through the area. We began to set our sights on nearby areas like Modderfontein and Frankenwold, where major institutions like the AECI chemical company and the University of the Witwatersrand held undeveloped land.

Although these visions, principles, and strategies were all drawn from ACO brainstorms and community workshops and were acceptable to the ordinary residents we worked with, other players in Alex opposed us because our ideas did not overwhelmingly serve middle-class interests and because they were linked to the Alexandra Accord and Joint Negotiating Forum. In Chapter 12, I describe the local resistance generated by the Accord. But the wide range of competing and opposing organizations in Alex also deserve some discussion.

Competition and opposition in Alexandra

Building a strong civic in contemporary South Africa is an uphill struggle, especially if the civic tries to unite people across class lines and other social barriers within one particular community, and in a manner that is non-party-political. We were an organization biased toward the needs of poor and working-class people, the young and old, women and men alike. But we could never afford to leave out more privileged residents, nor could we exclude those who were not interested in politics or community. We were capable of mounting impressive protests, but we also had to be very capable when it came to negotiating development and democratization of local government.

If we failed in any of these respects, there were other organizations, our competition and our opposition, ready to take advantage and woo away our supporters. In a high-profile, extremely poor, and very diverse township such as Alexandra, there were myriad tensions between organizations, and these even affected relations between progressive political allies.

The ANC, for example, due to logistical difficulties, only launched its Alex branch in December 1990. The SACP had strong latent support, and their structures in Alex were in a close partnership with the ANC. The PAC and AZAPO remained effectively dormant.

Alex ANC branch leadership was initially won by Popo Molefe, a popular UDF leader who came to Alex from Soweto in 1985 and in 1994 became the first premier of the Northwest Province. More than 500 people attended the launch at Rev. Sam Buti's church. Although I was nominated as branch chairperson, along with Popo and Sipho Kubheka, I stood down on the grounds that I was more committed to building the ACO at that stage. Sipho was not in attendance, so Popo won by acclaim. Meanwhile, Obed Bapela moved from ACO to join the ANC branch executive.

We initially saw ourselves as part of one democratic movement family, and ACO even helped to get the ANC launched (we gave assistance, just as we would have with the PAC, had they asked us). But the ACO and ANC now had to begin to come to terms with their respective roles, particularly because the local government negotiations were progressing rapidly.

With the ANC back, some argued, it should take its rightful position as the primary representative of the disadvantaged. Others, however, felt the civic was better placed for this responsibility because of its strong record and tight organization. During the following months, tensions between the ACO and ANC became quite serious turf struggles, leading later (in early 1992) to the formal realization that we had quite different power bases in Alex and that we also had a different perspective on political strategy.

Even though our executives were almost all loyal ANC members, ACO's relations with the local ANC began to degenerate quite a bit, basically over who was representative of community interests and who had the most appropriate development vision.

Consistent with the apartheid intention of dividing blacks along ethnic lines, our opponents sometimes alleged that ACO had a base only among immigrants, especially Xhosa people from the Transkei whom Moss had encouraged to come to Alex. But in relation to the mass of Alex residents, there were not that many recent immigrants. According to one survey in 1990, 56 percent of the total adult population had lived in Alexandra for over twenty-one years, 22 percent between eleven and twenty years, 13 percent between four and ten years, and only 9 percent between one and three years. Of those who moved to Alex at some stage in their lives, only 5 percent were from the Transkei or Ciskei. It was gratifying that 48 percent of all residents indicated that they intended to stay in Alexandra.

Even our establishment opponents, such as the Sandton and Randburg Councils, recognized our legitimacy. According to one confidential report ("Local Government Negotiating Initiatives") by the Urban Foundation, "Relative to most civics, ACO is very powerful: its leaders are exceptionally competent, and there is a very fluid flow of information up and down its extensive organizing structures. ACO is, without question, the most representative single body in the township."

Actually, we could never hope to adequately represent the entire community of Alex in our negotiations or struggles, but we could always *try* to. But Alex is an extremely diverse and complicated township. It was always a challenge to emphasize the unity of people with such varied backgrounds, especially because rival civic and political bodies sometimes attempted to organize class-based segments. Chapter 9 considered some of the tensions around privatized housing which led to the founding of Alexandra Land and Property Owners Association, and the next chapter covers the war with Inkatha.

In addition, some other small lobby groups (the Alexandra Builders' and Allied Traders' Association [ABATA], along with the Alexandra Industrial Association and the Alexandra Builder's Forum) spoke out against ACO: "The small contractor is being deliberately disadvantaged especially that ACO which sits in the two committees and Joint Negotiating Forum, is party to the submission of the proposal to TPA. What about ACA?"

What about the ACA? The Alexandra Civic Association was generally a feeble distraction, but often turned venomous. ACA leaflets issued during the tragic 1991 violence said the following:

 * MAYEKISO BAPELA AND THE ALEXANDRA CIVIC ORGANIZATION ARE SELLOUTS WHO ARE NOT WORKING FOR OUR PEOPLE
 * THE ZULUS AND THE ALEXANDRA RESIDENTS HAVE BEEN LIVING IN PEACE TOGETHER FOR YEARS
 * THE ALEXANDRA CIVIC ORGANIZATION HAVE STARTED TAKING

THE LAW IN THEIR OWN HANDS AND ARE CAUSING VIOLENT OUT-
BREAKS IN ALEXANDRA

* THE SQUATTERS AND SHACKS THAT MAYEKISO BROUGHT INTO
ALEXANDRA ARE CAUSING FILTH, CRIME AND DISEASE AND ARE
MAKING IT DIFFICULT TO STOP THE VIOLENCE

As the Urban Foundation reported of ACA, though, "No elections or
general meetings have been held since 1985, and the civic still does not
have a phone or office—let alone visible structures."

Along with the ACA, the builders, led by Darkie Rametsi, felt threatened
by the ACO's community-controlled approach to development. Rametsi is a
former teacher, employee of Dipac construction company, and public
relations officer of the Alex Council. In a letter he wrote (as the chairperson
of ABATA) to the Joint Negotiation Forum Secretary in October 1991, we
see the vanity of the petty bourgeoisie:

> The sad situation is that the Joint Negotiating Forum for Alexandra is
> busy pursuing other organization to go public on some hot-embarrass-
> ing issues which no rightful thinking community can endorse. The cause
> of all this is your organization's tight close-door policies.... May I be
> so kind to inform you that this may be our last letter to you, sir, because
> we are aware also that you do not even acknowledge letters that come
> from Black people especially Alexandrans—unless of course there is
> a white face. Do we sound like racists? No, we are telling the truth.

Perhaps it was inevitable that serious political tensions would emerge
from the petty bourgeoisie. The ANC was "vacillating between two ideologically conflicting readings of the spatial ordering of Alexandra," according to Justine Lucas, a Wits University social anthropologist who, through
participant observation, wrote a paper on "Civic Organization in Alexandra
During the 1990s." One interpretation, she argues, is that this is a unitary
township where there are conflicts between shack dwellers and residents of
formal housing. "This concurs with ACO's position, and makes political
sense if ANC and ACO are in alliance rather than competing for power."

But the other position, Lucas argues, is closer to the ACA's view: that
Alexandra was "unchanging over time" and was recently "invaded by
outsiders who, by moving uninvited into yards and refusing to pay rent, are
upsetting the 'natural' spatial order of the township, embodied in the concept
of property rights."

This second position was not well-grounded in reality. In Lucas's study of two yards in the Lusaka section of Alex, the ACO perspective was borne out. In one case, "members of the former landlord's family have largely incorporated the idea of a yard committee into their understanding of social relations in the yard, and the participants in the yard committee have likewise adjusted ACO's model to accommodate landlord-tenant continuities, leaving those who oppose the reintroduction of a landlord marginalised." This was a yard where ACO's yard committee was not even particularly strong, but where good social relationships existed because our model was a good and logical structure for solving problems.

In a second study, Lucas discovered very strong social bonds within our ACO structure. In a single yard in Lusaka, Lucas recorded a women's committee, a burial society, a resident *sangoma*, and three shebeens (people who tried to drink alone in the yard were persuaded to share). There was also a tough defense unit and a local justice committee. "The yard comprises a moral community within which thieving and crime are not tolerated." As both a social and political unit, this case "fits perfectly with ACO's conception of a yard. People frequently stressed that they were 'united' and spoke about their 'brothers' in the yard." As Lucas concluded,

When a committee was first introduced in 1986, it made perfect sense for people to organize themselves into a structure based on an ideology of equality, which provided mechanisms for social order, since their common experience of being tenants had already established these ideas in principle. Later, when shack-dwellers moved into the yard, they found a structure and model of social relations in which they were easily accommodated. The result is that the yard today is a bounded unit in which the political is inextricable from the social.

Not all yard structures were as tight as this one, and some ACO structures in transitory areas such as the Mozambique freestanding shack settlement did not function effectively. As is the case in any mass-based organization, on rare occasions mafioso or other unsavory characters infiltrated the structures temporarily. But the sense of unity, development, democracy, and accountability which is so central to ACO's ideology clearly had a grounding in the yards. This meant that even under several periods of ferocious attack from Inkatha in the early 1990s, the ACO retained its support and integrity.

11
From Protest to War
(1990-1993)

The most difficult chapter for me to write, and for the reader to consider, covers the war we suffered through in Alexandra during the early 1990s, in which the apartheid regime was able to distract our attention through its various frontmen.

The political roots of violence

The way the *Sunday Star* described the situation in Alexandra prior to the bloodshed of 1991 was fairly accurate:

This was the township that throughout the 1990s bloody battles on the Rand had been an outstanding example of peace and harmony. For years Xhosa and Zulu, ANC-supporter and Inkatha-supporter, had lived together cheek by jowl in the Alexandra hostels with no friction at all. There was also none of the friction between residents and hostel dwellers that has proved so fatally divisive in almost all other townships on the Rand. Hostel dwellers were involved in activities and were free to patronise community shebeens, which they often did. By the same token residents were regular visitors to the hostels.

To get a clear understanding of why, over the next two years, more than two hundred people lost their lives, thousands were injured, and thousands more were displaced by invasion of their homes, requires us to go back to the tensions between ACO and the security establishment. I think that many of the roots of the violence are to be found in this conflict, which firmly set the security forces against Alex residents.

If anyone in Alex believed that 2 February 1990, or even de Klerk's November 1989 commitment to disband the Joint Management Centres, would have an immediate effect on security conditions in Alex, they were badly disappointed. The Alexandra Joint Management Centre appeared to very quickly turn itself into the brand new "Alexandra Advisory Committee" with its very own "oliekol" (oilspot) subcommittee. Remarkably, in early 1990 the "223rd meeting" of this brand new Advisory Committee was held. (Seven months earlier, the JMC had celebrated its 200th meeting anniversary. So it was not too hard to discern the security force name-change strategy.) They continued to watch us closely, and knew, for example, that Moss had visited Lusaka, Zambia, twice in the space of a fortnight in 1989 to consult with the ANC.

In early 1990, Alexandra Advisory Committee minutes noted:

> Mayekiso is stirring and trying to rally the community. He has applied for accommodation in Alexandra, and the councilor was advised that he should be refused as long as possible.... One of the problems is that as General Secretary of NUMSA, he is in a strong political position and the government is consequently unwilling to touch him unless absolutely necessary.

Through our own intelligence network we received the minutes, and we decided to test the Advisory Committee on whether ACO leaders could return from our temporary accommodation in Hillbrow to Alex. In early 1990, Richard Mdakane, Paul Tshabalala, Obed Bapela, and I went to the Council and requested accommodation in the brand new Queen's Court apartments. We negotiated with Prince Mokoena, head of the Management Committee, who at that stage wanted to act like a good guy in front of us. He said he needed approval from the town clerk and from the housing councilor, Dennis Tao. The clerk, Willie Khumalo (the former AAC yard chair), even gave us the keys to several four-room apartments, and drove us to the flats to look around. We negotiated so that we would have rooms on upper stories, in order to reduce the threat of assassination.

We were to move into the apartments on the following day. But during the night, another set of keys was given to other people, rogue characters in alliance with other fractions within the Council under the JMC's influence.

The following day, I was surprised to find my flat occupied. We caucused, and decided that this could be some sort of a JMC ploy to get us into a fight with these people. It would have been bad publicity for us. Khumalo later told us, "Hey chaps, I'm in real trouble. Not long after I gave you the keys, the security police showed up. Then Mike Beea was told to put his own people in those places. Those people were told that some thugs [the ACO comrades] would come and try to take their rooms, and they must fight." Khumalo then thanked us for not trying to evict the intruders, because that would have played right into the security forces' plans.

As for those apartments, the Council ultimately wanted to sell them as part of their free enterprise campaign. ACO started a counter campaign to have the authorities rent them instead. Because of this issue, the security committee reported, there was "a growing feeling of rebellion in the air—the whole climate appears to be turning."

The pressure then intensified. At an Advisory Committee meeting in April 1990, Colonel George Ruthven, commander of the Alex police, was quoted as saying, "There has been a lot of intimidation of the councilors. The councilors want the police to wipe out these troublemakers without any formal charge being laid." Ruthven later tried to explain away what he meant to the *Star*: "An army youngster took the minutes. They are trained to 'wipe out' the enemy. This was not my meaning." (Ruthven had once publicly stated that the "chief problem" in Alex was the "population explosion among blacks," so whatever it was he did mean was bound to be disturbing.)

The minutes of the Advisory Committee's April meeting show that any means available to demobilize activists would be considered:

> Lieutenant Twiname noted that concrete evidence is necessary against Mayekiso before he can be accused of causing a war. The community will not help in this regard.... Mr. Burger mentioned under correction that a certain Benny Kutumela, who had been shot, was the troublemaker in this taxi war situation. He had been causing trouble while supporting Mayekiso. It is presumed that AMSTA [Alexandra-Midrand-Sandton Taxi Association] destroyed him. In retaliation, the Treasurer of AMSTA was later killed.... Lieutenant Twiname said that Mayekiso is not getting the political gains he should be and is trying to initiate a propaganda war.

In May 1990, the *Sunday Star* exposed the new face of security force operations in Alex by revealing the Advisory Committee as a rehashed JMC.

Moss then indeed turned up the rhetorical heat with the following statement to the *Star*:

> We have been aware of the councilors' attitudes toward eliminating activists in Alexandra and we have heard stories of hit squads. It is clear that the Advisory Committee is operating in the same sinister and devious way that the JMC operated. The central figures on both structures are Colonel Holland-Muter and Steve Burger. It is also a continuation of the methods used by the Alex JMC until their "disbanding" in November 1989—methods which included spying on community leaders, monitoring their movements, establishing informer networks and distributing fake pamphlets.

ACO continued to be a serious thorn in the security establishment's side. One set of Advisory Committee minutes from March 1990 noted, "Unless contact is made with all the community-based organizations, the ACO will take over and run Alex as in 1986." In May 1990, ACO was termed "underground" and "subversive," even though we were operating above ground from Alexandra Development Fund offices.

A security force representative at that Advisory Committee meeting said he viewed ACO not as part of the (now unbanned) ANC, but instead as affiliated to the "Fourth International." The Fourth International is a Trotskyist group whose associates in South Africa were the Workers Organization for Socialist Action, which was extremely hostile to the South African Communist Party. Moss, by then, was on the central committee of the SACP, which goes to show how hollow the analysis by the security forces was.

Moreover, according to minutes leaked to the press, the Advisory Committee also intended that Mike Beea's Alexandra Civic Association be revived in order to split the community.

This was a time of enormous tension, as each side continued to test the other's strength. Ours was growing, the regime's decaying. But the state and its allies still had a variety of weapons at their disposal.

In April, for example, Aldo Mogano, twenty-two, leader of the Alexandra Youth Congress, was assassinated. In June, sixty-seven of our civic members were arrested during a meeting at which ACO was discussing how to support an ANC recruitment drive, but the arrests were on the completely erroneous grounds that we were having a people's court. And then in August and September, the Inkatha Freedom Party began its Johannesburg-area attacks on communities and at train stations, leaving hundreds of black residents dead on the East Rand and in Soweto.

Thankfully, Alex was quiet during the worst of the 1990 violence. It was not until later that year that ominous signs began to emerge from the hostels, as our ACO comrades began to move out under threat. In March 1991, we finally understood just how badly the security situation had deteriorated when over one hundred of our residents were murdered by a new alliance of the Alex Council and Inkatha mercenaries from outside Alexandra.

The timing of the first attack—on 8 March, in the form of a Friday night Inkatha raid on a street committee meeting in the Freedom Charter area— was just a week after the mayor of the Alex Council had lost a major power struggle to ACO.

The first Inkatha attack

Alex had been a quiet community during the worst battles between Inkatha forces and East Rand communities in August and September 1990. At the grassroots level, there were no major conflicts between Inkatha and the ANC, and indeed members of both organizations were brothers and sisters within the civic association. And all, including those with Inkatha leanings, were in the campaign to have the councilors resign.

Soon, however, Inkatha hostel dwellers were coerced into fomenting a deadly war. First, they were harassed by other Inkatha members from outside Alex, who called them "weak." As we heard of this, ACO leadership took all possible measures to avoid the war spreading to Alex from the East Rand.

But the Alex Council used Inkatha as its last resort. Prince Mokoena wrote a memo to his councilors saying he was fed up with the Alexandra Civic Organization. ACO continued to press for all councilors to resign, and we continued with our marches on their houses demanding this, arguing that the councilors were still a crucial part of apartheid. Since the ANC would not take the councilors as members while they still held their apartheid positions, in the end they all joined Inkatha—obviously for protection.

Just before the agreement between ACO and the TPA was to be signed, a deadlock emerged over the control of land in the Far East Bank. As discussed in Chapter 9, it turned out that the TPA had already awarded the land secretly to the Alex Council for development. ACO insisted that the people of Alexandra control the land, and develop it for the poor. Because of the deadlock with the rent negotiations, the TPA decision on the land going to the Council was rescinded overnight. The TPA must have wanted the Alexandra Accord very badly, since they then gave the land to the Sandton Council to manage as an agent. We were satisfied, because with the Alexandra Accord, ACO now had a prominent role in a negotiating forum to decide what to do about the land.

But since Mokoena and the Alex Council had viewed the land as a gift from which to make bucks, when it was taken from them overnight their plans were ruined. Before, Mokoena was bragging that he had the land, and that he would sell it to the big developers. Everyone had heard this. Now he called Moss and told him, "I'm going to hit you."

We then sensed that a massive eruption of violence would come to Alex. During the week before it started, the ACO office was getting reports that more and more Inkatha people were arriving by bus and taxi. Mokoena whipped up the hostel dwellers' emotions, and made it appear to them as if Xhosa people wanted to fight the Zulus.

Then, for two weeks during February 1991, the security police put me and thirteen other civic leaders in detention without charge. They raided our offices three times, even while we were negotiating with the TPA. I went on another hunger and water strike, and was finally released.

This episode is worth a brief digression. The security policy had picked me up—under their detention-without-trial powers—just after I arrived back from holidays in the Transkei. I had been away when, in mid-January, there was a spontaneous, unorganized march to the homes of councilors, where angry residents dumped trash and emptied buckets full of night soil. I was initially blamed for the march, but eventually the police released me without filing charges.

In the meantime, I was placed in Johannesburg Hospital because of my hunger strike. The black nurses there warned me that in the same section there were three other hunger strikers: white racist members of the Wit Wolve (White Wolves) militia who allowed only white staff to treat them. On my first night, I slept on a separate floor. The following evening, the three paid me an unexpected visit at 8 p.m., introducing themselves with an air of aggression. They had come because they had heard an ANC member was nearby, and we chatted for three hours.

To the surprise of everyone, since this was the first time they had ever met their enemy face-to-face (and vice versa), we actually had a cordial chat.

They put their point of view across, even writing out in some detail their demands for full-fledged apartheid and for the banning of all Communists. They invited me to have breakfast the next morning. We continued talking, and agreed to disagree about nearly everything. I was released that day and reported back to the ANC's legal department at Shell House, since this was one of the first such contacts with the far right. With the ANC's Jeremy Seeber, I returned to visit the three in the hospital and tried to help them understand that they would have a chance to prosper in a non-racial South Africa. I doubt that I convinced them, and upon returning to Alexandra found that whites with much the same beliefs as these three were working closely with the police and with Inkatha to destabilize the township.

But back to the main story. The violence started on a Friday night, 8 March, in the Freedom Charter shack area. All of a sudden Inkatha members were observed grouping just behind Madala Hostel. They had red headbands, preparing for war with the community. They began shooting people, without asking whether they were ANC supporters or not. Residents who came under direct attack fled to the stadium and arms were rounded up from the township's nooks and crannies. This defense was not something organized by any structure, just by residents in the streets after they realized that people could be killed if they left themselves undefended.

We called many tens of thousands of residents into the stadium the next Saturday morning, to the point where it was nearly full. Winnie Mandela came in. Moss, Winnie, and Popo Molefe told the crowd not to be aggressive but to defend themselves if attacked. Negotiations were underway among the community organizations, Inkatha, and the police.

But more than sixty people died when, in the following hours, fighting broke out again. People were shot dead at point-blank range, were killed by sniping or stray bullets, or were wounded by bullets and then hacked to death. Alex became a killing field that weekend.

The police-Inkatha alliance

All of this unfolded just a month after Nelson Mandela and Gatsha Buthelezi had signed a peace accord in Durban. But the accord did not stand a chance against what came to be known as the Third Force, a sinister, shadowy group of white provocateurs within the security establishment who worked closely with Inkatha leaders to foment violence.

Our suspicions mounted because the police seemed to consciously avoid taking weapons from Inkatha—only one AK-47 was confiscated during the worst week of bloodshed, 8-14 March. Moreover, ANC leaders were not allowed to hold a mass rally in Alex on 16 March to tell their followers about a local peace agreement with Inkatha, because Alex had been declared an "unrest area."

Yet on 17 March, a huge Inkatha rally was held in Alex, with the Inkatha warriors (known as "impis") bussed in from across the region. The police allowed this because they believed the situation had "stabilized," as they said afterward. After the rally, the Inkatha impis ran wild and eight people were killed. Patrick Banda, coordinator of the liberal think tank IDASA, later described the scene:

> As the police were escorting the Inkatha members after the rally, hundreds of community members were injured and property was destroyed. Two youths were shot and killed by the riot squad as they were attempting to protect their homes in the shack dwellings not far from the area where the rally was taking place. This action angered the community and two Inkatha members were killed as a result. The other reason why the community believes that the police are conniving with Inkatha is the small number of arrests that are made.

Banda described "an unidentified group of not more than 10 black and white men operating after 9 p.m. when the curfew comes into effect." Bands of assassins were now specifically targeting ANC and ACO activists, Popo Molefe announced.

A few nights later, on 27 March, another gruesome massacre occurred. As people mourned their dead at a house vigil, Inkatha impis broke in and killed thirteen more of our comrades, including one of the most talented activists in Alex. The police had done a special tour of the area shortly before, but failed to prevent the attack or to arrive at the scene in a timely manner.

The head of the Alex Clinic, Dr. Timothy Wilson, summed up the linkages between police, Third Force, and Inkatha in the clinic's 1990-1991 annual report:

> The evidence on the activities of agents of the South African Government in using Renamo to destabilise Mozambique, in running the notorious Civil Cooperation Bureau inside South Africa, and in distorting evidence of attacks on the Alex Health Centre all make people at least query the good faith of the South African Police. The apparent

inability of the police to take any effective action against violent crime in Alex only makes things worse.

At the end of May, the police had the audacity to subpoena clinic employees to furnish details of patients treated during the violence, and one doctor was arrested for resisting and "obstructing police duties." The clinic was the subject of some direct attacks by groups of white and black outsiders, according to Wilson:

> They appeared to be white vigilantes attacking a symbol of resistance to apartheid. And are the new black thugs being used to attack a symbol of stability in an attempt to destabilise the society and impede progress toward a new and democratic country? Are primary health care facilities to be subjected to the same destruction as those in Mozambique?

Meanwhile, the police had encircled both the Inkatha-controlled hostels and a shack settlement nearby with razor wire, supposedly to keep the two sides (hostel occupiers and community residents) separated. The settlement became what was termed in the press a "laager of death," since residents were now unable to escape Inkatha's abduction, torture, and even murder. Two shack dwellers who were abducted and tortured by Inkatha managed to jump out a second-floor Madala Hostel window. A week after public complaints about the razor wire laager were aired, the police still had not removed the deadly fencing from the shack settlement.

Only in 1995 was it finally revealed that a security branch sergeant in his mid-twenties, Gary Leon Pollock, had deliberately fomented friction between political groups. "I was at all times acting under instructions from my senior officers and with their full knowledge of the actions I was carrying out," he told the Supreme Court. And he alleged that there was "an obvious cover-up for covert police actions" underway. He admitted to having planted guns on MK (the ANC's Umkhonto we Sizwe army) members in order to turn them into *askaris* (turncoats), to having sabotaged a bus full of ANC supporters, to having warned the Inkatha Freedom Party (IFP) about impending police raids, to having delivered arms and ammunition to the IFP in Alexandra and—to top it all off—to having, while employed by Anglo American's security division, bugged the conversations of Cyril Ramaphosa, F.W. de Klerk, Pik Botha, and Roelf Meyer.

Anatomy of a massacre

The vigil massacre on 27 March is revealing about the roles of the police and Inkatha. According to witness testimony in the trial, the police had been requested to provide protection for the area because vigils were becoming common targets for assassins across the Johannesburg region. The police refused, but agreed to send patrols by. Initially, at 9 p.m., a gang of 200 men walked from an area controlled by Inkatha to the vigil. Police came, and then returned at 11 p.m. and 1 a.m. But when the shooting occurred a bit later, police were absent. In fact, they responded with utter disregard when residents ran to the station just 800 meters away, even as gunshots were ringing through the night.

The human element sometimes is missing when technical reports of rampant violence are aired. The vigil was for Jane Ramokgola, the forty-one-year-old wife of Wellington Ramokgola who had been killed during an attack on her yard on 11 March. Ramokgola lost three sons and six other family members that night, and was completely distraught when he talked to the *Weekly Mail*:

> What can anger help? I don't know what my life will be like from now. This is going to take a long time to forget. I don't know what will happen tomorrow. They can even come now and finish me off. The more I talk of these things, the more I become confused. I'm already weak in spirit. I can't talk further about this.

Ramokgola was unemployed, having been fired by Barlow Rand in 1989 for taking part in a strike. He now faced a funeral bill of at least R13,000.

One wants to know, how exactly could a dreadful event of this sort occur? The police finally got around to an investigation, because all of South Africa, and even the U.S. State Department in Washington, clamored for something to be done. Arrested soon after the vigil were several men led by Gibson Mbatha, a twenty-eight-year-old man who was known to be active in the Alex Inkatha branch.

Mbatha was arrested because an AK-47 said to be used in the massacre was found in Madala Hostel. One of Inkatha's former members testified at the trial that he quit the organization because it was responsible for the violence in Alex. He recognized Mbatha as one of twenty-five men who went to the house to carry out the attack.

Another witness testified that earlier on the evening of 26 March, Mbatha had appeared at a shop and confronted this woman's boyfriend with the threat that if he did not join Inkatha he would be killed. She was then inside the vigil and saw Mbatha lead the shooting massacre, at one point crying out to three companions in Zulu, "These dogs are not yet dead." The incident terrified even the most callous, battle-scarred residents.

The *Sunday Star* later carried a story about how in late April one of the vigil massacre survivors, eighteen-year-old schoolboy Oupa Sehune, was arrested on the street because another student comrade with him was carrying a gun. He was then taken by the police into Madala Hostel one Sunday night and told he had to fight Inkatha with a panga. The cops called out, "Here's a member of the ANC, come and get him!" After twenty minutes of this, the police then took Sehune into custody inside a Caspir, where he was beaten up.

The newspaper gave police spokesperson Captain Eugene Opperman information about the incident, but he failed to follow up on it in a timely manner. A clinical psychologist whom Sehune visited following the massacre—which he survived by lying quietly underneath a dead woman's body, covering his head with her beret—attested that his subsequent experience was "a highly sophisticated kind of psychological torture, one of the most disgusting cases I have ever heard of."

The police "raid" Inkatha

The police finally got around to raiding Madala Hostel, and in April, Law and Order Minister Adriaan Vlok "made great play about banning dangerous weapons carried in conflict situations," as the *Weekly Mail* reported:

> The security forces had belatedly raided an Inkatha hostel in Alexandra and confiscated lethal weapons being kept there. Now these moves have been exposed as little more than a cheap publicity trick. The Inkatha weapons have been handed back—some of them still blood-stained, and many of them precisely the dangerous weapons which were supposed to be outlawed. A frightening pattern is becoming clear. While the police crack down on the ANC, the increasingly aggressive Inkatha supporters are allowed to get away with large-scale violence.

As public disgust with the police intensified, 2,000 police swooped at midnight on 3 May against four hostels, including Madala in Alex (the largest in the Johannesburg area, with more than 3,000 beds). But as Colonel Frans Malherbe admitted to the press even before the raid started, "We believe Inkatha knows what is going on. We don't know how much they know, but we know they are aware that some kind of operation will be conducted." The leaks meant that the operation was a failure, with only five arrests.

The authorities had other problems. Even weeks after the violence began, very few of the victims' bodies had been identified, because police stacked them on top of each other, four high, and allowed them to decompose at the Hillbrow mortuary.

Schools were also affected. One day in late April, children at the Gordon Primary School were struck with panic when armed boys with red headbands appeared. The children jumped out of windows, and twenty had to be treated at the Alex Clinic. To make matters worse, refugees were everywhere, in churches, neighbors' homes, even in parks in the white suburb of Bramley.

ACO and our regional civic body, Civic Associations of the Southern Transvaal (CAST), began to warn the police that arms would now be made available to residents if the violence did not stop. We also tried a legal route. On behalf of hostel dwellers who had been evicted (we had the names of 1,200 men), ACO requested an injunction by the Joint Negotiating Forum to force the police to evict Inkatha's invaders. But we got nowhere with it.

Prince Mokoena, meanwhile, bragged that he had recruited all Transvaal councilors into Inkatha. *City Press* carried Mokoena's denial that he had started the violence. Mokoena blamed it on a "love tiff" between a Xhosa and a Zulu—even after being reminded of a memo he had written four months earlier saying Inkatha should be brought to Alex in order to "crush" ACO: "If I have done a mistake by allowing Inkatha to Alexandra. I have done it because I am sick and tired of Civic Association, A.N.C."

Mokoena's memo

Mokoena was not able to keep his incriminating documents to himself. Creative grammar and all, the next paragraphs are taken directly from a letter written by Mokoena on Alex Council letterhead addressed to "all councilors," on 14 November 1990, at a time the mayor was readying the Inkatha attack on Alexandra:

> I am highly indebted to shower, the Mayor of "DIEPMEADOW COUNCIL" M.J. Khumalo with praises for endevouring [sic] to unite Black Mayors of the Transvaal. It is a phenomenon; his vision, his focus and his drive to establish an association of Mayors and Deputy Mayors. Mr Khumalo is a philanthropist— that for sure! Though the movement started three months ago, the first meeting took place at "TSAKANE TOWN COUNCIL." The second meeting at "BRAAMFONTEIN HOTEL" the copy attached.

My honourable Councilors, the attached copy is self-evidence. No agenda, no name of the association or movement. It is a voice crying—shouting for unity, saying since all black councilors are sharing the same objectives, same goals, and same hardships from "T.P.A.," who fuels the civic association with energy to humiliate black councilors. That is my view, that is the way I see it.

While the "U.S.S.R.'s" powder-keg is being prepared for C.A.S.T. laboratories to bombard all black councilors, that is my summary.

This is my own interpretation from the attached copy. I am taking my hat off for "COMRADE KHUMALO," I have my greatest respect for him. People in the struggle call each other comrade, although it is a Russian phrase. So that makes all of us. We may not like to say it because it makes us feel naked.

"DR ROLIHLAHLA NELSON MANDELA" the man we cried for years and decades for his freedom, his release became so symbolic to all black people of this country. Where are we today? Hardly a year, who are we today? A.N.C. is worse than Verwoed's [sic] Government. The card carrying members in Councils are speech-less shattered whilst INKATHA card carrying members walk with pride and pomp.

When they step into a train commuters use windows for exits, they threw themselves out of a fast moving train, than to wait and see what "INKATHA" members will say to them. They cannot even wait for "INKATHA" to greet—fly out is the best medicine.

Facts are facts. This may sound like a mockery, but it is a fact, which is hard to swallow. In the light of new evidence I mean the writing is on the wall. We as councilors we have a duty to revaluate [sic] ourselves.

The deranged Mokoena later told *City Press* that he was a former Wits University business lecturer, owned thirty-five kombi taxis, and held unused licenses for a bakery, supermarket, bottle store, garage, and stationery shop. Some of this was probably true, because he added, in response to our demands, "What's the point of resigning? People will think I'm doing so because I've made my fortune."

Clean-up goes dirty

Even though the July 1991 *Weekly Mail/Guardian* "Inkathagate" revela-tions of financial and logistical relations between Inkatha and the state left egg on many securocrat faces, they did not stop the killings. Violence had now gathered a certain momentum irrespective of what was happening at Alex

Council offices (or Mokoena's hideaway), at South African Police headquarters in Pretoria, or at Inkatha's Ulundi base in the homeland of kwaZulu. Inkathagate followed the threat in May by spokesperson Musa Myeni to deploy 100,000 impis in Soweto and 150,000 elsewhere. So Inkatha needed to clean up its image a bit. Suzanne Vos, the irrepressible spokesperson from the thriving Sandton branch of Inkatha, observed that the violence had caused "an enormous accumulation of refuse in the township." A clean-up campaign would, Vos said, "demonstrate to the people of Alexandra that Inkatha was deeply concerned by the living conditions of the community."

On 3 August, ACO leader Mary Ntingana recounted to the *Sunday Times*, "Crowds arrived waving banners. None of them had spades or brooms. But some had bin liners, which they used to hide weapons. They didn't clean their hostel, but marched down the streets chanting and singing. That was when the trouble started."

A different version from Inkatha's Humphrey Ndlovu: "We didn't carry spades or brooms because we needed neither. You can pick up the rubbish by hand. A few carried sticks because they are used to doing so. We intended to start cleaning outside the hostel and finish off by cleaning the hostel itself and holding a braai, but we were attacked by ANC members without provocation."

There were, however, reporters at the scene (such as Hubert Matlou from the *Weekly Mail*) who confirmed Mary's version:

> As I was walking down Roosevelt Road, word was going around that the armed Inkatha group was attacking Stjwetla, a shack settlement near the edge of the township overlooking the Jukskei River and regarded as another ANC stronghold. As we followed the procession, a white terrier lay bleeding and gasping on the side of the road after being hacked by the chanting Inkatha group. There was no sign of the group having cleared the garbage which was piled in heaps on both sides of the road. The plastic garbage bags carried by the men in the procession were either empty or nearly empty. The armed procession ignored heaps of rubbish as it moved down 17th Avenue, turned into 16th Avenue, and flowed back to Roosevelt Road. As it was passing by, I saw a very quick, brief attack with bricks being launched on the 11th Avenue shack settlement. Police moving in Caspirs took no action to apprehend the culprits except to shout "Stop! Stop!" A man was stabbed with an assegai as the group moved up the road after the attack.

Self-defense as a necessity

Under these conditions, any respect for the authorities vanished entirely. Newspapers were now revealing the tight links between the security forces and Inkatha, which police spokespersons had habitually denied. ACO had other sources of information which confirmed that the security forces had indeed imported Inkatha gangs from Natal and from within the SADF itself (the Fifth Reconnaissance Regiment) to carry out massacres. We were vindicated in our arguments, but this did not make residents feel any safer.

The point was made again in November 1991, when our comrade Jama Makhosi, who had sometimes served as my bodyguard, was shot by professional assassins as he entered our office. The assassins used the hostel as a base, witnesses told us. In fact, any pedestrians who ventured anywhere nearby were in continual danger of being randomly shot at from the windows by assassins living in the hostels. The murderers of Comrade Makhosi were never apprehended.

One resident, Peter Hlahatsi, commented to the press, "Police are not willing to protect us from the carnage that has fallen on our township, and neither does the ANC defend us. The only option left for us is to defend ourselves." Another resident, Sello Mothibe, added,

> The ANC must send Hani and MK [the ANC's Umkhonto we Sizwe army] to defend us against these people. We are not protected here in Alex. We don't have guns. We use petrol bombs, sticks and stones against people who are armed with rifles, shotguns, pangas and spears. We don't see what the ANC is doing to protect us. They must give us guns to protect ourselves. Didn't you see the AWB [the white extremist Afrikaner Weerstandsbeweging], even women, on TV the other day? Didn't they say they were training to protect themselves? So why can't we?

In mid-August 1991, after another twenty-eight people were killed by Inkatha in the wake of the "clean-up," ACO called for the formation of self-defense units. At a press conference, our spokesperson, Keith Madonsela, accused the police of offloading men with red headbands on 10 August. Then, according to residents, four white and two black men attacked a shack settlement at 20th Avenue. Others confirmed this in press interviews. Later, several balaclava-clad white men driving in a Caspir and minibus without registration plates killed eleven residents of the TB shack settlement across the Jukskei River from Old Alex.

The police remained extremely hostile, of course. Philemon Mauku, an executive member of our ACO hostel committee in 1990 before being forced out when Inkatha moved in, testified, "People who were not Inkatha members were forced to leave the hostel without their property. Some were killed, and some who were Zulu-speaking people were forced to join them." Philemon was a good comrade, a strong organizer in the Nobuhle Hostel, where I met him. He was instrumental in setting up the hostel committee, and became deputy chairperson of the area committee. He was a hard worker.

But Philemon was arrested in September 1991 with two AK-47s he had acquired to assist a self-defense unit in the township. In prison he quickly became a voice for the Marxist Workers' Tendency, a rather divisive group of Trotskyists within the ANC that independently formed the Philemon Mauku Defense Campaign. In doing so, the Tendency manipulated the insecurity of some residents of the Helen Joseph women's hostel—in my view, in order to make organizing inroads into Alexandra. The ANC was especially affected by these new organizers, and viewed the Tendency as a structure bent on destroying the local ANC branch. During Philemon's trial, Obed and I testified in his support.

ACO leadership maintained support for Philemon as an active member who needed help. However, we decided not to support the Tendency's campaign. Instead, I encouraged members of the community to go to give him support. In May 1992, Philemon was found guilty and sentenced to five years. His attempt to use the "necessity defense"—that he had no other choice but to take up arms for the community's sake—did not impress the Old South Africa judicial system. The magistrate, PJ Fourie, was not sensitive to community problems and needs.

"My crime was wanting to protect the community. We took a resolution to form defense, and arm the people," Philemon told the Tendency newspaper *Congress Militant*. "I put it clear to the state that as they fail to protect us, it was our responsibility for us to get arms for self-protection."

The violence continues

In late 1991, as Inkatha solidified its hold on the area around the mens' hostels, protection rackets grew. Fees of R5 to R100 were being demanded by Inkatha to leave residents alone. Terror for those who did not pay continued, as one person was killed, a woman gang-raped, and nine others hacked by men wearing Inkatha T-shirts one December weekend. On that occasion four Inkatha followers were arrested. But plenty of other individual shooting incidents never received any attention from the authorities.

In March 1992 another huge conflagration occurred around the hostels. In late February Inkatha had failed to come to a peace meeting. Then on Saturday, 7 March, almost exactly a year after the first Inkatha attacks, a heavily armed funeral march for an Inkatha man left the Madala Hostel and was stoned as it proceeded along 17th Avenue. One Inkatha supporter was shot dead. As *City Press* reported, "Enraged Inkatha supporters retaliated by butchering a man in Vasco Da Gama Road. Another man—walking along First Avenue—was hacked to death two hours later." The ANC blamed Inkatha for its provocation, since the police had assured the ANC that the marchers would be unarmed.

Over the course of the next week at least eight more people lost their lives. By Saturday, 14 March, Inkatha was ready to march again. ANC officials were watching very carefully as the police were now forced to prevent Inkatha members from carrying weapons. For three hours, negotiations over the weapons took place at the hostel, with the police offering full protection for the Inkatha march to the cemetery.

Humphrey Ndlovu, Inkatha's regional leader, drove into central Johannesburg to get approval for the deal—police protection in exchange for leaving the weapons—from a top KwaZulu official, but when he returned and explained the arrangements, they were deemed unsatisfactory by the assembled Inkatha members. Hundreds of hostel dwellers broke away from the police barricade and marched up Fourth Avenue, leaving several dead residents in their wake. Ndlovu now admitted that the Inkatha men were beyond his control.

Nevertheless, the next day an ANC funeral attended by 1,200 supporters went off without incident, and received a police escort for which ANC leaders were grateful.

A peace meeting the following week raised everyone's spirits. But these were dashed by more incidents, such as a double necklacing and continued deadly sniping from Madala Hostel. By now, 5,000 of our residents had fled their homes in the vicinity of the hostels, an area called "Beirut." Some card-carrying Inkatha members living in the area also fled, as hostel dwellers questioned their credentials and loyalty.

A report from the *Weekly Mail* in late March gives the flavor of the brutality in early 1992:

Pillaging had become more brazen as the hostel dwellers carried people's household goods into the Madala Hostel in broad daylight. But it was not only the looting that drove the residents away. Last week, snipers at the hostel shot at people walking past and even at those in cars. On Thursday morning last week, three men who walked past the hostel were harassed and dragged into the hostel in full view of residents. They found an ANC card on one of the men called Marobi Mkwanazi and later in the day the police found his body in the hostel. The other victim had been stabbed while the third managed to escape. On March 13, Reverend Sam Makgalemele was driving home from town when, near Beirut, the rear window of his car was smashed and two men demanded that he let them in. They forced him to drive to the hostel but he managed to escape when they got out to open the hostel gates.

The violence was so blatant that Inkatha began to distance itself from its members in Madala. "There are people in that hostel who do not belong there, there are elements who are out of control," conceded local official Lucas Koza. For diplomatic reasons, Obed Bapela, who was now the ANC's regional general secretary, accepted the position that the men who were driving residents from their homes were not Inkatha members but instead "thugs" with no ties to the hostel. The ANC and other groups participating in the Alexandra Peace Forum called for a stayaway for Thursday, 26 March, in order to force authorities to remove the unknown people occupying the shacks and houses near Madala Hostel.

However, the rally that day very quickly got out of control. Appeals to the crowd by ANC leaders Popo Molefe, John Nkadimeng, and Ebrahim Ebrahim to allow them a visit to government in order to demolish Madala Hostel were ignored. Popular ANC sports leader Steve Tshwete was even heckled. Soon, three-quarters of those assembled at the stadium were hiking up Selbourne Road to Madala in order to tear the hostel apart brick by brick. A line of police at the top of the road fired on the protesters, leaving nearly one hundred residents injured. Later, there was fighting between hostel dwellers in Madala and those in Nobuhle Hostel.

Tensions over a march

In mid-1992 I filed a report to my ACO executive on our relations with fraternal organizations, in which I tried to explain the differences between the ANC and ACO over the big 26 March protest at Madala Hostel. The following is an excerpt:

> The main problem was the march that the ANC organized with the Alexandra Peace Forum, from which ACO withheld participation. The march and stayaway occurred to protest the killings. The reasoning behind this was good, but ACO believed that the timing was wrong. The situation was extremely volatile, and there was the possibility that our people would be open to attack by Inkatha.
>
> ACO knew that if a massacre followed, we would take some of the blame. We argued against the march in view of the lack of consultations that had occurred, and the danger that something would go wrong.
>
> In the Peace Forum meetings the ACO was blamed for not taking part, and was alleged to be non-representative of the community. After our views on the deficiencies of the action were tabled, the ANC and other progressive structures still insisted that the march go forth. On grounds of bad planning, lack of consultation, and bad timing, the ACO and its structures sent a formal letter distancing the ACO from the stayaway and march.
>
> The stayaway and rally at the stadium were successful, drawing 40,000 people. Following the rally, thousands of people began to make their way to the hostel, and engaged in skirmishes with the police who were intent on stopping them. The police used a heavy hand, and some one hundred participants were injured.
>
> The anger of the crowd was great, and the desire to demolish the hostel could not be quenched. But there was no way to channel that anger into any action actually feasible at that time.
>
> The danger of an Inkatha massacre in the event of a community attack on the hostel was clear. Inkatha, after all, had suffered deaths and many injuries a few weeks earlier during a funeral march, and ACO received information that there were Inkatha plans to get revenge on that particular day.
>
> The ANC also released the information to the Peace Forum the day before the march. At that point, the magistrate also banned the march. The next day the magistrate's banning order was announced at the stadium, but it simply served to provoke the assembled masses to march anyway, and not to the Council but rather to the hostel.

Never-ending war

More sniping occurred from Madala in subsequent days, and targets included children at the MC Wiler Lower Primary School on Second Avenue. It was clear to everyone now that Madala was the base for these attacks, and that official denials or not, Inkatha was the driving force. Inkatha leader Ndlovu continued with the bluster, though: "No member of Inkatha owns a gun. We are a party of peace and have always been for peace."

The day after the march, displaced residents occupied the Alex Council offices demanding the demolition of Madala. The following Wednesday, another stayaway occurred (this time impromptu) and another march to Madala was repulsed by the police. The South African Press Agency reported: "At one stage the sprawling township threatened to explode into open warfare as thousands of residents squared up to a large contingent of police in the streets."

Seven people were killed in clashes, but the police remained studiously ignorant. Regional police commissioner Major-General Gerrit Erasmus stated that "despite intensive investigations" it could "not be substantiated" that Madala was the base for attacks. Erasmus said the police had raided Madala on four occasions in early 1992, and had only come up with one AK-47, one rifle, and one homemade gun.

By early April the ANC, the ACO, and our allies were again blaming the police for collaboration with Inkatha. Frank Chikane of the South African Council of Churches said that police were "perpetuating" violence. South African Police spokesperson Craig Kotze responded that this was nonsense and that instead, ANC and Inkatha leaders should "get together to spread the message to their grassroots." This, of course, had been tried.

Ultimately, what was really needed, in our view, was responsive, democratic local government, which would, through both political legitimacy and physical protection, end the reign of terror in Alexandra. Our ideas on how to bring this about are the subject of the next chapter.

12
The Drama of Local Government Negotiations (1990-1993)

In this chapter I try to explain some of the complexities of local government reform. There were furious debates underway between Alex civic activists, other Alex residents, and officials from nearby white suburbs. There were also profound disagreements within the Johannesburg area civic movement over the main negotiating forum (the Central Witwatersrand Metropolitan Chamber). And later, there were conflicts surrounding the national process of local government reform. In short, local government negotiations were among the most important terrains of struggle during the transition, even if the media often neglected them. This chapter offers the view from my ACO office.

"One city, one municipality"
Local government negotiations in Alexandra were one of the factors that can be held responsible for some of the violence described in the last chapter. The subsequent metropolitan-level debates were so divisive that they seriously threatened civic unity within our region. While ACO was generally successful at the local level, the same was not true of our position in the Johannesburg metropolitan area. Yet at the national level, the Alexandra negotiations ultimately shaped, to some degree, the final form of local government transition to democracy agreed upon at the constitutional negotiations in Kempton Park in December 1993. The story is complex, and so perhaps it is best to start with some basic principles.

Without doubt, the most important element of our local government reform strategy was the demand, made across South Africa by the civic movement and later the ANC, for single non-racial cities with single tax bases. This very directly reflected the material interests of township residents.

In Alexandra, like all townships, our workers are employed mainly in white areas. This means that the taxes that employers pay do not come back into Alexandra but instead go to the white municipality. Similarly, the small wages that are paid to workers do not circulate, by and large, in Alexandra. Instead, they go out to the white areas where the shops are mainly located. In turn, the municipal taxes paid by those white shops, supported by consumer goods bought by blacks, are again funnelled into the white municipality, not into Alexandra. This is the political economy of apartheid geography.

So the worker/consumers sell their labor-power and buy their most expensive commodities in the white areas, but do not in return receive tax revenues to help support what Marx called the "reproduction of their labor-power" (those aspects of shelter, food, clothing, recreation, and so forth that allow us to regain our energies to work some more). Instead the tax revenues form the basis for the reproduction of the bourgeoisie in the white suburbs of Sandton and Randburg. That is why Sandton could budget tens of millions of rands for a new civic center in 1993, while in Alex there was a huge deficiency of municipal services, including sewage, paved streets, electricity, water reticulation, garbage collection, and recreation.

This immediately brings me to a related point. The ACO insisted that *the community must be directly involved* in addressing the deficit of municipal services in Alexandra, and that this must be done with the first principle being that of *affordability*. People must have as basic human rights shelter, clean water, and a clean environment, and, in this rich country with a surplus of electricity generation, sufficient (and appropriate) sources of energy. These rights must be targeted to people's income levels, although it is clear that to do so effectively will require research and consciousness-raising. We want to see more of what Marx termed "use-values," and much less emphasis on the provision of goods and services by the free market, according to their so-called exchange-value.

The rent boycott was a key weapon, but it was by no means elevated to a principle. *In other words, no civic association ever argued that people should not pay what they can afford for municipal goods and services that they use.* But the rent boycott was, and is, a vital political tool. We argued that people must not pay their rents and service charges, because these payments support the Black Local Authorities.

However, ACO leadership also recognized that for municipal services to continue to be made available, the rent boycott would have to end at some point. After extensive consultations with the community, we were willing to use an "interim services charge" to ensure that the limited services provided in Alexandra were not turned off completely. But as was the case nearly everywhere, that rent boycott (along with the threat of mass action) was our main leverage in the negotiations. That leverage led us to sign and begin to implement the Alexandra Accord.

Gains and losses in the Alexandra Accord

Our negotiations with the Transvaal Provincial Administration, its lackeys on the Alexandra Council, and other authorities went through several stages, and in the early going they nearly derailed. Following the Soweto Accord of August 1990, many civics went to the bargaining table with local authorities and made demands for one city, one tax base, and also for development resources. When gains were made in some areas, we found, losses quickly piled up elsewhere. Alexandra offers evidence that the local negotiations were as painful and contradictory as those occurring in the national constitutional deliberations at Kempton Park.

In November 1990, what was to become the Joint Negotiating Forum was established as the main vehicle for the democratization of Alexandra. The Forum included the TPA, the Alex Council, (mainly represented by Steve Burger and Willie Khumalo), the Sandton and Randburg Town Councils, the Central Witwatersrand Regional Services Council, Eskom, the Rand Water Board, and the Development Bank of Southern Africa.

The real power broker in Alexandra continued to be the TPA, the unelected, bureaucratic agency led by National Party boss Olaus van Zyl. On 27 February 1991, the Alexandra Accord was signed by the TPA, the Alex Council, and the ACO. The Accord included our agreement to campaign for the end of the rent boycott in exchange for several concessions:

- resignations of the remaining members of the Alex Council;
- write-off of R12,4 million in arrears on rent and service payments;
- affordable charges for future rent and service payments;

- improved services and installation of services where they did not exist;
- hostels upgrading;
- creation of an Alexandra People's Fund for community development based on a R2 per household contribution from those renting Council houses;
- development of the Far East Bank for low-income housing; and
- investigation of non-racial local government with a common tax base.

As described in Chapter 11, the Accord was nearly sabotaged by the TPA, which tried to grant control of the Far East Bank land to the Alex Council just days before our planned signing. "Whilst the Accord commits the parties to a future non-racial local government, the [Far East Bank] development strategy submitted by the TPA is totally submerged in apartheid ideology," we concluded. "The only deduction that can be made is that either there was no effective communication between the TPA representatives at the negotiations and the Directorate of Physical Planning, or there is a deliberate ploy to undermine the Alexandra Accord."

As noted, the TPA backed down, made Sandton its development agent, and gave the Joint Negotiating Forum decision making power. Although in retrospect the TPA retraction was the catalyst for Prince Mokoena's fury and the subsequent violence, at the time the decision was acceptable to ACO on the grounds that it would speed the creation of a non-racial municipality, promote community participation, and limit corruption in development which under the Alex Council would otherwise have been rampant.

But violence broke out within a week and was the overriding reason that our plans for local government reform were stymied. The TPA's role in all of this was dubious, and not only because of the near-derailment when the TPA tried to give land to the Alex Council. In addition, when the ACO tried to publicize the agreement at a press conference in early March, the TPA negotiators failed to arrive as promised, and instead sent the five Alex councilors who had not yet resigned. TPA intentions may have been to project the Accord as simply between ACO and the Council, instead of ACO and the TPA. It was only in October 1991 that the TPA got around to appointing an administrator in place of Mokoena and the other councilors, and it still retained the old councilors on contract as "advisors."

These kinds of experiences were dispiriting to ACO leaders and staff. We attempted to keep up with all the details, assisted by the Planact team. We felt that even minor victories were worthwhile, and—with the expectation that the TPA would play games—we avoided romanticized negotiations. But pursuing our broader political demands independently of the flawed negotiations remained just as important, because it was obvious to ACO's constituents that Mokoena and the other councilors were the most significant immediate barriers to local democracy.

We were not, in short, simply a talking civic. Negotiations were accompanied by civil disobedience, mass action, and other forms of organizational development in which our constituents could participate. On the day the Accord was signed, a non-violent sit-in against Mokoena and the Council commenced, led by several dozen ACO women. Richard Mdakane explained to the press, "We are putting pressure on the councilors to resign because they are not serving the needs of the community." As *City Press* reported, "The 24-hour-a-day sit-in has crippled the running of the council and is regarded as a 'coup' against Mokoena and his council."

Not only was Mokoena prevented from using his office, but town clerk Willie Khumalo's office was also disabled by the occupation of his secretary's office. Khumalo was also stymied when Mokoena, now working from an office in the white suburbs, celebrated Sharpeville Day (21 March 1991) by mistakenly locking the women and Khumalo in the Alex Council building. Khumalo finally persuaded another councilor to unlock the door. Said Mokoena, "I was only exercising my democratic rights [to lock the door]. The office is mine and it has been left open for more than three weeks."

Mokoena that day also turned the cops on the ACO women. Mavis Tshabalala was beaten up; she reported that a cop "slapped me in the face twice and pulled me by the dress." Lillian Kgoele was kicked, and, as she told the newspapers, "As a result I fell and rolled down a flight of 13 stairs. The other policeman laughed." Several women were then charged with trespassing, but another group immediately replaced them.

A week later, a month after it had begun, the sit-in was called off in order to pursue other strategies. Popular pressure continued; Mokoena's flat was attacked many times, and he ultimately left the township. However, before he quit, he made the unsubstantiated claim that people involved in the anti-Council campaign had offered him the role of administrator of Alex if he paid them "protection" money—a ludicrous assertion.

Implementation of the Accord would be difficult under circumstances when Mokoena and others trying to hold onto illegitimate power did so until the bitter end. Nevertheless, Alexandra residents' rates payments increased by 37 percent and Eskom reported 82 percent payment of its bills by the end of 1991.

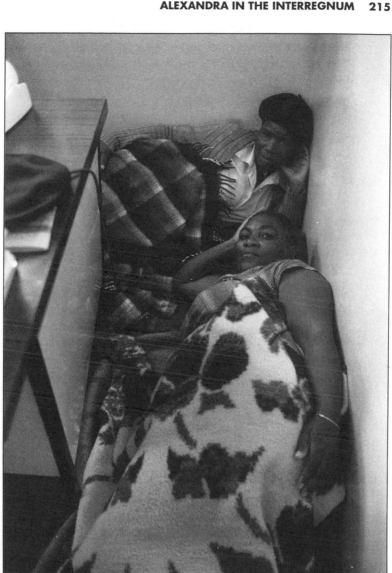

An overnight at Mayor Mokoena's office during the March 1991 occupation. The sit-in was well organized, with women holding down shifts to cover for each other during the entire month. *Photo: Anna Zieminski, author's collection.*

These were nowhere near the Accord's goals, but then again neither was the promised delivery of better township services. It was impossible to get people to pay more until they saw substantive improvements.

Finally in October 1991, when funding could at last be guaranteed by the Regional Services Council, Mokoena was heard from no more. Sandton assumed responsibility for refuse removal, fire and ambulance services, and personnel training. Randburg took over rent collection and financial administration. But fully-unified administration and non-racial local government would have a much longer wait.

We were running into dead ends in many of our negotiations. At our biannual ACO congress in November, our leaders interpreted the implementation problems in larger terms: "It is not clear how far negotiations can proceed before metropolitan and national negotiations advance." Even in mid-1991, Moss had explained this to the press:

> There must be negotiations at local, regional, provincial and national level, but following the leads at national level. White municipalities and the government are rushing to say they must be autonomous and they are doing it in a way that will pre-empt national negotiations and decentralise power. Power has always been centralised, so why are they trying to change that now? It will create the equivalent of mini-tricameral parliaments. If we don't change direction now, we may have a monster on our hands.

Local resistance to the Accord

Meanwhile, opposition to the Accord appeared in Alexandra, at the same time the ACO was attempting to consult extensively about the agreement. An explanatory booklet was produced in popular form and had been widely circulated by mid-1991. Many workshops and meetings were held in our offices. All ACO structures participated in the process, and other progressive organizations in the township—ANC, ANC Women's League, ANC Youth League, COSAS, SACP, COSATU locals—were continually informed of the developments. The issues, however, were often so nitty-gritty that not all activists and ordinary residents were able to stay abreast of all developments. And since ACO was seeing the emergence of many opposing political interests, it was perhaps inevitable that the Accord itself would come into question.

For example, Darkie Rametsi of the Alexandra Builders' and Allied Traders' Association claimed that residents were rejecting the Accord in mid-1991. In addition, the Alexandra Land and Property Owners' Association and Mike Beea of the Alexandra Civic Association voiced their disapproval of the Accord—not on any technical or substantive points, but rather on the grounds that they had not been consulted.

More surprising was opposition from Obed Bapela, who went from being a central ACO negotiator of the Accord in December 1990 to the Alexandra ANC branch's Publicity Secretary. He claimed the ANC was not consulted, even though there had been briefing sessions on negotiations with all our fraternal organizations, and informally there was complete overlap between our two leaderships.

And then there was Prince Mokoena's refusal to give up power until the bitter end. Even though two of his councilors opposed him, Mokoena withdrew what he claimed was Council support from the Accord in the last week of July 1991. (This was amusing, since in late March Mokoena had told the *Weekly Mail* that the Accord "is the best thing that has ever happened in my career as a councilor.") The Council had not met on the issue, and ultimately remained a signatory.

In withdrawing his personal support for the Accord, Mokoena argued that ACO no longer had community backing, nor did Moss. "Those Sandton whites are hobnobbing with him because they think he has a constituency," Mokoena told *City Press.* "They'll be shocked to learn that he hardly has a house permit in Alex. He has two houses outside Alex and he owns a flat in Hillbrow. That proves he and his ACO comrades have no constituency in the township." Whether or not this could ever constitute proof of an organization's constituency, Moss in fact did have a permit for his rented house on 27 7th Avenue, where our brothers and sisters stayed, and he had recently bought a house in the Joe Slovo area of Alex. While at the time he was living in Hillbrow for security reasons, it was in a rented flat.

The arguments of anti-Accord politicians ultimately relied neither on lack of consultation nor on opposition to the Accord's contents, but instead on personal vendettas or devious political agendas. This was demonstrated by the lack of constructive suggestions about improving or replacing the Accord.

The only detailed public complaint about the Accord from Beea and Mokoena was that it would result in the Far East Bank being developed by white companies. Beea cried, "We do not need white developers in the township dictating terms to us and making a mockery of residents here," and for once we completely agreed. But, as part of our attempt to guard against this possibility, the Accord included clauses ensuring community participation. We had the feeling that Beea had never bothered to read the Accord.

I will be the first to admit that the Accord was by no means 100 percent in the interests of all Alex residents. Negotiations are always a process of give and take, but we got about 80 percent of what we sought. The Accord was never a Bible, but it was nevertheless an historic document which served as a starting point from which more substantial goals could be achieved.

Problems with the Metro Chamber

In August 1990, the Soweto Accord was signed as a means of ending the rent boycott, restoring services, transferring houses from the state to the people, and establishing the Central Witwatersrand Metropolitan Chamber, or "metro Chamber." By implication, though, the Chamber included many more areas outside Soweto, including Alexandra, the so-called colored and Indian areas, and even, it was initially proposed, East Rand towns. But the Soweto Civic had failed to consult with the ACO or other civics on this accord which would decide so much of our future. (Some of the Soweto Civic's advisors in Planact had a much different strategic perspective on the costs and benefits of the Metro Chamber than those of us closer to the ground and to campaigns for grassroots democracy in Alexandra, and this and similar conflicts opened up serious strategic differences between technical advisors and community organizers which would persist for several years.)

Had ACO leaders been consulted, we would have made clear some of our political problems with the Chamber. For one, all the municipalities of the subregion were there, including the hated black councils. Why would the ACO build a militant campaign to force Alex councilors to resign on the one hand, and then on the other sit with these same puppet councilors side by side, with equal status, in a Metro Chamber we had no role in the formulation of?

Instead, our ACO position was that black councilors were simple stooges with no ideas of their own for the future of the metropolitan area. In contrast, the white councilors had a limited legitimacy: they had actual (although racially-defined) constituents who had real needs and aspirations that had to be taken into account. Not so black councilors, who were there only by virtue of our mass boycott of apartheid elections.

We would also have wanted to see much more research on facets of local and metropolitan governance, from constitutional issues to service delivery issues, before committing to the kind of decision-making forum that the Chamber represented. Also, we in the civics needed much more thinking on the implications of the Metro Chamber for the national liberation struggle. Our hope was to continually strengthen the prospects for a national solution, because local apartheid was a national problem.

The Metro Chamber ran the risk of actually weakening progressive initiatives at the national level by engaging in the exercise of constitutional metropolitan change. At the local level, we always avoided negotiations that had constitutional implications, whether or not these conflicted with the program of the national liberation movement. In other words, ACO proceeded with such negotiations without the aim of arriving at new constitutional decisions. Instead, hand in glove with our comrades at the national level, ACO tried to work on building the future non-racial system as the old one decayed and fell apart.

In sum, there were six political problems that ACO had with the Chamber:

• the principle of consultation was trampled on (by our own Soweto Civic Association comrades);

• there was an unacceptable involvement of black councilors in the Chamber;

• the involvement of the Sandton and Randburg white councils threatened to relieve them of their direct responsibilities to Alexandra workers and consumers;

• there was fear that the Chamber would lead to a premature metropolitan government;

• there was fear that the Chamber would have constitutional implications that would preclude the national political negotiations; and

• there was still an unacceptably strong element of the status quo, whereby people were represented according to race.

From local to metropolitan reform

If the negotiation and implementation of local government reform appeared difficult in 1991, then getting to the metropolitan scale would be nearly impossible. Intense battles across the Joint Negotiating Forum table were the rule, not the exception.

ACO leaders reported back to our structures regularly, and we finalized our position on metropolitan government at an ACO Central Committee meeting of 300 yard, street, and area committee representatives in February 1991. On the other side of the table, though, problems surfaced which had serious implications for the reform process.

The problems were mainly reflected in byzantine maneuvering over the geographical boundaries which we would be negotiating about. The main negotiators, including the ACO, met at the Development Bank in January 1991, at which point the idea of creating a giant non-racial municipality in Johannesburg's northern suburbs came under serious discussion for the first time. But Sandton's representatives immediately got cold feet, and instead began promoting the option of joining Johannesburg and Soweto in the Central Witwatersrand Metropolitan Chamber.

Sandton's participants often seemed to us to represent the degeneracy of white English-speaking liberalism (while, in contrast, many Randburg officials were characteristic of *verligte* Afrikanerdom and the "new" National Party, and were slightly more realistic). Sandton councilors argued that the northern subregion would not want to be cut out of the entire Johannesburg region's multi-billion rand tax base. Other white officials countered that as the richest subregion in South Africa, Sandton and Randburg would easily have the economic capacity to generate a tax base sufficient to support Alex.

But Sandton's pro-Metro Chamber camp quickly came up with a more original (if dubious) objection to the northern subregion: it would be immoral for them to ignore the northern suburbs' financial obligations to Soweto. So vehement were the debates over whether or not to join the Metro Chamber that even a year later, those Randburg councilors who took a pro-subregion posture ran the risk of the kind of mockery expressed by Sandton councilor Frederick Ehlers:

> Quietly, they tell you that "Jo'burg is stuck with Soweto, so better we stay out." They dangle big-fish-in-little-pond status before the eyes of ACO and dismiss the economic dependence of the suburbs on Jo'burg. Their idea is that the Regional Services Council will be retained as a toothless metropolitan government, to redistribute its levies, mainly paid by Jo'burg businesses to the "Subregion." I hear that Jo'burg businessmen have a pile of rotting fruit and fish for anyone who sells them down the river like that.

That pile would not intimidate ACO, of course (and selling Jo'burg businesses down the river was part of our tradition). But our position was not limited by self-interested concerns. ACO straddled the two different camps with two consistent arguments of our own: (a) redistribution of the entire region's wealth was desirable, of course, but (b) the most effective way to go about this was to go as a united, non-racial, bottom-up subregion into a metropolitan authority. This was especially true, we believed, where coordination of electricity and water were concerned. But we soon began to understand the real reason Sandton was pursuing the Metro Chamber route: as a red herring, to deflect attention from imminent local change, and indeed simply to slow down change.

While the Randburg Council ultimately agreed to help implement an agreement with Alexandra, Sandton's participation was nearly foiled by bureaucratic bumbling and procrastination. The worst offenders were then-management committee chair Meyer van Niekerk and town clerk Sybil Mostert. According to an anonymous councilor quoted in the press, these two "unilaterally rejected an appeal to help rebuild the [Alexandra] township's failing administrative infrastructure." Van Niekerk's excuse was that "ACO is trying to intimidate us and pressurise us into a single administrative and financial unit. They say we should defy the law. But things must be done in the proper, legal way."

Van Niekerk, a self-described "liberal-democrat," still wanted to work hand-in-hand with the Alex Council. Yet "The fact that it's practically comatose, with only five councilors still in office, and that the mass-based ACO is doing all the running, seems to have escaped him," a *Star* reporter commented with rare honesty. "It may be a case of political arteriosclerosis. But his caution, his habit of playing by the rules, is seen as reluctance to change. The least that is expected from white South Africa is gestures of intentions to change."

Another Sandton councilor, Liz Clogg, defended van Niekerk: "That Sandton should be castigated for refusing to accept that the town clerk of Sandton should run both Sandton and Alexandra on a part-time basis is ridiculous. The administration of each is patently a full-time position, and province clearly needs to appoint a full-time town clerk in Alexandra." But proving Clogg wrong, councilor Andre Jacobs became the Alex administrator in 1992 while retaining his Council responsibilities in Randburg.

The limits of white democracy

Infighting is not just a "black thing," and township politicos were not the only ones who saw in the Accord opportunities for troublemaking. For the Accord touched off racial strife in surrounding suburbs, and these often had serious class implications. Many white politicians and residents of Sandton and Randburg feared the day when they would have to take responsibility for reversing the drain of tax funds through which they were subsidized by Alex workers and consumers, and when they would surrender the precious buffer strips comprising vast tracts of land which poor citizens urgently needed for housing.

One Sandton Council tactic was to spend R20 million on a combined civic center, library, and art gallery, which ACO viewed as a vulgar move to deplete their coffers prior to democracy. Even Sandton Councilor Peter Jardine complained, "It's as if it's an opportunity to spend money before someone grabs it to spend on something basic."

In March 1992, when two Sandton councilors suggested the merger of Sandton, Randburg, and Alex, prominent representatives of the Sandton Chamber of Business, the Sandton Civic Foundation, and the Sandton Federation of Ratepayers who sat on the Sandton Council's constitutional committee immediately expressed opposition, although they patronizingly stated how "extremely encouraged" they were about "the general attitude toward assisting Alexandra." Also opposing her two colleagues, Councilor Clogg noted that because of Sandton's higher land values and lower rates, there would be no advantage to a merger.

Some of the growing unease in Sandton was due to the feudalistic way in which the "ruling group" of councilors—as Bruce Stewart termed himself, Willem Hefer, Peter Gardiner, and others—made decisions. By this time, even a management committee member, Councilor van Niekerk, was "out of the loop" and was denied briefings on well-advanced merger talks. The chairperson of the Ratepayers' Federation was correct in saying, "This group is autocratic and does not understand that democracy is not simply a one-way channel for giving out bits of information."

In our view, Hefer was the most enlightened and rational of the lot, perhaps because of his experience of working with Alexandra on the health clinic. But that would not win him brownie points with other councilors. Three of them walked out of a Council meeting when he was elected to chair the management committee.

One of Hefer's most vigorous opponents was Clogg, a prolific and eloquent writer of letters to the editor as well as a permanent nonruler. Of her Council colleagues, she complained in November 1991 that "information is extracted by questions—with the same difficulty as extracting the proverbial hen's teeth—or from the Press where, for instance, we recently saw for the first time the management committee chairman's views on a future local government structure. Our views on this matter have not so far been bought."

The more Clogg found out about the concessions Sandton was forced to make through the Joint Negotiating Forum, the more furious she became:

> This is a living example of how totalitarianism, loudly spouting moral platitudes and claiming sole care for the common good, rises like a phoenix from the ashes of democracy, however limited that may have been. The foetus of the new dispensation, at least in Sandton, is developing features that bear a remarkable resemblance to the defunct governments of Eastern Europe, and those becoming increasingly unfashionable in the rest of Africa.

Councilor Gardiner labelled Clogg and other opponents "right wing councilors stirring up racist feelings." She responded that "the Sandton Council, faced with decisions of the greatest importance to our ratepayers, must be among the most ill-informed groups of decision makers in the country."

But what was Clogg's constituency? Only 30 percent of Sandton's white voters came to the polls in February 1992, for example. Those people elected, by a vast margin, the representatives of reactionary ratepayers' organizations. One new councilor, Melanie Stewart, was fully against the Joint Negotiating Forum and ACO. But it is revealing that the white voters had no way of reaching their own political party councilors in Sandton except by voting them out. In the future, the civic movement in black cities, towns, and rural areas must be able to help white ratepayers' groups relate better to our problems, and perhaps also build unity on issues of common concern.

Another reflection of growing discontent among our white neighbors was when nearby Linbro Park residents turned away from Sandton and in May 1991 voted in a referendum to change incorporation of Modderfontein, the Anglo American Corporation's chemical company-town across the N3 highway from Alex. A ratepayers' association spokesperson complained of Sandton, "They use us as a dumping group for all their problems, be it litter or squatters." Modderfontein's plan was to become a "high quality" residential area. "We don't have confidence in [Sandton councilors] fighting against unfavorable plans for the area," griped the ratepayers' spokesperson, presumably referring to local democracy.

Other Sandton residents were panicking, and in mid-1991 four neighborhoods attempted to transform into "security villages"—a "mink and manure laager"—with privatization of the roads, a single access road with patrol point, electrified fences, and round-the-clock security patrols. Moss responded,

> Rather than enclosing themselves from the reality of a violent society, whites should be addressing the real reasons for the violence and offering more permanent solutions. This should be a time of increased openness. Whites should be involving themselves in truly de-racialising their areas, whereas this trend is a racist attitude designed to counter black presence in these areas.

Some white residents of the Douglasdale neighborhood (where the trend began) seemed to agree with Moss, telling the press that the security complex would "destroy the area's friendly character." But in reality, given the limits of white democracy, very little having to do with the unification of black and white South Africa could be described as friendly.

Sandton and Randburg's metropolitan strategy

ACO leaders were continually reminded, as we negotiated the Accord, that the metropolitan negotiating forum would be the basis for a fully reorganized local government system. This forum was the Central Witwatersrand Metropolitan Chamber.

In supporting the Metro Chamber, the white councils had embarked on a divisive strategy. Our view was that the approach to regional unity should have been bottom-up, not top-down. This is important to understand. Sandton, for example, was able to argue in the Metro Chamber that the problem of Alexandra was not their problem, but had been imposed by apartheid. That argument would allow them to duck their own responsibilities for addressing redistribution of wealth according to the single tax base demands of Alexandra workers and consumers who were in effect subsidizing Sandton. The Sandton solution, therefore, was to remove the debate from that bottom-up local level where we were prepared to fight and win our demands, and instead to try to get it resolved in a top-down manner through the Chamber.

Prior to 1992, therefore, ACO opposed using the Chamber. After much struggle, however, Sandton and Randburg joined the Chamber, while there was still little agreement between various civics on the way forward.

Therefore, ACO agreed—under protest—to enter the Chamber in early 1992. Our principles of refusing to negotiate with the puppet Alex Council, however, remained the same as when we opposed the Chamber.

Sandton and Randburg believed that the Chamber met their interests better than local-level negotiations with Alexandra. This, in our opinion, was because the Chamber essentially clouded issues, rather than dealing with them specifically. The Chamber had the status of a "talk shop" for some of its members, and this inhibited progress. It was one reason the Chamber soon broke down.

More generally, though, as Metro Chamber chairperson Frederick van Zyl Slabbert put it, there was "a crisis of delivery." The puppet councils had promised to do many things for the people, especially in Soweto. But since conditions were not improving, the people of Soweto individually and unilaterally reduced their services payments to 30 percent by early 1992. This crisis of delivery justified our position that you could not discuss anything meaningful with the black councils. Indeed, nearly everyone eventually realized that the full and final resignation of the puppet councilors everywhere was a precondition for progress toward democratic cities in the New South Africa.

From local to national, and back

National-level negotiations on local democratization began when Moss led a delegation from the South African National Civic Organization (SANCO) to a meeting with Local Government Minister Leon Wessels in mid-1992. SANCO was founded in March that year, and as its first elected president, Moss lobbied Wessels for such a meeting. ACO's experience was considered an important precursor, partly because of Moss but also because the main technical support came from Planact's Andrew Boraine, who left the Alexandra negotiating team to work at the national level.

Eventually, the national Local Government Negotiating Forum, which was led by SANCO and included other ANC Alliance partners, stitched together the principles for the eventual establishment of non-racial, democratic local government. This was ratified in a deal by the multiparty constitutional negotiations, after some heated controversy, toward the end of the process in December 1993.

There are many provisions of the national negotiations to consider. SANCO and the ANC Alliance agreed that in each locale, delegates from the "non-statutory" side would gain a 50 percent say in local government decisions prior to formal elections, working with delegates from the parties who, under apartheid, held office in white, "coloured," and "Indian" areas. In some areas that could not reach agreement of this nature, there were other options for joint governance in the interim period.

The main compromises made for local government elections, scheduled for November 1995, were that existing local authorities would get 30 percent of the unified local council seats, and that a one-third minority vote in a council would be sufficient to block major decisions. Adding in their proportional vote to the initial 30 percent, representatives of the white areas have been granted disproportionate power. For example, they can even veto budgets that provide infrastructure and goods to black townships. When the Conservative Party holds power in a white town but gets a tiny percentage of the total vote, and the ANC wins 90 percent of the overall vote—which is not unrealistic in dozens of small towns—things are obviously very unfair.

On the other hand, in a few "white-dominated" cities such as Johannesburg, the large number of domestic servants and new inner-city residents can give an absolute majority to the ANC, and thus local democracy can proceed rapidly with a more representative council. Yet another situation is in the Western Cape, where smaller African townships are favorably biased because they get 30 percent representation automatically, despite the fact that they do not account for such a high percentage of the local population (the colored community predominates in the Western Cape). One other serious problem is the lumping together of white, colored, and Indian constituencies as a single bloc, as a result of the fact that, traditionally, they have all been ruled by white-dominated town councils.

Why these complications? One reason is the threat of counterrevolution, even civil war, and hence the need to give concessions so the white right wing, rather than resorting to lawlessness and terrorism, will be part of the process. Another reason is to promote reconciliation at the local level. At one level it is good to build trust, given our conflict-ridden history and the need for peace, democracy, and development. I am in no position to second guess whether the approach taken by our negotiators will succeed in this respect.

But we must never forget that ordinary people on the ground expect delivery, most of all. To them, the election means political representation, which will assure them of goods and services denied by apartheid and an improved standard of living. So if the local-level deals stall delivery, especially in the townships of smaller cities and towns, then we have a big problem.

There were at least two foreboding signs that quickly emerged after the deal was signed. First, the Conservative Party-dominated towns boycotted the January 1994 local government summit at the World Trade Centre, still demanding a racist *volkstaat* of their own. Second, when he spoke to the summit, F.W. de Klerk failed to make good on a commitment to write off the R1,8 billion in black township arrears. He passed the buck to the new structures, thus—in the view of the civic movement—double-crossing our delegation. How typical of de Klerk and his fraudulent, deceitful National Party. The problem of who would pay for the arrears would continue for a long time to come. And this led to other major controversies over how colored areas would be treated when the arrears were finally written off.

But there were other signs for hope. First, some of the flaws in the local government deal could be corrected by the first democratic parliament, especially to ensure that long delays and hitches in local dealmaking could be remedied. Second, during the negotiations, the NP was driving drunk. As Billy Paddock of *Business Day* put it, Local Government Minister Delport (Wessels's replacement) was "fighting for all local governments to take on the flavour apparent in his province." Here he was very badly mistaken, because he did not realize that his lily-white Port Elizabeth was not like other cities, where domestic workers live in suburbs, not only in townships.

For the civic movement, the negotiations process was good training for governance. Within months, we had permitted many of our leading comrades—the cream of our civic crop, like Richard Mdakane, Dan Mofokeng, Mary Ntingane, Benny Kutwane, Max Mamase, Trudy Thomas, and hundreds of others—to become candidates on the ANC's local and provincial government lists. We also released several civic cadres—Moses Mayekiso, Winnie Mandela, Henry Fazzie, Kgabs Mosunkutu, Father Smangaliso Mkhatshwa, and others—to the national Parliamentary list.

When a child leaves the home, it is always painful. But when there are many more children in the household, the gaps will be filled in naturally. And when we set our comrades free to help build a democratic government, they will reward us by adopting policies and programs to empower the civil society from whence they came. At the time, I counseled many of our

SANCO leaders not to throw up their hands in despair that civic cadres were leaving, as if that would decimate us.

But some final questions: Would the people buy the new local government deal? Would rent and service boycotts end? Would civics retain the respect we have traditionally enjoyed among most township residents? After all, when he was SANCO Southern Transvaal leader, Dan Mofokeng said this: "Once we have seen the creation of non-racial local government structures, that decent services are being delivered and there is a visible program of upgrading, we will take a conscious decision to pay."

This was a consensus position, and reflected our experience. When the Soweto Accord was signed in August 1990, and the Alex Accord was signed in February 1991, most township residents showed good faith and began paying their bills. But after three or four deeply disappointing months of the status quo—no change in living conditions—the ordinary resident resorted to the old standby, nonpayment. Why should they pay for something they didn't see? Especially during such a sharp economic crisis.

This understanding had nothing to do with a so-called culture of nonpayment, nor of our proud legacy of ungovernability. Instead, what should be clear, after all these years of struggle, is that you cannot separate what is political from what is economic. A political vote without economic empowerment and social justice is as inadequate as the old black councils. If local governments do not deliver, our civics, still critical, well-informed watchdogs, will begin to bite again.

All these debates encourage us to step back and make an assessment of how the civics related to our constituency during the transition period. We are assisted in doing so, in the next chapter, by looking at some criticism of the civic movement by outside academics, political commentators, and staff of the large development agencies.

13
"Institutions that Themselves Need to Be Watched Over": A Review of Intellectual Attacks on the Civic Movement (1992-1993)

During the long and often bitter transition, the civic movement came under enormous fire from academics, establishment political commentators, and other township-watchers. Some of the specific criticisms of civics during our formative 1984-1986 period I evaluated and rebutted in Chapter 5. Others concerning civil society were considered in Chapter 8. In this chapter, I review a second wave of intellectual output on civics, which covers our development during the early 1990s. (I initially published this chapter in the journal Urban Forum in 1993, and endnotes from that article which amplify my arguments have been omitted here.)

Introduction: Idealism and realism

Looking at some of the intellectual arguments about civics is interesting, because we must always review our situation from a critical perspective, and often, fresh viewpoints are useful in doing so. In this chapter, I consider contributions from various intellectuals, who can be divided into two broad camps.

First, intellectuals of the economic status quo (Lawrence Schlemmer, and Nedcor/Old Mutual scenario planners) were enormously idealistic during the transition, in that they promoted a vision of a successful capitalist-oriented social contract in which civics play a neutral "developmental" role. Second, a group of more cynical writers (Jeremy Seekings, Kehla Shubane, Blade Nzimande, "Ben Jacobs," Shalto Cross, Bruce Boaden, and Rob Taylor) argued that civics were on the wrong track, were on a short-lived track, or had fallen off the rails entirely.

I should begin by noting that not all analysts of the civic movement were overly critical or overly idealistic. For example, there was an excellent description of civic movement development in Thozamile Botha's *Theoria* article entitled "Civic Associations as Autonomous Organs of Grassroots Participation." And in the same journal, Mark Swilling, a strong civic movement advocate, set out the factors for why civics were one of the most important sectors of our society even before the national launch of SANCO:

• the existence of about 2,000 civic associations countrywide, several regional civic federations, and a uniform value system and organizational structure;

• the recognition accorded to civic associations by the apartheid regime and development agencies;

• the far-reaching reorganization of local government that civic associations were, at the time, negotiating in some ninety localities countrywide; and

• the conclusion reached by analysts from Latin America, Africa, North America, and Eastern Europe that South African social movements are probably the most well-organized and effective in the world.

Too few analysts have brought these basic facts into their studies of township politics. Yet at the same time, critics of civics (from a variety of persuasions) were rarely answered, due to their difficult jargon and the obscure journals in which they publish. Therefore, my objectives in this chapter are to set out an entirely different position—that of a civic movement leader aiming to engage the critical arguments one by one. I will try to do the following:

• defend civic associations and their participatory-democratic processes;

• contend that in spite of problems, the civic movement is here to stay, and is well-positioned to play a crucial role in power struggles in the future;

• examine the rise of cultural analysis of the civic movement, and explore its implications; and in the process,

• evaluate some of the main dynamics, strengths, and weaknesses in the civic movement at local and national levels.

The recent decay and future demise of civics (Seekings)

The most ambitious article about the civic movement published during the early 1990s was in the authoritative *South African Review* book series by Jeremy Seekings, a University of Cape Town sociologist (Seekings also compiled an extensive and useful bibliography of writings about civics). The importance of his article is reflected in the fact that when the capitalist magazine *Financial Mail* launched a broadside attack against the South African National Civic Organization in September 1992, at the time of SANCO's bond boycott threat, it resorted exclusively to Seekings's analysis:

> The civics' prominence masks their limits. These include weak organization of membership, uneven levels of consciousness, variable leadership and dubious accountability.... When they made national political concerns their priority or adopted uncompromising tactics, support for the civics declined, says Seekings. Civics have moved beyond their essential watchdog role and are now "institutions that themselves need to be watched over."

The subtext is clear: don't worry, fellows (bankers in particular), for the civics are not going to threaten the established order.

Seekings's original article is indeed a harsh indictment of the civic movement. In writing a comprehensive overview of the civics' development, however, Seekings advances many unsustainable generalizations.

First, there are numerous interpretive and factual errors amidst the deluge of information. Having correctly observed that the formation of a national civic was delayed for nine months beyond the 1990 disbanding of the UDF (reflecting the natural unevenness of our grassroots movement, not simply "the weaknesses of civic organizations"), Seekings's concluding paragraph to a section on "Regional and National Co-ordination" is as follows:

> A further problem involved the continued divisions between civic organization in coloured and African areas. Even an apparently united regional civic structure like Civic Associations of the Southern Transvaal [CAST] has revealed significant weaknesses. The Soweto Civic Association did not affiliate, and protracted disagreement about participation in the Central Witwatersrand Metropolitan Chamber led to the resignation of some CAST officials.

How many errors can find their way into a single paragraph? Soweto Civic was always affiliated to CAST. And within CAST, civic divisions were never an issue along "coloured and African" lines. Indeed, the only tensions among CAST civics I can determine were over participation in the Metro Chamber. Yes, there were deep differences between the Alexandra and Soweto civics on this issue, and yes, Soweto was supported by civics which happened to be from "coloured" townships such as Eldorado Park, En- nerdale, etc., but it is extremely pernicious of Seekings to imply these were racial differences. Indeed, these differences were by no means "significant weaknesses," but were instead political-strategic differences that we cele- brate as evidence of our maturity in accepting diversity. Finally, only one CAST official ever formally resigned, and according to his resignation letter, his decision had nothing to do with the Metro Chamber.

Second, a central argument is profoundly wrong: that civics exist because credible political parties in recent times were preoccupied with national issues. This position negates civic mobilizing based on non-partisan work of various sorts, as well as in contesting national political ideas (a topic I return to shortly).

From this false start, Seekings attempts a class analysis of civic leadership, which he says "was generally broad-based in terms of occupation, although professions (including professional activists) and white-collar workers pre- dominated. Traders and other businessmen, blue-collar workers, and public sector employees (including teachers) were rarely involved." As a result, he goes on, "Support [for 'radical' civics] was generally weak in shack settlements and among backyard shacks, in hostels, and in the newly developed extensions to townships. This pattern of support reflected civics' leadership, predominant ideology, and concerns."

Seekings's incorrect argument on the class character of civic leadership is derived from a 1984 Soweto Committee of Ten internal critique. The Committee of Ten was hardly typical, and no other examples are given to prove that civic leadership "rarely" includes blue-collar workers. The Alex- andra Civic Organization executive, for example, includes many blue-collar workers and is broadly representative of the various layers of the community. My experience is that this is common of most civics' leadership, and if this is not the case in some township or other, SANCO and regional civic bodies are aiming to provide educational support (and pressure) for holding proper elections so that a representative leadership emerges.

As for the character of popular support for civics, it must be recognized first that communities are not homogeneous. Naturally, there are social tensions within and between layers of township residents. The goal for civics is to represent the interests of the entire community (especially in local-level negotiations), but this cannot be achieved merely through slogans. The civics must establish structures throughout the community, and must engage in vigorous education campaigns to actually pull this off; there have rarely been resources sufficient even to attempt this, much less succeed.

As a result, if in some shack settlements, for example, civics are not prevalent, this is rarely an issue of petty bourgeois leadership or the civics' "predominant ideology," but is instead largely because of problems relating to the severe poverty of shack dwellers. Rare is the civic body that has gained the resources necessary to meet shack dwellers' needs for adequate water and sanitation or for informal loans to build shacks, for example, much less gain access to formal houses. This is a temporary problem, I hope, for in many townships civic associations are still new organizations, and in time our demands for "housing and electricity for all," for example, will appeal to residents across the board. In Alexandra, the civic has been well-organized throughout the township, in shack settlements, in Old Alexandra council houses, in fancy East Bank private homes, in the women's hostel, and even in the mens' hostels until Inkatha kicked out the civic's hostel leadership in 1991.

The future of civics, Seekings suggests, is shaky. There are many reasons why this may be the case, but Seekings bases his argument on just one: the next generation of local government will be legitimate, and political parties will have more time and resources to take up local issues:

> If post-apartheid local government institutions enjoy popular legitimacy and elections are contested by a range of credible political parties, what space will there be for civics?... There is little reason why civics will not come to resemble existing ratepayer or civic groups in white areas, playing a very limited role lobbying local government councilors.

Once again, cynicism leads to poor analysis. The civics will still have a major role to play in the post-apartheid South Africa, given the fact that problems created by apartheid geography will remain over the next decades. The current restructuring of the economy is already causing so much havoc that nearly all local governments today have insufficient resources to ensure that development (jobs, housing, education, health-care, etc.) reaches large parts of our townships. The credibility of local governments that were popularly elected but denied adequate resources by central government may be thrown into question.

There is still, at the time of this writing, no guarantee that the future local government structure will be so thoroughly democratic as to allow and empower people to actively participate in and control local governance and development. The civics will therefore play a watchdog function with respect to political education, and in the process experiment with alternatives in building participatory democracy. This is a crucial learning process to go through, for even in the wealthy United States, formal democratic rights have not solved socioeconomic problems. There, community groups have emerged in most poor and working-class areas to address bread-and-butter issues. South African civics will also continue to play this role, and at a more sophisticated political level. Throughout the world, there are few examples of community self-organization and political-ideological development as advanced as the South African civic movement.

Without question, there is a bright future for civics, and for the many people who will emerge from the communities with new visions for our movement's evolution. One reflection of this future is the degree to which civics have been involved in national-level debates, discussions, and negotiations about the optimal form of local government and development policy that will strengthen the civic movement. Thus, the next section deals with the complex relationship between civics and political processes.

Civics and politics (Shubane, Nzimande and Sikhosana, Stadler)

As a national force, the civic movement sat proudly at various negotiating tables in the early 1990s. Civics took an active role in local government restructuring, in the National Housing Forum, and in negotiations with banks and other businesses on behalf of township residents, and on behalf of the struggle for peace and democracy more generally.

The big question of where, politically and ideologically, to locate civics was answered by Seekings: "Civics stressed their supra-partisan objectives, and there was widespread (but not universal) in-principle agreement over the respective role of civics and parties. But most civics failed to convert their rhetoric into reality." Tellingly, Seekings provides no citation of even a single civic (much less "most") which failed to practice non-partisan principles.

A more philosophical argument is advanced by Kehla Shubane in *Theoria*, concerning the political prospects for civics and other organs of civil society representing the disenfranchised. Shubane was an advisor to big capital's Urban Foundation and the parastatal Independent Development Trust, but he was also a political prisoner and prolific commentator on civic issues. Civics, he claimed in 1992, "do not have any significant positive impact on the policies adopted by government":

> Their relationship to government is invariably marked by antagonism. The influence which each exercises on the other is cast in conflictual terms. It is this relationship, structured by the nature of the South African polity, which lies at the root of the argument, advanced in this article, that in South Africa the level of conflict excludes a true civil society among the disenfranchised.

> It is easy to appreciate why an institution like the family would constitute a part of civil society whatever the prevailing political arrangement might be. In this sense, the disenfranchised do enjoy civil society. If, however, overtly political formations like trade unions, civic associations, etc. are considered, such formations are not as easy to locate. Rather, they should be positioned within the liberation movement, which projects itself as an alternative authority to the apartheid state.

First, it is incorrect, even bizarre, to say that political conflict "excludes" organs of civil society from emerging (this whole book rebuts the last sentence of Shubane's last paragraph). Second, the family is much better considered within the realm of the private rather than within civil society. Third, the liberation movement is a broad creature, and the civics have certainly been (and will continue to be) part of it. But the civics are creative enough to locate themselves where they want to with respect to different ideological positions.

As Shubane recognizes in his other writings (such as a paper for an Urban Foundation strategic planning booklet), our movement's basic position remains that civics are not party-political. True, during the apartheid era, we never ducked our responsibilities as part and parcel of the liberation movement. And as the election approached, civics first endorsed the *program* of the ANC (the Reconstruction and Development Program) because it was in keeping with the civic movement's needs and aspirations.

This led to SANCO's endorsement of the ANC for the first democratic election, following negotiations with ANC leaders in November 1993.

Indeed, political issues will always be discussed within the civic movement, and debates will rage. It would be naive for civics to leave to political parties all discussions about the economy, social policy, local government constitutional structure, national political negotiations, and so forth. And yet there is still no contradiction when the civic movement pledges that it will not actually contest elections.

With respect to the political process, how then does Shubane imagine civil society will be built from the grassroots? This is an important issue, for Shubane argues that one of two key impediments to building a vibrant civil society—"structural limitations arising from colonialism"—"could be resolved by decolonizing South Africa in ways which benefit all." ("All" in Shubane's vocabulary cannot include most whites, whose standards of living have to a large degree been bolstered by apartheid.)

But the other impediment, Shubane goes on, is "more difficult to resolve." Here he speaks of "liberation-dominated politics," and in particular the difficulty in "institutionalising the notion of *legitimate and loyal opposition* in politics." This is a refreshing change from those such as Blade Nzimande and Mpume Sikhosana, who would collapse the civics into the ANC. But Shubane's interests are not primarily in civics and other working-class organs of civil society, but are rather in seeing a plurality of political parties emerge from the liberation movement.

Would civil society naturally emerge if there were many political parties? Perhaps, but civics, unions, and other organs of civil society will definitely remain even if there is a single progressive party in South Africa. What is more interesting is the opposite argument, advanced repeatedly by Natal-based ANC/SACP intellectuals Nzimande and Sikhosana (their positions and my rebuttals were reviewed in Chapter 8, and were published in *Mayibuye, Work in Progress,* and the *African Communist*). Nzimande and Sikhosana claimed repeatedly that civics (as part of an imagined *bourgeois* township "civil society") were weakening the drive not only toward the democratic stage of the revolution, but also toward socialism. As a result of this hotly argued viewpoint, the democratic movement witnessed quite a debate about the radical pedigree of the notion of civil society. My own contribution—stressing *working-class* organs of civil society as part of the process of building a socialist movement— need not be repeated here. But Nzimande's final contribution to the debate (in the *African Communist* in 1992) contained a new twist. Ever since negotiations with the ANC began, the apartheid regime attempted, Nzimande insisted,

> to separate civic and socio-economic issues from political-constitutional questions, which might have the effect of depoliticising civic and trade union struggles and channelling political struggles through the negotiations process only. The regime understands full well that these civic, trade union, and socio-economic struggles were the engine of our struggle in the 1980s.

Although Nzimande's article included a convincing critique of sunset-clause concessions and other constitutional compromises that were underway in late 1992, he also expressed anxiety that an all-powerful apartheid state was running roughshod over divided and confused grassroots forces. This was a theory which really had very little to do with reality. Were civics "depoliticized" after 2 February 1990? Civics, on the contrary, stayed more politicized than ever, and also more focused, more unified in our strategies, and more sophisticated. The same was true of COSATU, what with all the stayaways and marches at the heart of mass action. Without the involvement of independent organs of civil society, those actions could not have happened.

If the apartheid state was hoping to weaken the progressive forces by giving the civics greater status in negotiations, as Nzimande suggests, it was insane. The demise of the black councils proved that the civics were more effective than ever before. In the National Local Government Forum, civics also led the progressive forces (including political parties) toward interim arrangements on service delivery and development, even prior to the finalization of the national constitutional arrangements.

A final comment is useful regarding the anticipated power of the first democratic state. A number of intellectuals tried, in the early 1990s, to advance beyond either/or arguments about a strong state and a strong civil society. It soon became clear that you can't have the latter without the former (although the former East Bloc showed that the reverse can easily emerge). But it is important to specify in which way the democratic state should be strong.

As I noted in Chapter 8, some commentators, like Friedman in *Theoria*, remained locked into a status quo agenda, desiring a strong, hopefully liberal state, but, in addition, straightjacketed against supporting civil society by an irrational distrust of civic associations. A more helpful vision, even if aiming ultimately to "generate the conditions for [capitalist] accumulation," was put forth by Alf Stadler:

The conditions for a civil society minimally require that all citizens are entitled to equal respect and participation in political affairs. In contemporary society, this can only be achieved through economic and social policies which seriously address inequalities in access to jobs, housing, health, services and education—as part of the economic and social rights of citizens.

Faults in the civics' own national organization (Jacobs)

If, through rebutting Shubane, Nzimande, and Sikhosana, we have a more useful conclusion about civil society and political parties, the next question that logically arises is how to strengthen the civic movement so that a potentially strong democratic state stays slim, and does not either ignore or repress civil society. The answer, by most accounts, is to overcome the unevenness in national and regional development of the civic movement, which necessarily entails building a strong though flexible and accountable national body, the South African National Civic Organization. But, as with the case of the formation of national trade union bodies, plenty of introspection is required on this very crucial issue.

One of the most eloquent and thoughtful articles on SANCO's development during the transition was by "Ben Jacobs," in an article entitled "Heading for disaster?" in *Work in Progress*. (Jacobs preferred the use of a pseudonym for his own reasons.) Notwithstanding the extremist title, the article was well-informed about internal dynamics and problems in the civic movement. As an insider in the formation of the national civic body in late 1991 and early 1992, I believe it is an article to be taken with the utmost seriousness.

Jacobs's critique of SANCO flows from a central claim which I also believe to be true: SANCO's unitary structure is much less desirable than a federal structure. Indeed, I attended the SANCO launch in Port Elizabeth in March 1992 with a mandate from Civic Associations of the Southern Transvaal to support a federal structure. The delegates debated this topic openly and with integrity, and in the end CAST was the only affiliate that supported the federal position.

Jacobs provides the reason that convinced most delegates to the SANCO launch to go the unitary route: "SANCO could not be a federal organization if it supported a unitary state (the contrary example of COSATU was ignored)."

What was the rationale here? There was the fear, well-founded in many instances, of some delegates that the apartheid regime would use divisions and unevenness within the civic movement to structure local government (e.g., the Thornhill Commission) or development projects (IDT site-and-service schemes) and policies (the De Loor Housing Task Force) in a top-down manner in its interests. On the other hand, there was also danger with a unitary structure if the leadership was incompetent. The solution is to always maintain communication, accountability, and the long-term interests of the entire civic constituency at heart.

But Jacobs was correct in demanding more recognition of local autonomy. Jacobs argues: "The "C" in SANCO denotes the singular, giving rise to the absurd notion that a civic (which represents local interests) can be a single national body." True, the name should have been South African National Civics Organization. But the point is to advance beyond a debate over simple unitary versus federal autonomy, and to try to define exactly how a *tight* federal structure, with bottom-up policies, would combine local autonomy with what is needed from the unitary vision: the ability to provide a national framework from which all of us can identify the road ahead on various issues. A tight federal structure would permit this, and the struggle for SANCO in the years ahead is to move in this direction. Several problems will be overcome if we take this route.

For example, while it may be useful to have a SANCO national office gaining resources from funders who desire to support the national, this should not prevent (or compete with) local civics raising their own funds. SANCO should not have national membership cards—local civics should have cards (and charge a small fee to members), and should pay a minimal affiliation fee to their provincial offices so as to make the structures self-supporting. The provincial SANCO in turn should then contribute to the national office. Finally, for administrative and communication purposes, there remains a need for a strong national structure. But the optimal approach is tight federal, not tight unitary or loose federal.

This is clear if one considers the vital need to structure campaigns and national policies in the optimal manner. Indeed, provinces and zones exist in large part to coordinate events. Jacobs slates SANCO for ignoring regional diversity and neglecting "the fact that grassroots struggles are about different issues in different areas." This is too strong a generalization, and Jacobs backs it up only by citing SANCO's call for a national bond boycott. He argues that "It was appropriate in some of the main metropolitan areas," but not in others where banks never made loans or where civics were in the process of negotiating with banks for new loans. Jacobs ignores the fact that the boycott was in the first place about ensuring *national* democracy (by pressing the banks to pressure the government, following the principles of the successful ANC international financial sanctions campaign).

By its nature as a national formation, SANCO represents a diversity of regional interests. Apartheid-capitalism has created vastly uneven development between town and countryside, and SANCO must be sensitive to those differences. But to conclude that a national bond boycott was an inappropriate response simply because of uneven development, is to imply that all conditions everywhere must be equal if any national policy is to emerge. That will never happen. Instead, a key objective of the bond boycott was to get the banks to come to the bargaining table to at least open up the possibility of further loans, concessions, and a banking Code of Conduct which will apply to comrades in both urban and rural areas. Addressing uneven development was, in fact, a primary goal of SANCO's bank negotiating team.

In sum, Jacobs has done a service by pointing out the fact that our SANCO constitution is not a good constitution. Having said all of this, however, there is no justification for the conclusion that SANCO may be "heading for disaster." The rationale is contained in Jacobs's concern: "With SANCO up and running, what is happening on the ground? On the one hand, one hears local leaders saying things like, 'We cannot do anything now. We are waiting for SANCO National to decide on the direction'—which never happened in pre-SANCO days. On the other hand, some areas ignore SANCO and carry on as if nothing has changed."

There are clearly flaws in the existing system, but my own fear is that Jacobs's proposal—an ideal type of "loose federations at regional and national levels"—may weaken the civic movement, and may well lead to personal, regional fiefdoms and baronies along the model of KwaNatal (Buthelezi's loose federalism), or the political tragedies unfolding within so many countries now being torn apart by regional ethnic or political divisions.

Finally, SANCO must be a stronger organization, and that requires a strong organizational structure. Reasons why SANCO has been weak include overlapping leadership with other progressive forces; tensions that exist between some local civics and ANC branches (and other political organizations); and the capacity and resource problem. As a result, building the civic movement through loose federalism is utopian.

One other reason for a tight federal structure, as I explain next, is that the anti-civic ideologies that have been sprouting at the national level require a national-level response.

Civics and the culture of poverty
(Schlemmer, Nedcor/Old Mutual)

The final two sections of this chapter are about method and ideology of analysis. The reason to focus on this is that while many of the previous arguments in one way or another weakened the civic movement by confusion, this reflected the confusion of the authors. In contrast, there appeared a much less confused political move afoot by liberal pragmatists from big capitalism's camp, who attempted to shoehorn the civic movement into thinking about the overall problems facing black society in South Africa in a way that lowered our expectations.

This is known as the "culture of poverty" analysis, and its application by, among others, Lawrence Schlemmer of the Urban Foundation and researchers of Nedcor/Old Mutual (the single largest financial institution in SA), represented a very disturbing intellectual development. The central issue is, as might be expected, one of *class*: those writers who suffer from what I call a "culture of privilege" appeared willing to do anything in their power, even floating reactionary and untenable ideas to the civic movement, to maintain their own wealth, assure the continuation of an extremely exploitative form of capitalism in South Africa, and lower the political willpower of the civic movement to gain our socioeconomic objectives.

Schlemmer, whose work stems from a biased reading of the United States experience, admits that "until recently the idea of a culture of poverty was thought to be outdated. But it is now being revisited, especially since other ideas didn't adequately explain barriers to development within poor communities." Schlemmer believes that "People who are very poor also often have unrealistic expectations about the future. This is usually a way of escaping from reality." He goes on to distinguish "social action" (also called the politics of protest) from "community-based development" (politics of development). Schlemmer's analysis has already been attacked from the grassroots (in this case by a Civic Associations of Johannesburg comrade at an Urban Foundation seminar):

> Lawrie [Lawrence Schlemmer] spoke about the sense of futility and frustration that are supposed to result from social action and protest. I don't

think this is really the case in South Africa. Many people feel that the changes of the past two years have come about because of these pressures. They feel they have achieved something through mass mobilization.

Such criticism can be advanced even further, beyond what the civic movement has achieved in the past through politics of protest. My point is that Schlemmer's distinction between social action and community-based development is a false dichotomy, because protest is inseparable from development. After all, the civic movement is, even after formal political liberation in 1994, still dealing with intransigent (mainly white) bureaucrats steeped in the culture of privilege, many of whom have shown themselves to be—

• profoundly corrupt (the Department of Development Aid wasted hundreds of millions of rands, much of which was linked to fraudulent schemes of individual bureaucrats);

• linked to the security establishment (typical was the role of the Development Bank of Southern Africa in the reconstituted Joint Management Committee in Alexandra, which threatened activists' lives as late as 1990; later, agents from the National Intelligence System began monitoring "foreigners" from Southern Africa in the civic movement in 1994, especially in central Johannesburg, which was these deluded agents' self-proclaimed role in the Reconstruction and Development Program);

• extremely supportive of the most undemocratic forces in South Africa (again, the Development Bank has placed billions of rands in the hands of BLAs and homeland dictators);

• utterly incompetent in carrying out their own development policies (two examples include the Urban Foundation [UF], whose development subsidiaries lost R11 million on a turnover of R17 million in 1991, in part due to ill-advised land speculation, and the Independent Development Trust, which tried to pump billions into township credit and loan guarantee schemes and by all accounts failed miserably);

• miserly in their visions of development (again, consider the undemocratic, non-participatory IDT/UF "housing policy," which in reality was a site-and-service "toilet policy," offering R7,500 grants in a developer-driven process); and

• trickle-down, free-market oriented in their socioeconomic philosophy.

These are characteristics of the establishment development agencies which civic activists confront daily, and it is for this reason that protest can never be separated from development. For that matter, even with the advent of democratic government, protest remains an essential part of the development process, in view of the uncooperative role of bureaucrats.

Protest, however, is unfashionable among social democrats aiming for "social contracts." The most sophisticated intellectual approach to the civic movement (and the oppressed community in general) was that of the financial capitalists Nedcor and Old Mutual, who mastered the art of the "compact."

A fairly well-balanced group of researchers, led by the charismatic Bob Tucker (then Perm managing director), developed "Scenario Planning" as a means of probing future "prospects for successful transition." The exercise was guided by Pierre Wack of Shell Oil. Among the researchers, Maude Motanyane, Mamphela Ramphele, and Sheila Sisulu supported the Scenario Planning exercise by "analysing changes taking place in the black community." In doing so, they considered the analysis generated by consultant Bruce Scott (a Harvard business professor) "a useful framework for understanding the dynamics of 'underclass' development in a process of desegregation." What did they learn?

Perhaps most importantly, they discovered an 'underclass': a "community of the careless," a "dreadful society" in which "undesirable behavioural traits ... cease to be viewed as 'deviant' and instead become the norm." They dwelled upon the often-cited problem of the "culture of boycott," which allegedly emerged in politicized townships. They observed that mistrust, suspicion, and economic deprivation remained entrenched in townships. And they concluded that this so-called "collective victimisation" was leading to "dependency" and a "culture of entitlement," and, moreover, that this "culture" was inimicable to democracy in the new South Africa:

> Inferiority complex formation results from constant degradation. This leads to mediocrity, aggressive denial, and intolerance of criticism. In the late 1960s, the Black Consciousness Movement recognized the formation of an inferiority complex among blacks as one of the greatest constraints to their becoming active agents of history. The sense of victimization and its use to justify a lack of self-accountability and a culture of entitlement pose serious problems for the future. It may become difficult to wean people from the negative attitudes and behavior patterns flowing from such a culture.

The argument carries fundamental flaws. To compare black political thought in the 1960s with conditions forged by progressive organizing and demands of the 1980s and 1990s is silly. Township organizing in the 1980s did not make even a bit-part appearance in the Nedcor/Old Mutual analysis of black "survival strategies," unfortunately; nor for that matter was it included anywhere in the Scenario Planning exercise. Except: "The power struggle conducted between the government and its security forces on the one hand and the black community on the other during the 1970s and 1980s eroded the relationships, institutions, standards, and discipline on which any successful community depends." The opposite is truer: struggle strengthened not only our survival strategies but also our vision of a future society free of apartheid and socioeconomic despair.

No doubt, township activists were out to destroy the apartheid system, and went to great lengths to do so, many thousands losing their lives, *but not because of an "inferiority complex."* It was because they felt legitimately entitled to a democratic political system, and in particular political empowerment of the oppressed, redistribution of South Africa's wealth, and restructuring of the economy in the interests of poor and working people.

Nedcor and Old Mutual are, it seems, satisfied with a democratic political system only if it specifically *does not* lead to political empowerment of the oppressed, redistribution of wealth, and restructuring of the economy in the interests of poor and working people; this led their analysts to construct a method for dealing with political demands which treats them as cultural weaknesses.

In contrast, the civic movement argument is that a democratic government must be responsible for subsidizing the living standards of people so that they have at least the basics that are essential for a decent life: housing, education and child care, health care, basic household goods, electrification, clean water, sewage services, essential clothing, etc. This is a well-developed notion in many advanced capitalist societies (and practiced in Scandinavia without too many inferiority complexes forming).

What is crucial is that demands for these entitlements, and the political movement to support the demands, emerged not from weak township consciousness and organization, but rather, in the mid-1950s (when the Freedom Charter was drawn up) from very militant anti-apartheid forces, and from even stronger township civic forces in the 1980s.

So no one should be surprised when Nedcor/Old Mutual and their hired hands characterize those of us demanding minimally decent standards of living as having inferiority complexes and a sense of victimization, as highly dependent, and as unable to develop a culture of democracy.

When development goes sour
(Cross, Boaden, and Taylor)

Finally, consider the use of "culture of poverty" analysis as a means of explaining why establishment development plans go sour and establishment agency philosophies are rejected. Many development plans went sour in the interregnum. Someone had to be blamed, and when establishment agencies could not legitimately blame the community itself (for this would make it difficult to rationalize continuing with development work at all), those such as the Independent Development Trust and Urban Foundation easily cast blame upon the civics. For example, Shalto Cross, coordinator of rural development for the IDT, set out this argument:

> The language of development, and much of the limelight, is currently dominated by civic and service organizations which are in the process of transforming themselves from organizations of struggle into vehicles for the delivery of development. This is a rich area for study, and the wide bounds between the most ruthlessly tribunite and cynically populist of these, and those with less selfish and more genuine commitments to the arduous process of social reconstruction and self-reliance, will provide a broad field for the next generation of social historians.

Who are the ruthless and cynical? Cross believes that:

> the most obvious proponents and standard bearers of civil society, namely many of the civic and service organizations which now offer their services as development intermediaries, acting on behalf of the rural poor, may provide more an obstacle than a help. This essentially arises precisely because of their predominant concern with the political, which ... leads directly to an understatement and misinterpretation of those more hidden forms of social organization, as represented by social and religious movements, which can most ably perform these functions.

The "culture of poverty" ideology is important to his explanation. Cross approvingly cites Adam Ferguson's 1767 *Essay on the History of Civil Society*: "The great object of policy ... is to secure to the family its means of subsistence and settlement; to protect the industrious in the pursuit of his occupation; to reconcile the restrictions of police, and the social affection of mankind, with their separate and interested pursuit."

Now it all becomes clear: Cross seeks not a vibrant civil society able to defend poor and working-class people's interests through ongoing struggle, but rather an explicitly *civilized* society with "a common sense of nationality, and internalised sense of civic order ... "such as new religious movements, all within the broader "developmental" context, of course, of "a shift toward manufacturing industry combined with a breakthrough into major new export markets."

A similar position with respect to the supposed gatekeeper role of civics and service organizations was adopted by Bruce Boaden and Rob Taylor of the Urban Foundation. Boaden and Taylor denigrate the civic (the Community Committee, an allegedly "elite group") of St. Wendolin's, a township between Pinetown and Durban:

> The manipulation of the community by its leadership became problematic, as evidenced by the inability of those most in need of housing to gain access to even the most rudimentary of formal houses. Acquisition of sites on a site-and-service basis for the erection of informal housing was discredited by the leadership. The presence of a development agency made it possible to gain credibility for the leadership in terms of attracting resources. The fact that those resources were not used appropriately was not considered to be the fault of the leadership.

We are asked to believe, from the representatives of big capital, that a large community is "manipulated" by its civic (one well-structured, with eight functioning area committees and countless street committees) and by (democratically elected) civic leadership, who in turn are misled by the development agency, a university-based service organization. (In reality, the organization, Built Environment Support Group, has a well-respected working methodology characterized by community capacity-building.) Boaden and Taylor complain that St. Wendolin's was "over-serviced and over-surveyed" by this "interventionist agency" with its "own agenda."

In reality, the civic leadership's opinion was that the UF was aiming to build middle-class housing. This opinion was based on extensive experience with the UF throughout the Durban area. (My source on St. Wendolins is former civic leader Musa Soni, whom I worked with in Johannesburg at Planact.)

Boaden and Taylor did not reveal in their article that the UF attempted, unsuccessfully, to acquire St. Wendolin's land from the Catholic Church, which formally owned it on behalf of the community. Nor did they reveal that there was no UF consultation on the housing process. The site-and-service scheme was rejected because the plan did not fulfil community expectations of decent standards. (This was in 1988, and it is no surprise that after hundreds of efforts by establishment agencies to make the horrid site-and-service philosophy work, in July 1992 SANCO adopted an official policy position calling for a moratorium on IDT and UF site-and-service schemes.) Community members were so opposed to the UF that they occupied the St. Wendolin's Development Centre (a UF Informal Settlement Division workshop), leading to the center's shut-down.

Rather than admit their own failings, Boaden and Turner explain consistently with a "culture of poverty" analysis that St. Wendolin's was the victim of "a sense of helplessness born of years of dependency fostered by the political system," complicated by "a dependence on the church as the purveyor of goods and services" which "created an atmosphere of expectation in relation to the further development of the area," such as "the expectation of subsidy which would deliver large numbers of sites and formal houses at virtually no cost to the end-user."

While it is interesting to note the difference between these authors and Cross in terms of their respect for religion, the community itself disproved the Boaden and Taylor "helplessness theory" by constructing their own school at St. Wendolin's. So while the "culture of poverty" analysis may appear tempting as a means of shifting blame for development gone sour, in this case the analysts protest a bit too vigorously, apparently because the community *was not dependent enough* ... on the UF.

Conclusion

The civic movement is like a young child, beginning to crawl, learning about basic needs, trying to articulate demands, viewing the world every day with fresh eyes, increasingly aware of what it means to survive and prosper, and in a halting way developing a strategic niche in broader society. She needs nourishment and continual encouragement if an independent mind is to be developed, if her limbs and muscles are to grow strong, and if she is going to reach adulthood and change the world. We must watch carefully, with an always-critical eye. And if a false step or two are taken, we must not write her off as terminally uncoordinated or confused. Her problems in life are not derived from her culture or from her uncertain sense of the future, but rather from the diverse elements around her that pull her to and fro. All these are her challenges, and if we are to understand her sometimes unsteady trek through life, it will be because we relate to her goals and objectives and have a profound sympathy for these. And finally, those that fear the child's development must be identified, for some of their prescriptions for her future may be very harmful indeed.

What is striking in the previous pages is that a spirit of sympathy for the civic movement is generally not in evidence in the literature reviewed, and there must be a reason for that. I have focused in the last sections of this chapter on ideology, because the unveiling of civic movement commentators is only complete once the methodology employed is clarified. (In addition, the institutional affiliations and lack of township experience of some of these writers also provide *material* explanations for why they think about the civic movement in the way they do.)

Looking back through this review, we see that one commentator uses faulty description to undermine the civic movement, others toy with situating civics within political processes (leaving the real class issues as bland side dishes not even tasted), another rips the organizational form and early development of the national civic movement, while others attempt to downplay all of the above through simply characterizing the stage ahead as one of moving from protest to development via social contracts, unproblematic except for those pesky civics who actually attempt to represent the community.

But of all the writers, none at all contest (or consider) the idea I discussed earlier: that civics grounded in an ideology of working-class civil society can help build a strong socialist movement through experimenting with new relations of production in the future, and by concretely challenging the modalities of capitalism in the present. It would be good to have this discussion in a fresh round of research and philosophizing on civics in the coming period.

Meanwhile, if this review of civic movement analysis has picked up the salient intellectual trends, then it appears we must continue working very hard in the realm of the ideological. For here lie hints of the real interests behind the characterization of civics as "institutions that themselves need to be watched over." What should be clear is that it is the watchers who also need watching!

PART 4
TOWARD AND BEYOND
LIBERATION

14
The Civic Movement's Agenda
(1993-1995)

In this chapter, I describe how the national civic movement matured as a leading progressive force within South African society. To put this in context, though, I first return to the debate over how working-class interests are advanced during a slow transition to democracy, within both civil and political society. Then I discuss some of the gender and generational forces within and around the civic movement. Finally, I relate our movement's arguments on behalf of what we called "people-centered development," and show how these paralleled the ANC Reconstruction and Development Program.

Does working-class civil society
require a working-class political party?

In July 1992 I moved, temporarily, to the United States to train as an urban planner. For many years I had wanted to study professionally so as to begin to fill the huge gap created by apartheid. I had initially wanted to become a lawyer, but realized that there were quite a number of black lawyers coming through the ranks, and that as community activists our main lack was in the field of planning. I met progressive recruiters from the Pratt Institute in New York, a community-oriented university specializing in planning, architecture, and the arts. Politically, this was a time when ACO was developing well, many of our leading comrades were taking roles in negotiations, and I was feeling more urgently the need to upgrade my skills so as to specialize in restructuring Alexandra when apartheid finally fell. I began courses at Pratt, only returning to Johannesburg in April 1993 to attend the funeral of Chris Hani, the great SACP leader who was assassinated. Then, with the pace of change finally picking up, I decided in May 1993 to take a fifteen-month leave of absence from Pratt to play a role in the transition.

I quickly found that the old debate over civil and political society had again engulfed the Left. Comrades from civics and unions were again asking, with a new intensity, whether the working class was being represented effectively by the ANC and its Alliance partners. This was partly because so many aspects of negotiations were being conducted so secretly, and partly because many of the public statements of ANC leaders represented concessions to big business and the apartheid-era bureaucracy. At one point, Joe Slovo was forced to concede, before a huge crowd of trade unionists who had marched to the site of the negotiations outside Johannesburg, that the ANC negotiators had begun to change their ideology once they put on fancy suits.

Of course, it is not the garment that makes the man, so to speak, and plenty of trade union or township negotiators wearing jeans have had a hard time in negotiations. The main thing was to maintain firm ideological principles. Even for activists like myself who supported the ANC throughout, there was sometimes a sense that too much was being surrendered to the Nats and too much latitude was being given to Inkatha and the security forces. Such is the nature of negotiations.

Alienation began to rise, and a growing chorus demanded that the Left consider forming a workers' party, perhaps along the lines of the Brazilian PT (which had grown from the powerful unions, and was distinct from the old-style Communist Party). Worker delegates of the National Union of Metalworkers (NUMSA) passed a controversial resolution at their congress in July 1993 calling for "new forms of organization that will unify the working-class organizations and parties that will take forward a program to implement socialism."

This debate is worth recalling in detail, because it sets the stage for much of what I believe should happen in civil and political society even after the transition period, into the next century. Unfortunately, the NUMSA resolution was vague and open to misinterpretation. NUMSA should have been clearer about what "new forms of organization" its workers had in mind, and why such forms could include a new working-class party. The underlying objective, NUMSA's resolution noted, was to unite the Left, namely people who endorse the following: control of the means of production by the working class for the benefit of society as a whole; democracy; internationalism; anti-imperialism; and non-racialism. (Gender relations were not, unfortunately, addressed.)

This objective offers an all-encompassing socialist vision, which is worthy of pursuit under any conditions. But there were fundamental differences between the various socialist parties active in South Africa (and between these parties and independent socialists). The formation of a workers' party implied collapsing the South African Communist Party, the Trotskyist Workers Organization for Socialist Action (which itself had suffered severe splits since its formation and later became the Workers' List Party), and other groups into a larger and more coherent force.

But in reality, what would it take to give a working-class party the necessary degree of unity and social weight, given the Left's fragmentation and the fundamental differences that existed within the socialist movement? Why not instead put that effort into reinvigorating the SACP, with its tens of thousands of members? One answer is that the NUMSA resolution reflected disillusionment with the SACP, since the party had failed to come up with an independent program that would unite all sectors of the working class. Regrettably, as if to illustrate exactly this concern, in responding to NUMSA in the *Weekly Mail*, leading SACP intellectual Jeremy Cronin did a disservice to progressive debate. He compared the workers' party idea to a National Intelligence Service document which advised the National Party to "prolong the negotiations" by splitting the ANC. This misrepresented the NUMSA congress resolution, which was really a plaintive call for a safeguard against the anticipated failure of the first democratic government to meet popular aspirations.

NUMSA workers may have jumped the gun in this. But their call for a workers' party could not be ignored in light of lessons from other parts of the world. The Brazilian Workers' Party, for instance, led by the charismatic metalworker Lula, nearly won the national election with an extremely radical program in 1989. Yet according to the book *Without Fear of Being Happy* (a Workers' Party slogan), the strength of the Brazilian model was based on the "privilege of lateness." As a result, "the Workers' Party grew from a relatively 'blank slate,'" according to authors Erwin Sader and Ken Silverstein. The lack of a strong Brazilian Communist Party tradition meant that the

Workers' Party was really a diverse popular movement, including even some wealthy churches, and so not just a workers' party.

Sadly, after the narrow 1989 defeat, both the Workers' Party radical municipal program and its socialist, anti-imperialist content deteriorated. This resulted, I am led to understand, from the general economic crisis and from World Bank policies which forced Workers' Party mayors in more than a dozen cities to resign from their party through frustration at not being able to implement meaningful reforms at the local level. And it was also reflected in the Workers' Party's much more moderate position in the 1994 elections, which they lost badly.

Since the Workers' Party claimed a pluralistic social movement membership which closely resembled our 1980s UDF, this led comrades to ask whether the Workers' Party-type popular-socialist ideology could be sustained within an electorally oriented political party under conditions we face today. Alternatively, should that ideology instead be more deeply developed and ingrained through working-class instruments of civil society, as I had argued? After all, other workers' parties in the advanced capitalist countries have had an even poorer record of maintaining socialist objectives during the twentieth century. In contrast, organizations within civil society have not necessarily liquidated their radical politics, in the manner working-class political parties seem to.

Regardless of the answer to this question, there was no doubt among members, friends and foes alike, that the SACP, as a working-class political party, would have to do more to advance a working-class program that would distinguish it from the ANC in specifically advocating the end of the capitalist mode of production. Following its unbanning, the SACP gained high quantities of membership—and it continues to evolve into a mass party today—but a concerted effort was required to produce more quality cadres who could articulate the socialist vision. But I had confidence, in part based on the SACP's excellent Central Committee Discussion Paper, "The Role of the SACP in the Transition to Democracy and Socialism," released in May 1993. In addition, the SACP seemed to take seriously warnings about corporatism (deal-making between elites) that emerged in various state-business-civil society forums.

Most importantly, the SACP seemed to be willing to support our notion of working-class civil society, by endorsing the "development of a vast network of democratic organs of popular participation in both the economy and the political system and the leadership of the working class." My view was that in light of the SACP's openness, all socialists should join and help transform the SACP into a mass working-class political party—instead of throwing up our hands and forming something new and fragile. This was not terribly controversial, for Moss and many leading trade unionists had gone into the SACP. But it was only after the 1994 election that the SACP began to really attack the conservative elements within the Government of National Unity, and by implication within the ANC itself. By this stage, Cronin was playing a very important role in challenging neo-liberalism.

All of this discussion and dissent was to be expected, for while the national struggle was being brought to a successful conclusion, debates over the class struggle were now heating up. But we were only beginning to understand the gender struggle, and meanwhile the youth were losing most of their struggles.

Women and power within the democratic movement

The civic movement is notoriously patriarchal. While women do the bulk of the civic work at the grassroots level, they never seem to be permitted leadership status, whether in their local civics, in their regional groups, or at the national level. This is not much different, of course, from what happens at the top ranks of big business, the judiciary, the media, and so forth, yet it will cripple the civic movement—and indeed nearly every branch of South Africa's progressive movement—if not addressed.

At SANCO's national office, this was always recognized, even if lethargy prevented us from addressing the problem. Finally, a conference was held in January 1994 in Durban, where eighty women and men from civics gathered for what was our first opportunity to talk openly together about gender roles and conflicts. To start, the SANCO women talked about themselves, by themselves. They came up with recommendations, such as a gender desk and specific conferences for women, aimed at dynamizing the civic movement.

When the women presented these ideas to the plenary the next day, temperatures at the already-humid beachfront hotel soared. I chaired the session, and did most of the sweating! My role was to harmonize competing interests, as far as possible, and to do so by promoting a frank and honest discussion. Our male comrades were not used to hearing such forthright criticism of their personal and political domination, and their resentment nearly prevented them from hearing the proposals for change. But in the end the men adapted, and we left surprisingly refreshed, with a better understanding of what we have in common, what still divides the sexes, and what we must do in future.

Moving to democratize the society and state, and to build our working class organizations, SANCO leaders have realized we cannot be effective if we don't walk on two legs of equal length and strength, rather than limping along for macho reasons. If in the future we look back at our trail, we must see footprints of similar depth, otherwise we will have veered off course.

After all, in many of our township struggles during the last decade, male and female cadres acted with equal bravery and stamina. Even in exile, the liberation movement sent women to the front for combat, and also depended upon their crucial role in providing education, health, nutrition, welfare, and the like.

Surely the best traditions of gender equality can continue. The roots of women's oppression in society, community, family, and in relation to partners must be unveiled. How, then, do we go about this?

One opportunity comes through the fact that roughly 30 percent of those elected for the ANC's parliamentary seats are women. But has this gone far enough? SANCO's national, provincial, and local executive boards are nowhere near this number. Nor had such gender representation been achieved elsewhere in ANC leadership.

We must also go beyond mere quotas and address the most concrete problems faced by all women. The Interim Constitution does this by challenging the oppressive features of traditional law. The Reconstruction and Development Program offers special support for women in land reform, education, housing, and many other areas. And ANC policy on health recognizes reproductive rights, which should empower women greatly in their hidden struggles against sexual domination.

But are these goals short-term in nature, and if they are won will we just as easily lose them over time, as has happened in many third world countries facing socioeconomic crises? After all, working-class women have much of their time taken up by domestic work and child rearing, which patriarchal society long ago defined as unfit for men.

So I wonder if we are going about things correctly. We in the civics have often been guilty of asking women to play what has been termed a "triple role": first, to take a lead in community organizing and delivery of community social services, second, to handle traditional family responsibilities, and third, to find a job or income-generating activities.

For a woman, trying to play all these roles while rarely being rewarded with local, regional, or national leadership in our movements is especially frustrating if the men are only drinking beer and reading the newspapers. We, as men and women in the civic movement, must therefore confront head-on outmoded traditions where women take the main role in reproducing the extended family and mobilizing the community.

But even if we succeed here, this may not be enough. We must also go beyond this, to understand what Friedrich Engels called the "world historical defeat of the female sex," namely, the advent of the nuclear family under the capitalist economic system. The family became more oppressive as a unit, Engels argued, so that emerging class society could pass on wealth from one generation to another.

For women today, the circulation of wealth is not only bound up in family relations, but also in conforming to a *Cosmopolitan* magazine style. Capitalist society very subtly persuades us to imitate some degenerate Western varieties of women's identity, which stress mainly power and status and fashion and money.

I am no authority on these issues. But I do think that we who consider ourselves progressive must get away from the individualism, consumerism, and egoism that characterize some female "role models" in South Africa. Because ultimately, I am certain, it is only by linking our political and socioeconomic struggles with those of sexual equality that we can move to a higher stage of liberation.

For civics, this means being part of a movement in which the nuclear family is condemned as the vehicle for passing on wealth and class power, especially because of its oppressive implications for women. We must force society to re-order how our social wealth is generated and shared.

I think that this can be done, in part, if we place a much higher priority on social struggles through which women's lives can be less burdened, more liberated. This means highlighting women's concerns in every facet of our demand for the satisfaction of basic needs, in housing, health care, education, welfare, and so many other areas. Our emerging civic agenda has enormous room for new and more gender-liberating directions in these struggles, but if men continue to dominate we will probably never fight the good fight.

A generation lost?

I have always been concerned about the need for civics to provide leadership roles to the younger cadres in our communities. As a young person myself, and as someone who tried to bridge the gaps between civic and youth politics during the 1980s, I feel an enormous social weight bearing down on young people. The danger is that this weight is creating marginalization, criminaliza-tion, and ostracization. Let me try to illustrate in a personal way the dangers of what amounts to a frontal attack on youth.

As I have already indicated, I grew up in rural Transkei, received Bantu education in the Ciskei, and then migrated as an unem-ployed youth to Johannesburg's "Dark City," Alexandra Town-ship, in the early 1980s. In Alex, I supported insurrection, ungovernability, and the total overthrow of the existing law, order, and capitalism. The government sent me to rot in prison for three years, on charges of high treason, sedition, and subversion.

By virtue of this background, I am a leading candidate for membership in the so-called lost generation of township youth. By virtue of my age and gender, I am often judged, even when walking innocently in the downtown streets, as a public enemy, a danger to society. The English definition of "youth" is harmless in itself, but in South Africa the "youth" are all black and bad, while "teenagers" are all normal white kids.

Clearly, my generation has a public relations problem. Here is how respected Durban poet Ari Sitas describes stereotypes of South Africa's own Khmer Rouge, the lost generation: "The tyre, the petrol-bomb, the knife, the stone, the hacking: death. The media picture is of young men, hungry men, with hardened features and red eyes."

For white teenagers, tires and petrol are used to go to the cinema, restaurants, or dating. The knife is a tool used on a mountain hike or for cutting steak roasted at a braaivleis. Rugby balls are thrown on the sportsgrounds (not stones on the killing fields). Hacking is for the golf course. The young men are generally well-fed with softened features. (Over time, though, I have seen them become hardened, hungry torturers, with bloodshot eyes.)

For generations these teenagers were socialized as decent white citizens, respecting property, embracing individualism and the nuclear family, and accepting the established order—including apartheid and exploitation.

In contrast, black youth organized, developed a collective con-sciousness, engaged in civil disobedience, and thought hard about how to develop democracy and socialism for all generations. Many of us spent the decade from 1984 to 1994 staying up all night in self-defense units, digging trenches against police vehicles and marauding Inkatha mobs, defending homes, families, communities. Yet if reporters had taken the trouble to talk to us, they would have found our aspirations are like everyone's: a good life, stable family, decent home, access to cultural amenities and recreation.

In his book *Heroes or Villains?* Jeremy Seekings puts it well: "Teenager is a term devoid of political meaning; youth is laden with it." In other words, society is still very sick, and youth are still its main victims. But instead of really making society healthy—through jobs, education, housing, health care—the youth are simply blamed and marginalized when they continue to reflect the illness.

So why are the symptoms of depraved black youth—the gangs of young tsotsis dressed to kill—not attributed to their roots in the failure of society? Why are youth seen as the cause, not the effect, of the breakdown of the family system as working hours get longer while unemployment worsens, the feeble education, the vulnerability to AIDS and other diseases incurable at under-resourced township clinics?

Looking back, I failed my annual exams three times. Was that the result of a culture of school boycott? No; the first time, in 1975, I shared a class with sixty students, had to cross a river on my daily ten kilometers barefoot walk to school, had no classroom supplies or books, and missed alternate days as I took turns looking after livestock with an elder brother. In the early 1980s, I failed twice again, and this time superficially because of student boycotts. But the reasons for the boycotts were the same conditions that existed all over South Africa: lack of qualified teachers, resources, etc.

This background did not prepare me for a degree in chartered accountancy, but neither did it prepare me to be a rapist, murderer, or anti-social tsotsi. What my background, and that of most youth, has prepared me for is a lifelong political struggle for socioeconomic justice.

It is amusing that many from my generation are now teaching. The *verligte* development agency bureaucrats say they are interested in learning how participatory democracy works in townships. Big businesses like Nissan are trying Japanese methods of shopfloor participation in order to understand from young workers how to improve production efficiency.

Nevertheless, it seems that generically, young black men have become the enemy of self-appointed guardians of bourgeois law and order. Though we have a political integrity and sensibility that should be celebrated, we will have to fight for our very survival. White adults, on the other hand, have somehow managed to change their ideological stripes and no one seems to remember who was really the lost generation while I did my time in jail.

If they have not done so already, civics must take heed of the resource that our next generation of leaders represents. Visionary democrats of our community organizations and activists from the youth movement have much in common. At the grassroots level this often leads to working alliances. At the national level, it is for SANCO to assist the process by which civics expand and continually renew their energies by working with and drawing in the revolutionary youth.

People-centered development

I was fortunate to be able to take a break from my studies in New York and spend nearly a year at the Johannesburg urban service organization Planact, from November 1993 until September 1994. This was, personally, an opportunity to get more experience working in a professional non-governmental organization (NGO), one at the cutting edge of township development yet also immersed in the friendly, non-racial atmosphere of trendy Rockey Street in Yeoville. It also allowed me to maintain my links to Alexandra, where I was elected President of ACO, as I mention in the next chapter.

However, I often found myself at odds with white-collar professionalism, which I felt was usually oriented toward the deradicalization of the grassroots. This was especially true when our time and energy were wasted on arcane details of technical agreements rather than popular mobilization for the planning and implementation of development. At times negotiations are a product of democratic decisions taken at the grassroots level, but at other times they are hijacked by service organizations that should be serving, rather than negotiating on behalf of, the community-based organizations. Few would disagree with this principle.

For NGOs, which were often guided by white, middle-class staff (mainly with very strong student anti-apartheid credentials), sorting out the technical details were important, and I don't mean to downplay the progressive input made by NGOs. But there were many disagreements about strategy between the NGOs and civics that flowed from professional arrogance and community vulnerability. I had hoped to serve as a kind of bridge between the two, and in some cases, such as with SANCO's head office and with a few civic groups working on development finance, I think I helped to reconcile styles. Relations improved, but overall it was a difficult hybrid role for me to play.

My position is that people in communities generally know what they want. As professionals, we should be in a position to establish development plans in a way that is as community-driven as possible. In part, this means taking already-existing popular campaigns and turning them into broader policy frameworks, and only at that stage allowing the technical experts to fill in details the community may have missed.

In our broad campaign for "people-driven development" (a slogan SANCO adopted at our launch), we had to come up with a national policy framework, a "SANCO Reconstruction and Development Program," which would feed into COSATU's and the ANC's similar Reconstruction and Development Program efforts during 1993. COSATU had paved the way, by negotiating with the ANC that it would help to develop a broad socioeconomic strategy, the Reconstruction and Development Program, and this eventually became the ANC's campaign document. SANCO's RDP was taken into consideration in the later drafts of the ANC RDP, which was issued as a final campaign document in early 1994. In some areas, such as housing and local economic development, SANCO's RDP was the basis for the ANC policy.

SANCO is normally non-party-political, but in November 1993 we agreed to endorse those parties which, during the 1994 elections, would support our aims, objectives, and policies, and which claimed a democratic, anti-apartheid legacy. The PAC and two small Trotskyist parties never offered a full-fledged people-centered development program, and very little of their campaigning had to do with civics, so only the ANC got the endorsement.

RDP stands neither for Revolutionary Dictatorship of the Proletariat nor for Reactionary Doctrine of the Populists. The final ANC Reconstruction and Development Program was drafted in late 1993 and early 1994 by all of the ANC's major progressive allies, led by COSATU. The ANC built a large tent in which most progressive organizations helped to forge this RDP, and as a result it came to be adopted as a mass-popular program with the status of the Freedom Charter.

So many of our people lack jobs, housing, basic health care, literacy and education, decent clothing, cultural and recreational facilities, child care, and so on. In addressing the spiral of poverty and underdevelopment in our country, the RDP's emphasis on basic needs, as a "first priority," is to be welcomed by poor and working-class people:

No political democracy can survive and flourish if the mass of our people remain in poverty, without land, without tangible prospects for a better life. Attacking poverty and deprivation must therefore be the first priority of a democratic government.... The first priority is to begin to meet the basic needs of people—jobs, land, housing, water, electricity, telecommunications, transport, a clean and healthy environment, nutrition, health care, and social welfare.... Attacking poverty and deprivation is the first priority of the democratic government, and the RDP sets out a facilitating and enabling environment to this end. The RDP addresses issues of social, institutional, environmental and macro-economic sustainability in an integrated manner, with specific attention to affordability.

The biggest immediate challenge is to make the state accountable, democratic, and powerful enough to help civil society prosper and meet basic needs. The integrity of the state is crucial for this. A common problem with many countries' development strategies is the loss of that integrity. The RDP makes clear that this should not be South Africa's fate:

Relationships with international financial institutions such as the World Bank and International Monetary Fund must be conducted in such a way as to protect the integrity of domestic policy formulation and promote the interests of the South African population and the economy. Above all, we must pursue policies that enhance national self-sufficiency and enable us to reduce dependence on international financial institutions.

The RDP on the civics

The RDP spoke eloquently of our civic movement's contribution to the broader struggle:

A wide range of trade unions, mass organizations, other sectoral movements and community-based organizations (CBOs) such as civic associations developed in our country in opposition to apartheid oppression. These social movements and CBOs are a major asset in the effort to democratize and develop our society. Attention must be given to enhancing the capacity of such formations to adapt to partially changed roles. Attention must also be given to extending social-movement and CBO structures into areas and sectors where they are weak or non-existent....

Apart from the strategic role of government in the RDP, mass

participation in its elaboration and implementation is essential. Within the first nine months of 1994, the RDP must be taken to People's Forums, rallies, and meetings in communities.

In the course of 1994, trade unions, sectoral social movements, and CBOs, notably civics, must be encouraged to develop RDP programs of action and campaigns within their own sectors and communities. Many social movements and CBOs will be faced with the challenge of transforming their activities from a largely oppositional mode into a more developmental one. To play their full role, these formations will require capacity-building assistance. This should be developed with democratic government facilitation and funded through a variety of sources. A set of rigorous criteria must be established to ensure that beneficiaries deserve the assistance and use it for the designated purposes. Every effort must be made to extend organization into marginalized communities and sectors like, for instance, rural black women.

Trade unions and other mass organizations must be actively involved in democratic public policy making. This should include involvement in negotiations ranging from the composition of the Constitutional Court to international trade and loan agreements. Education about trade unions and other mass organizations should also be promoted in school curricula and through publicly-funded media....

Institutions of civil society should be encouraged to improve their accountability to their various constituencies and to the public at large. There should be no restriction on the right of the organizations to function effectively. Measures should be introduced to create an enabling environment for social movements, CBOs, and NGOs in close consultation with those bodies and to promote donations to the non-profit sector. This should include funding of Legal Advice Centres and paralegals....

The RDP national coordinating body must also ensure that the structures of civil society are involved in the program. It must ensure coordination between the various ministries, parastatals, labor groups, civics, and other organizations. It must link with existing sectoral and development forums at the national level, in order to establish effective systems of coordination. Similar bodies should be established at provincial and local levels. In addition, provincial and local development forums are important vehicles for ensuring the participation of local communities and interest groups in the development process. Development forums must be strengthened through the provision of adequate resources.

Avoiding "market-centered development"

If we maintain the integrity of our policy-making process, so that South Africa is ruled from Pretoria, not Washington, DC, then we will avoid the market-centered development favored by international financial institutions. The World Bank, I would argue, is incompetent in meeting basic needs. A 38 percent "unsatisfactory project completion" rate on recent projects, according to the Bank's 1992 "Effective Implementation" report, is just one example. Sadly, though, there are many glaring examples of third world leaders—even committed leftists like Michael Manley of Jamaica, the Nicaraguan Sandinistas, and more recently Jean-Bertrand Aristide of Haiti—failing to keep the World Bank and IMF at bay. In South Africa, the World Bank adopted a strategy of working with the ANC as early as 1990. Everyone expected the ANC to lead the first democratic government, so this was to be expected, but the Bank's record was so dismal in the third world that the civic movement suggested extreme caution in any negotiations. The Bank's friendly attitude was not meant to uplift the poor, but to confuse us for the purpose of future exploitation. Many of our comrades resisted this, became more aware of the World Bank's agenda, and remain cautious of dealing with the Bank.

In our civic movement, we adopted a flexible counter-strategy. When faced with a Bank mission, the Civic Associations of Johannesburg, for example, came up with a proposed "protocol" to regulate the Bank's activities and ensure that the Bank followed our movement's non-racial, non-sexist philosophy. The Bank was surprised by this, and told CAJ that this was not standard operating procedure. The protocol was rejected.

We do not need World Bank financing, nor that of other international agencies which will impose conditionality and exploit us. Let us not take foreign loans when there is plenty of domestic capital available (hundreds of billions of rands—"paper chasing paper"—in the stock market). Let us not take dollar-denominated loans from foreign banks to build houses which cost rands (not dollars). Let us not borrow when the rand is declining, which (according to a study by the Centre for the Study of the South African Economy and International Finance of the London School of Economics) has meant that "South Africa has paid a premium, as large as 83 percent (fourteen percentage points) on one measure, to raise funds from international capital markets, relative to the cost of borrowing on the domestic market."

Let us instead follow the RDP advice in this matter: "The RDP must use foreign debt financing only for those elements of the program that can potentially increase our capacity for earning foreign exchange."

Promoting local economic development

Finally, there is scope in a democratic South Africa for great advances in what we are terming "local economic development." In most areas of meeting basic needs, such as housing, there are many local linkages between production and consumption (such as use of local building materials and labor) which have thus far not been made, for two reasons.

First, the structure of production is highly concentrated, with most building material sectors controlled by three or fewer companies. This must be corrected by anti-trust action and by promoting local black businesses, perhaps through direct local government purchasing arrangements or outright state subsidies. The RDP endorses this approach, especially when the enterprises are worker-owned or community-controlled:

> In order to foster the growth of local economies, broadly representative institutions must be established to address local economic development needs. Their purpose would be to formulate strategies to address job creation and community development (for example, leveraging private sector funds for community development, investment strategies, training, small business and agricultural development, etc.). If necessary, the democratic government must provide some subsidies as a catalyst for job-creation programs controlled by communities and/or workers, and target appropriate job creation and development programs in the most neglected and impoverished areas of our country. Ultimately, all such projects should sustain themselves.

Second, our people can simply not afford the cost of most major commodities. Only 10 percent of the township population can afford to buy a house on the open market, even with a twenty-year loan. Yet if the state adopts appropriate policies, the demand for local production could be enhanced by use of subsidies. According to the National Housing Forum, there should be a 50 percent subsidy on each R25,000 house in order for those without housing at present to be able to afford housing. The RDP commitment to this large a level of subsidy is unmistakable:

[The democratic government] must allocate subsidy funds from the budget—to reach a goal of not less than five per cent of the budget by the end of the five-year RDP—so that housing is affordable to even the poorest South Africans.

Finally, it is particularly heartening that the RDP recognizes institutions of civil society as crucial implementing agents for development, supported where possible by a developmental local government. The central government must be committed to providing resources to make development affordable to all.

In turn, I know that civics and our allies in civil society are devoted to empowering an ANC-dominated government if it pushes forward the progressive agenda. We will strive to help the people's representatives overcome friction from redundant apartheid bureaucrats who attempt to block a smooth socioeconomic transformation. Indeed, it is our primary responsibility to guard against elements who want to shelve or stall the RDP. This means the civic movement must strengthen our own structures and help our people to understand, participate, and control the local development process.

This has been our position in the civic movement before, during, and after the formal transfer of power. In the final chapter, I consider some of the most important concrete challenges at local and national levels in carrying forward these objectives.

15
Conclusion:
The Future of the Civics
(1994-1995)

Let me return to the point where I started, on the streets of Alexandra. In 1995, even a year after the elections and five years since we initiated many of our development programs, not much has changed there. To some degree this is the result of a decade's legacy of manipulation and destruction by the apartheid security apparatus, the Third Force, and Inkatha. To some degree it is the logical outcome of the capitalist development principles foisted upon Alexandra by business and state agencies, which can hopefully be undone once liberation filters throughout the South African fabric. But the lack of progress also reflects an ebb in our own organizational strength, which in turn I trace to pressures which we will hopefully overcome in the future. For without civic power, even the first democratic state won't respect the popular will. More optimistically, though, a strong future awaits civics which demand and acquire the capacity-building support they deserve. If we gain access to resources to expand our work in the ways I have suggested, we will have enormous potential to shape the New South Africa, and also to contribute to a resurgent international popular politics.

Alexandra after freedom dawned

Tsediso is still outside the factory at 6 a.m. each morning, and still earns R15 profit after a hard day of selling peanuts. He still goes home to a huge family in a tiny shack, clean on the inside but filthy outside, with streams of rainwater and sewage runoff flowing around his tiny plot. The cows and goats still roam the streets around his house, the litter still blows in the dusty wind, the sewage still overflows, the shacks still proliferate, the diseases still spread, the women still do most of the work, the children still lack recreational facilities, domestic violence still occurs, unemployment is still pervasive, the crime rate is still rising, the prices of goods in the stores are still high.

And yet, as President Nelson Mandela told Parliament in his inaugural address in May 1994, people must have hope for a South Africa free from want, free from hunger, free from deprivation, free from ignorance, free from suppression, and free from fear. The elections were meaningful in restoring Tsediso's and other Alexandra residents' sense of citizenship and their hope for a truly free South Africa. But so far, our economic situation and the physical environment in which we suffer have not improved much. Prospects for market-led development remain nearly nil. And a year into the New South Africa, government initiatives for uplifting the township are halting, uneven, unremarkable.

If all of this is true even in a high-profile, well-organized, politically well-connected township like Alexandra, it is worse in most other parts of black South Africa. Alexandra should really be a model township, a model of reconstruction and development, a model of unprecedented levels of popular involvement in community planning, construction, maintenance. The fact that it is not, thus far, reflects several developments which we must consider frankly.

There are some positive improvements, of course, which must also be considered. There is more light on the streets at night, and electricity in shacks and old houses which never had power before. (Even here, though, this was accomplished in a way that mimics a concentration camp, with security-oriented high-mast lighting, and on the basis of cost-recovery, which leaves out many residents who cannot afford the hook-up fee). Some roads are newly paved (but continue to deteriorate quickly in bad weather because they lack stormwater drainage). Some new houses are being built here and there (but they are far too expensive for most residents). A few new freestanding toilets adjoin some of the older houses (but for most residents, ablution blocks are still a long way from the shacks, and the hated bucket system continues in other parts of the township).

What of the psychological differences between now and five or ten years ago? There is, without doubt, pride in our right to vote, our new citizenship, our potential to shape our country politically and economically. There is also a widespread belief that with democracy, our lives will ultimately change for the better. Even if the ANC must share power with the National Party and Inkatha, expectations remain high. Not even periodic warnings by the highest ANC leaders can dampen people's spirits for what is reasonably within grasp, namely, the basic goods denied so long under apartheid capitalism.

And here is a warning: *without* economic improvement that we can witness in our daily lives, faith in government will wane. Cynicism will breed, apathy will become widespread, internecine fighting will increase, and social unrest will reemerge on a wide scale. Without access to skills development, job creation, better education, and primary health care, comrades will feel increasingly desperate and become increasingly angry.

Emblematic of the dangers ahead was the upsurge in xenophobia and anti-foreign sentiment in Alexandra following the 1994 election. One of the difficult responsibilities I had as president of the Alexandra Civic in late 1994 was to try to talk some sense into people who blame unemployment, the proliferation of shacks, overuse of facilities, new forms of violence, and other social ills on Mozambican, Angolan, Malawian, Zimbabwean, and Zambian immigrants (many of whom are legally in the country after decades of formal migrant labor, and many more of whom recently came in search of jobs and are not legal). Ironically, these were (with the exception of Malawi) the frontline states that hosted us while we were in exile, and that were bombed and sabotaged by South Africa because of their liberated status and their geographical proximity to apartheid.

And more tragically, South Africa today continues to nurture more than our fair share of ex-colonial British, Portuguese, and other white castaways from these African countries, who drifted like deadwood down to apartheid South Africa and who have since been guaranteed their government jobs and pensions under the new democratic order, even as they join the fascist white right and further poison South African politics. These tens of thousands of mercenaries, soldiers of fortune, and parasites should be the first targets of xenophobia, not unemployed, oppressed blacks. But they are generally out of sight of the average township resident.

Most importantly, some of our Alexandra residents fail to see that we must solve excessive immigration not through vigilantism and harassment on the South African side of the border, but instead by creating a coherent Southern African economic region which is non-exploitative and which develops more evenly. I made it clear to the press that although a few opportunistic leaders of the Alexandra Property Owners' Association organized a march of 400 residents to the police station in January 1995, demanding immediate eviction of foreign residents, the ACO distanced itself from such misplaced emotions. But we need more than just statements; we need a process of education for Alexandra residents who take out their frustrations on a new South African "other," the foreigners whose nation-state borders often arose out of the figment of some colonialist's imagination in the first place. But I fear that this problem, which reflects blind frustration, will only worsen if progress on township development continues to stagnate.

Development at a standstill

We must move from blaming foreigners, and return to the more important causes of the failure of development to take root in Alexandra following the 1994 election. Overall, the state of Alexandra's development remains dismal. Residents remain oppressed and exploited in our work and as consumers. The delivery of services is still inadequate. The roads are potholed, demonstrating the low quality of work of the top-down development agencies. We remain without adequate transport. Our environment is a disaster and preventable diseases are rife. Here we blame not just ourselves for litter, but other, more fundamental, causes: pollution from nearby industries, the dumping of toxic waste by unethical companies, and on the part of local government, the lack of sanitation and clean water supply, soil erosion caused by inadequate civil engineering work, and the failure to maintain the ecology of the Jukskei River in contrast to its beauty when flowing through white residential areas.

The women's hostel is still overcrowded, and in general Alexandra women remain the most oppressed residents. Their safety is often threatened, especially when moving around at night. And they work overtime in the household, in the community, and when generating income. While women are the heartbeat of the civic, taking leadership at yard level, they are rarely in the ranks of the executive. When there are opportunities for education or travel, we in the civic have still not been effective in promoting women's interests.

Another key development issue is housing. In the old section of Alex, housing is still an appalling mess. The one-room dwellings are host to large families. The mushrooming of shacks is a contentious issue. We hear allegations that shack settlements are the result of leaders (including ourselves) bringing in their followers. This is untrue, and fails to confront the fact that we are centrally located in the economic heart of South Africa, so we receive waves of newcomers who are facing crisis in their home areas. In addition, our own sons and daughters desperately seek privacy, and therefore move into shacks.

For example, the Far East Bank continued to demonstrate how an undemocratic outside agency, in this case the Independent Development Trust, with its top-down site-and-service system, could continue to divide communities and undermine local organization. This area, which had so much potential for community-controlled planning, may simply continue to degenerate into a massive slum. The reason is simple: people are moving to this large field where there are only standpipes, outside toilets, some infrastructural connections, and gravel roads. Most of the new residents earn less than R1,000 per month, and simply do not have sufficient resources to build houses on the plots. The old conditions of squalid shack housing may well emerge in the new area.

It is not as if we in the civic movement are unaware of the solutions to these and other development problems. We know we need new systems to protect our scarce resources, such as land. Some civics begun experimenting with cooperatives and housing associations, which prevent speculation and ruiding of land and housing by the rich. In Alex, the ACO realized that we could not work solely within the township, but that we must acquire land for housing beyond the East Bank, in Modderfontein, Frankenwold, and even Sandton and Randburg. So much land is lying fallow while so many Alex residents are overcrowded. Yet official intentions for new developments in the area, such as Frankenwold, are to increase the supply of "non-racial" middle-class housing. Nevertheless, ACO continues to push for Alexandra-centered development to reverse apartheid planning. This means we must force Sandton and other traditionally white areas of the Johannesburg metropolitan area to finance the desperately needed infrastructure and services in black townships.

ACO's ambitions have not lessened. Our next major development must be a housing project, not site-and-service. It must be the product of negotiations with a new non-racial local authority that enjoys a unified tax base. The design must be compatible with the needs of women. Developments must be fully integrated, with new schools, creches, recreation, and health facilities. We must plant more trees and shrubs to beautify and cleanse the environment.

One example of the civic's continuing resolve, on New Year's Day 1995, was an effort to prevent the burning of tires and other debris in the streets. New Year's is traditionally the time when barricades go up and the roads are lit with fires. This time the civic leaders decided that this trademark of defiance in our struggle would have to give way to a more environmentally sound celebration which would not prove as damaging to the infrastructure or to our lungs. Even with just four days spent on organizing the ban, it was a successful campaign, with the streets 99 percent bonfire-free in 1995.

But ACO has faced its own internal struggles just to remain a powerful voice for the voiceless, a well-organized community group, a coherent office offering advice and support to residents, a source of information, and site of debate and knowledge generation. The challenge of maintaining a civic organization during the turmoil and distractions of political transition was one of the greatest I have faced.

The Alexandra Civic during the transition

What happened, then, to civic organization in Alexandra from the early AAC to ACO in the early 1990s, and beyond?

As I showed in Part Two, the enormous potential of the Alexandra Action Committee in the mid-1980s was truncated by blunt police and army repression. Our embryonic, latter-day Paris Commune was nipped in the bud, when our leaders were rounded up and tried for high treason and other layers of the civic were forced underground. There were, of course, agents of repression in Alexandra other than the armed white men in hippos and Caspirs, and we saw how the township came to play host to a small circus of sellouts, vigilantes, charlatans, and informants from within the community (some of whom are still active today), as well as shadowy security figures and smooth-talking white officials bent on co-opting black activists. But no ordinary Alexandra resident could fail to recognize who was on whose side. The AAC was the most popular organization in the township's history, and from the regime's standpoint, it had to be banned and broken in order for apartheid to carry on during the insurrectionary mid-1980s.

In the early 1990s, when the Alexandra Civic Organization picked up the AAC mantle, the civic again enjoyed a very high level of popular legitimacy, notwithstanding the increasingly more complex social divisions and class structure of the township. There were still strong residues of the regime's repressive organs, reconstituted as the Joint Management Committee and active within other state bureaucracies (like the Development Bank of Southern Africa). But it was an entirely different experience building community organizations in the early 1990s, because not only could civic leaders negotiate with the regime directly, but the enemy now included a much more sophisticated crew of development technocrats even more intent on co-opting us and forcing us to accept their capitalist agenda.

This new situation reflected not only the regime's weakness and acceptance of imminent power sharing, but ours. We spent countless hours in strategy sessions and smoke-filled rooms which would otherwise have been better spent doing grassroots organizing. The negotiations route was not necessarily the wrong one for ACO, but it challenged us to step up our organization-building work. These should not be seen as contradictory, for the more sophisticated social movements become, the more they have to do both, simultaneously, with greater and greater skill.

We occasionally stumbled due to an overemphasis on one side or the other. For example, one of our clearest weaknesses was retaining, training, and recruiting personnel. Our small office staff always grew when we encountered emergencies, even with nearly everyone having the status of volunteer. But over time, as our staff became vastly overstretched, our consultations, report-backs, education sessions, committee meetings, planning sessions, media publicity work, demonstrations, and other forms of organization-building faltered.

Political violence was also partly responsible for our problems. I think back to the cold-blooded assassinations of civic allies like Michael Dhlomo, the talented young activist killed in the March 1991 vigil massacre, and Jama Makhosi, a fine comrade and self-defense unit member who had been assigned to protect the ACO office but who was gunned down one morning in November 1991 as he bounded up the office stairs. I think of the way our civic hostel committees were hounded out of the two mens' hostels. I shudder in recalling the violent deaths of more than 200 of our residents during those conflagrations in 1991 and 1992.

Death was very close to our door during the early 1990s, whether at the hands of the apartheid regime's Third Force or Inkatha. We had every reason to keep our organizing on safe turf. The ACO office was moved twice, once into the center of Alex, and then (because of limited office space) to the outskirts of the township in Marlboro.

What did all of this mean for ACO as an organization? Most importantly, people were quite rightly frightened to come to meetings in the township during the worst periods of violence. And because of the violence, we had to take more care in running our campaigns in safe zones, away from the Beirut area, for instance. The most important priority on the ground was defense. This meant that our offensive strategies had to be put on hold. It made our reporting back to mass meetings extremely difficult.

But on the more positive side, we did survive both the mid-1980s and early 1990s attempts to liquidate our organization. And while negotiations proved such a distraction that I left the table in 1991 in order to return to organizing work, they did provide a site of struggle for some of our better-trained staff and leaders (working with experts from Planact). Indeed, the ACO staff and leaders gained great experience during the early 1990s, which is now being put to use in national, provincial, and local government. In 1994, former ACO president Moss Mayekiso became a national member of parliament, general secretary Richard Mdakane became the chief whip of the provincial Gauteng parliament, and deputy president Tex Molobi went to the Northwest Province to work in the local government department. In 1995, four more ACO leaders—general secretary Mary Ntingane, deputy general secretary Thabo Motlou, housing committee chair Goodwill Qhushwana, and ACO treasurer Buda Raja (representing our area committee in the Indian area of Marlboro)—left for elected positions in the metropolitan government. Yet with these departures, the civic movement lost years of experience.

This assessment of civic organizing in Alexandra rests upon what I hope are transitional problems, such as periods of repression, the time-wasting negotiating tactics of the dying regime, the incompetence of conservative development agencies, and our loss of cadres to jobs in government. But there is a final problem that may prove far more persistent: our perpetual difficulty in acquiring sufficient resources to run an organization, to ensure that good quality staff remain with the civic, and to promote the kinds of development programs and projects which give our residents minimal basic necessities, opportunities to control their own lives, and hope for the future.

Resources for the civics

Civic associations are expected to do an enormous amount of work, and most civics are very fortunate if they have only one or two paid, full-time staff members (as ACO managed through most of the early 1990s). ACO attempted a variety of fund-raising initiatives, including a membership fee of R5 per year. One of our more creative initiatives was to try to establish a community-supported fund that would have small but mandatory contributions from residents (R2 per month), who in turn could direct their individual funds to popular community organizations of all types by means of a (secret ballot) democratic vote. This system got off the ground briefly in Alexandra, as part of the Alexandra Accord, but was attempted with more consistency in other townships (such as Tembisa and eMbalenhle) and was later proposed as a national model by SANCO. (It is similar to fund-raising strategies that the United States consumer advocate Ralph Nader has successfully implemented.)

But international support has been the ACO's main source of funds. This was often based on community-to-community relations, such as the excellent friendship with the Chicago Sister-Community project. And we were always very grateful to the Dutch solidarity group Committee for Southern Africa (KZA), to a progressive Montreal-based development agency (CIDMA), and to the official Swedish aid agency (SIDA), for example, because they provided funds with no strings attached. In addition, after 1990, as the movement's view of the U.S. Agency for International Development began to change (and as U.S. AID needed to gain credibility quickly, and remained prohibited from giving money to the then-apartheid government), we also took money from the U.S. government for a couple of years. (With the election of the Government of National Unity, many sources of solidarity funds began to dry up.)

None of this is to deny the general problem that progressive organizations and governments have witnessed in the third world, which is that foreign funders often attach conditions to grants, use their influence for information-gathering and propaganda purposes, or even try to change the nature of the organization's politics. We were extremely conscious of this problem, and we often heard reports of these dangers from comrades in other community and sectoral organizations within the democratic movement. But in Alexandra (and in SANCO), to my knowledge, no such manipulative efforts were made, perhaps because of our legacy of self-direction.

Nevertheless, foreign grant funding creates dependency. And as citizens and taxpayers, our residents had every reason to demand that our own democratic government provide support to the civic movement, so long as the civics continued to be the primary instruments through which the popular will of the oppressed communities could be expressed. A civic which wanted to be the main representative of a given township had to prove its overall accountability and sensitivity. From SANCO's head office, we always encouraged civics to try to represent the multiple voices, identities, class interests, and other opinions that swirl through any community. We remained confident that no other kind of organization, in either Alexandra or South Africa as a whole, was doing as good a job as the civics in articulating community needs and leading negotiations for reform.

This is to say, therefore, that civics developed a convincing justification for financial support from the first democratic government, so long as there is no danger that such funding is used to create dependency or to buy support artificially. SANCO's Commission on Development Finance set out quite clearly this position in its April 1994 report, *Making People-Driven Development Work*:

> Capacity building finance does not lead directly to the building of infrastructure or homes. But it does lead to the building of confidence and of community organizations. These are essential.

> Because of the legacy of apartheid, capacity building will not be cheap. For small grants in its drought relief development program, IDT allocated 7.5 percent for capacity building, and this was insufficient. Capacity building costs will probably be at least 5-10 percent of the cost of the actual physical works of large capital projects, and up to 25 percent of smaller projects.

> Capacity building has become a popular part of the jargon of development agencies, but they tend to consider it to be visits by "facilitators" and a few weekend workshops. Capacity building does require this, but it also requires much more. It always requires hiring someone locally as a community organizer. It also means training in management, financial control, and bookkeeping skills that cannot be passed on in a weekend; these typically require one to three month courses. Capacity building demands support and training which continue after the construction is done to ensure that management and maintenance skills are learned. Capacity building support might include vouchers for special training courses, for example for bookkeeping or management.

> Finally, capacity building requires time—for long meetings where people learn to take control, for the initial slowness in all processes as people gain experience, and for the local recognition of what skills are needed and what further training is required.

In the future, capacity building finance must be seen as essential and as a right. We must curb the power of unelected gatekeepers. The challenge for the new government will be to develop mechanisms which are simple, quick, transparent, and efficient, while preventing corruption and ensuring broad participation.

A few months later, when the *White Paper on Reconstruction and Development* (the government's plan for implementation of the RDP) was released, civic leaders were pleased that at least this demand for capacity building finance appeared to have become official policy. In a chapter entitled "Consultation, Participation and Capacity-Building," the *White Paper on Reconstruction and Development* made several specific commitments:

Capacity-building is required in civil society to ensure effective participation in RDP implementation. Through initiatives such as Presidential Projects, path-breaking approaches to consultation, participation and local control will be explored. There will be financial support to civics and other community-based organizations during the course of an RDP campaign to establish Local Government legitimacy and hence improve both service delivery and user payments. Development projects such as those funded through the National Public Works Program (with a business-labor-community commitment to labor-based construction methods) will also contain a far greater training and capacity-building component, with women targeted as beneficiaries. The Public Service Training Institute will make its resources available to civil society in addition to the civil service. Increasingly, organizations of civil society will be involved in planning and policy-making through a variety of advisory boards, commissions, forums and other venues by which experience is gained and skills are acquired. The new approach to freedom of public information will also play an enhancing role in capacity-building....

Organizations of civil society should continue to have the choice of access to alternative sources of services such as policy research, so that they are not completely dependent on Government. In addition, community-based development organizations will receive more extensive financial and logistical support once representativity, accountability, and effectiveness are confirmed....

With respect to mass-based organizations of civil society—especially the labor movement and the civics—their role in the establishment of political democracy was central. They have also won very substantial improvements in the social and economic lives of their constituents. A vibrant and independent civil society is essential to the democratization of the society that is envisaged by the RDP. Mass-based organizations will exercise essential checks and balances on the power of Government to act unilaterally, without transparency, corruptly, or inefficiently....

The social partnership envisaged by the RDP does not, however, imply that mass organizations do not retain the right to their own interpretation of—and their own goals for—the RDP.

Civics will indeed develop their own, often different, interpretation of the RDP and its implementation. If funding support is delivered consistently with the intentions stated in the *White Paper*, civics in general, and SANCO in particular, should be in a good position to lead the local RDP process. This will involve upgrading our local organizations, guiding and controlling development in the interests of all residents, establishing policy positions on key issues, and playing a variety of other roles. SANCO will promote this process nationally, for our policy positions became official ANC policy and even government policy in some key areas.

SANCO also gave the new government an entire layer of staff, hoping that activists fresh from struggle, steeped in our culture of accountability, and familiar with the challenges of development and democracy, would strengthen the state without allowing it to become suffocating. SANCO conceded that the former civic leaders would no longer be able to retain their formal civic roles, as they must represent the interests of the government. SANCO maintained a firm position here, consistent with our policy on independence from the state. But that does not prevent us from using all our allies within the new government, influencing and pressuring them, and demanding from the state the resources which will allow our movement to prosper for many years to come.

Another important resource of the civics, and one that came under surprising threat in the initial months after liberation—surprising in view of the praise and promises for civics in the RDP and the *White Paper on Reconstruction and Development*—was the sense that SANCO had a role to play in policy making.

SANCO's struggle to influence
the Government of National Unity

The Government of National Unity, meanwhile, felt compelled to clamp down hard on grassroots protest in situations where wildcat strikes or land invasions or occupation of vacant housing or inner-city buildings threatened the sanctity of private property. There were lots of protests, mostly a function of reasonable expectations that were not being met.

Even where SANCO was not involved, the impression was somehow being created that civics had become an anarchic force opposed to reconstruction and development. For example, some conservative forces within the new government, as well as in the bourgeois press, began a hysterical campaign of blaming SANCO for what were termed "continuing rent and bond boycotts." The universal sentiment was for an end to rent and bond boycotts and a rapid increase in payment rates (which remained around 20 percent). But by now this was a red herring, since no one was calling for boycotts (aside from a few threats from so-called colored areas), and indeed SANCO leaders now stressed that not only should payments resume, some of the arrears would also have to be met by residents.

The nonpayment of rent and service charges was not the result of a civic-generated "culture of nonpayment," as many conservatives enjoyed arguing. Instead, nonpayment reflected the fact that economic circumstances in the townships continued to be extremely unfavorable, and residents did not experience any noticeable increase in household income with the 1994 economic upturn. Moreover, as Linda Mngomezulu, SANCO Gauteng spokesperson, put it in early 1995, "Only if the causes of the boycotts such as the low quality of houses and services were resolved, would the boycotts end." Meanwhile, SANCO took the decision to cooperate with the government, hoping to avoid the eviction of nonpayers at all costs.

An even more disturbing problem arose in the area of housing policy. Unfortunately, the new government did not immediately follow the housing policy guidelines of the RDP, and instead endorsed a compromise "incremental housing" policy that fell far short of SANCO's suggestions and the RDP promises. The deal for housing finance that government negotiators struck with the banks in October 1994 was particularly disappointing. Before the deal, if a family forfeited its house to a foreclosure, often through no fault of its own (losing a job, becoming ill, etc.), a bank had been unable in many cases to kick the family out because of community pressure. The government-bank agreement specifically stripped communities of the strength that pressure, by allowing the bank to give the loan to the government, which in turn would apply heavier pressure against individuals (the bank was let off the hook). In short, the deal made it impossible for grassroots forces to exercise their own countervailing power against bank foreclosures.

Sadly, the extensive experience SANCO had with the banks (two years of in-depth negotiations) was ignored by the small band of white men negotiating for both government and the banks. Therefore, in many areas the deal reached between the banks and government was a huge step back from what SANCO had negotiated in February 1993 (which had given borrowers more flexibility in loan repayments, and empowered community groups to monitor bank lending and services activity). The problem of bank redlining also remained outstanding, because the government-bank agreement did not prevent banks from discriminating on the basis of race, gender, or geographical area.

There were other areas of conflict. Some of the SANCO affiliates in the Eastern Cape, for example, were engaged in struggles against traditional leaders. President Mandela went to investigate in December 1994 and again in February 1995; the Office of the President issued this statement:

> The President criticized the leadership of SANCO for not doing enough to educate their membership about the important role that has been played by traditional leaders in the anti-colonial struggle. He cited great warriors like Hintsa, Sekhukhune, Dingane and many others who made colonial advance difficult by waging fearless resistance over decades. He referred to mistakes that were made in other countries by abolishing traditional institutions only to regret it later. The President reminded the leadership of SANCO that many traditional leaders had played an important role in the ANC election victory. It would be wrong for them to be ignored now that democracy had been attained, he emphasized.

> The President also pointed out that the process of democratization would necessitate that traditional leaders stay above politics. He called upon traditional leaders to respect SANCO just as they would expect SANCO leaders and members to respect them.

> President Mandela explained that the recent past bedevils the development of healthy relations between the communities and traditional leaders. He pointed out that many traditional leaders collaborated with the apartheid regime. Some even assisted the oppressive machinery.

The latent tensions between the civics and traditional leaders relate to the local government electoral process. The elections threaten the institution of traditional rule, and hence careful discussions must occur between the chiefs, progressive political parties, and organizations of civil society, including SANCO. In this case, President Mandela was careful to consult with SANCO, but there was always the danger of the civics being left out of crucial negotiations at the local, provincial, and national levels.

In short, the civics would face more and more resistance to our legitimate role as a social movement; as a force, in other words, that raised issues and embarked upon coordinated campaigns to counteract the power of big business and conservative elements within the state. This was spelled out clearly by two Urban Foundation intellectuals, Anne Bernstein and Jeff McCarthy, in November 1994 (right before the collapse of the UF and its emergency merger into the Consultative Business Movement). Not surprisingly, *Business Day* was the site of the debates.

On the one hand, they argued, "The difference between the functions of a local branch of a political party and a local community organization is clear. The local branch of a political party is there to promote support for the party and its policies. A local community organization exists to promote the interests of that community as perceived by the members of that organization." There is no problem so far.

But on the other hand, Bernstein and McCarthy continue, "It is more difficult to envisage a national local community organization with national policies and programs. It is hard to understand which particular 'community' that organization would represent." The implication of this argument is to liquidate SANCO.

This was made even more explicit a week later by the oft-quoted commentator Steven Friedman (in an article entitled "Having SANCO at the Table Will Be Bad for Digestion"), in his effort to prevent us from having representation on the government's new National Economic, Development and Labor Council. (Friedman apparently was backtracking on desires he expressed in 1991 and 1992 for "inclusivity" in government.)

Among other claims, Friedman argued that civics were not representative of rural, shack, or hostel residents. (This was also a criticism of allegedly "single-issue" civics, carried uncritically from Jeremy Seekings's writings, in the otherwise excellent 1994 book by Martin Murray, *The Revolution Deferred*.) He also claimed, "SANCO leadership is somewhat distant from many issues likely to be negotiated at the council. Trade and tariff policy, wage and productivity trade-offs and the like have not been the meat and drink of SANCO activity."

But SANCO's policy arms were stretched into these areas and many more, including the Trade and Industry Department's reference team on trade, a variety of small enterprise development task forces, the Southern African Development Community, and numerous local economic development initiatives. SANCO President Lechesa Tsenoli and Finance and Economic Development Department Chair Sandi Mgidlana responded,

> Surely the macro-economy has a bearing on the micro level? At the end of the day, the broad parameters set at the national level will either thwart or promote activities at the micro level.

> For example, we have ideas about the World Bank, IMF, and their engagement with us; how the economy as a whole must be geared toward addressing the basic needs of our communities; how the budget must be used to stimulate the economy without penalizing the poor and disadvantaged; how our national industrial policies must be in harmony with our regional, continental, and international goals.

As Lechesa and Sandi aptly concluded, "Friedman has done a sloppy job. The policy formulation environment in our country should not be polluted by this kind of shoddy work. He owes his profession an apology."

But more importantly, as Martin Murray wrote, "Without a distinctive political program of its own that would enable it to chart a course of action largely independent from political parties and state institutions, the civic movement risked marginalization and eventual disappearance as a viable social force." My contention, which I make on the basis of South African and *international* civic politics, is that exactly this sort of political program is now emerging among the world's leading social movements, from the Freedom from Debt Coalition in Manila to the Third World Network in Malaysia and Bombay, to SANCO in South Africa, to Latin American urban protest organizations, to the Zapatistas of Chiapas, Mexico. Everywhere, the ravages of the world economy are denuding the ability of nation states to make their own policy, and are intimidating even popular political parties like the ANC to cut loose from their progressive roots. With the South African economy still dominated by enormous conglomerates that have international escape routes, the ANC requires continuing critical support from the civics, trade unions, churches, and other bodies. But more generally, international civic politics is a real alternative to weak nation-states across the globe.

The future of international civic politics

The most important lesson of the pages I have written so far does not concern development and democracy in Alexandra, the township social movement, national politics, or even the prospects for socialism in South Africa. I believe that what we have learned over the last decade or so in the civic movement can inform the future of global progressive politics, which I firmly believe rests upon democratic organizing and mass mobilization from within working-class civil society.

As SANCO's first International Representative, I began to explore this idea by observing how anti-apartheid movements around the world became people-to-people movements. In South Africa, we realized how much we had to learn from similar struggles elsewhere. We understood that other social movements had adopted their own, equally effective strategies and tactics. But we also knew that we could transfer some of our own lessons in democratic organization and struggle, and establish permanent international linkages between the popular, progressive forces.

In places like Mexico City, I encountered similar social struggles to ours, particularly for decent housing. Even in a rich society like Holland, I found a squatter movement. And upon my arrival in Rio de Janeiro, Brazil, I was greeted by the news of a massacre of forty-two favela (township) residents by state police in a revenge attack the previous night, which quickly brought back memories of tragically similar Alexandra events of 1986, 1991, and 1992. I met a bereaved woman, whose family of eight was murdered, and I flashed back to the fateful night vigil in 1991 on Second Avenue, where fifteen of our best young community and student activists were gunned down. In the United States, the experiences in some cities reminded me still further of South African townships. We see flashy American images on the movie screens, but the dirt and grit of the inner cities is not so different from our own ghetto situation. Go to the South Side of Chicago, Alexandra's sister city, or to Watts, Los Angeles, or to East New York, in Brooklyn, and you find homelessness, unemployment, and crime to rival our own.

There are also concrete lessons on community development to learn from comrades in civic organizations across the globe, including the United States. In places such as Washington, DC, Chicago, New York, Atlanta, Pittsburgh, and San Francisco, I have worked with solidarity committees and learned a great deal about local government and local economic develop-

Back in the township for the first time after our acquittal, April 1989. From left to right: Mdakane, Tshabalala, me, Obed Bapela, and Moss. *Photo courtesy of the Star, Johannesburg.*

ment. We must put people to work, build decent housing and community facilities, assist informal businesses, initiate labor and building material cooperatives which can gain preferential access to construction contracts, and maybe start our own community bank. All these things have been done elsewhere by advanced comrades working in community development.

From the perspective of community mobilization, there are also tough civic associations in the United States ghettos, such as the Industrial Areas Foundation, the Association of Communities Organizing for Reform Now, Citizen Action, National People's Action, and others. Some of them draw inspiration from Saul Alinsky, who in Chicago helped develop organizing tactics from the 1940s to the 1960s. In turn, his students in the Philippines wrote manuals and handbooks which many of our leading South African civic comrades used in the late 1970s to help our movement get off the ground.

We have witnessed nine successful sister-community relationships with the United States alone, including one between the civic organization in Alexandra and the city of Chicago, as well as very impressive projects connecting St. Paul, Minnesota, with Lawaaikamp in the Eastern Cape, and Wichita, Kansas, with Thornhill in the homeland of the Ciskei. Other sister-community links have burgeoned with Holland and England. (A recent book on such linkages, Michael Shuman's *Toward a Global Village*, is highly recommended.) There are also many institution-to-institution linkages developing, ranging from universities and schools to farmer groups and rural craft cooperatives.

What all of this should make evident is that the daily struggles of people across the world have much in common. There is, in fact, a growing recognition that poor and working class citizens of different countries now have more in common with each other than they do with their own elites. We must develop a whole new approach, a "foreign policy" of working-class civil society. I hope South Africa will become a bastion of such thinking, because of the political solidarity that we have experienced in past years.

Unfortunately, of course, what we have in common with our sisters and brothers across the world is economic inequality and uneven development. Racial apartheid may become class apartheid, which is a phenomenon in many countries at present. The World Bank and International Monetary Fund impose very similar Structural Adjustment Programs on each country, aimed at lowering wages and shrinking welfare states and making conditions ripe for big international businesses. One very unfortunate result is a spate of "IMF riots," which have helped to topple many dozens of unpopular governments, but which as David Seddon and John Walton show in their 1994 book *Free Markets and Food Riots*, have not so far been sufficiently well-organized to replace corrupt regimes with anything better.

The common conditions that structural adjustment imposes on all of the poor communities I have visited must be understood in global terms. This will allow us to develop stronger links between the oppressed peoples, and to develop an organization (or organizations) that serve our interests in international fora. If we have common problems, we logically have common solutions.

From my visits to the United States ghettos, the *barrios* of Mexico, and the *favelas* of Brazil, I have a growing conviction that an international body devoted to linking civic associations can become a reality. There are many difficulties in organizing such a body, of course. While we cannot uncritically translate the local experience to the global, my view is that our processes of mass mobilization, democracy building, addressing local grievances, and building new institutions in the community can all be shared with our comrades in other societies. That is the subject of my future work, where I hope to join the reader in ongoing struggles for social justice and democracy.

Bibliography

Articles and books

Bernstein, A. and McCarthy, J. "High Time for Some Soul-Searching by Civic Organizations." *Business Day*, 4 November 1994.

Boaden, B. and Taylor, R. "Informal Settlement: Theory Versus Practice in KwaZulu/Natal." *The Apartheid City and Beyond: Urbanization and Social Change in South Africa*. Edited by D. Smith. London: Routledge, 1992.

Bond, P. "Township Housing and South Africa's 'Financial Explosion': The Theory and Practice of Financial Capital in Alexandra." *Urban Forum* 1, no. 2 (November 1990).

Boraine, A. "Managing the Urban Crisis, 1986-1989." In *South African Review* 5, edited by G. Moss and I. Obery. Johannesburg: Ravan Press, 1989.

Botha, T. "Civic Associations as Autonomous Organs of Grassroots Participation." *Theoria*, no. 79 (May 1992).

Callinicos, A. *South Africa Between Reform and Revolution*. London: Bookmarks, 1988.

Carter, C. "Community and Conflict: The Alexandra Rebellion of 1986." *Journal of Southern African Studies* 18, no. 1 (1991).

———. "Comrades and Community: Politics and the Construction of Hegemony in Alexandra Township, South Africa, 1984-1987." Ph.D diss., Oxford University, Oxford, England, 1991.

Castells, M. *The City and the Grassroots*. Berkeley: University of California Press, 1983.

Centre for the Study of the South African Economy and International Finance *Quarterly Report*, August. London: London School of Economics, 1993.

Cronin, J. "Workers' Party Plays into Nat Hands." *Weekly Mail*, 29 July 1993.

Cross, S. "From Anomie to Civil Society in South Africa: Reflections on Development Planning." African Studies Seminar paper, St. Anthony's College, Oxford, 1992.

Engels, F. *The Housing Question*. Moscow: Progress Publishers, 1979.

Frank, A. G. and Fuentes, M. "Civil Democracy: Social Movements in Recent World History." In *Transforming the Revolution: Social Movements and the World-System,* edited by S. Amin, G. Arrighi, A.G. Frank, and I. Wallerstein. New York: Monthly Review Press, 1990.
Friedman, S. "An Unlikely Utopia: State and Civil Society in South Africa." *Politikon* (December 1991).
Friedman, S. "Bonaparte at the Barricades: The Colonisation of Civil Society." *Theoria,* no. 79 (May 1992).
———. "Having SANCO at the Table Will Be Bad for Digestion." *Business Day,* 14 November 1994.
Gramsci, A. *Selections from the Prison Notebooks of Antonio Gramsci.* Edited by Q. Hoare. London: Lawrence and Wishart, 1971.
Jacobs, B. "Heading for Disaster?" *Work in Progress* (December 1992).
Jochelson, K. "Reform, Repression and Resistance in South Africa: A Case Study of Alexandra Township, 1979-1989." *Journal of Southern African Studies* 1, no. 16 (1990).
Kane-Berman, J. *South Africa's Silent Revolution.* Johannesburg: Institute of Race Relations, 1990.
———. *Political Violence in South Africa.* Johannesburg: Institute of Race Relations, 1993.
Lucas, J. "Civic Organization in Alexandra during the 1990s: An Ethnographic Approach." Paper prepared for the Albert Einstein Institution Project on Civil Society, University of the Witwatersrand, Johannesburg, 1994.
Marx, K. *The Civil War in France.* In *Selected Works* by K. Marx and F. Engels. Moscow: Progress Publishers, 1968.
Mashabela, H. *Mekhukhu.* Johannesburg: Institute of Race Relations, 1990.
Mayekiso, Moses. "State of the Civic Movement: Year-end Statement by SANCO President Moses Mayekiso." Johannesburg, 17 December 1992.
Morris, M. and Padayachee, V. "State Reform Policy in South Africa." *Transformation,* no. 9 (1988).
Murray, M. *The Revolution Deferred.* London: Verso, 1994.
Mzala. "Building People's Power." *Sechaba* (September 1986).
Nzimande, B. "Let Us Take the People with Us: A Reply to Joe Slovo." *African Communist,* no. 131 (Fourth Quarter 1992).
Nzimande, B. and Sikhosana, M. "Civics Are Part of the National Democratic Revolution." *Mayibuye* (June 1991).
———. "Civil Society and Democracy." *African Communist,* no. 128 (First Quarter 1992).
———. "Civil Society Does Not Equal Democracy." *Work in Progress* (September 1992).
Peires, J. *The House of Phalo.* Johannesburg: Ravan Press, 1984.
Petras, J. and Morley, M. *U.S. Hegemony Under Siege: Class, Politics and Development in Latin America.* London: Verso, 1990.
Sader, E. and Silverstein, K. *Without Fear of Being Happy.* London: Verso, 1991.
Sarakinsky, M. "From 'Freehold Township' to 'Model Township': A Political

History of Alexandra, 1905-1983." BA thesis, University of the Witwatersrand, Johannesburg, 1984.

Schlemmer, L. "Organizing Communities: The International Experience." *Strategic Planning for Civics*. Report on Workshop of Civic Associations of Johannesburg and the Urban Foundation Development Strategy and Policy Unit, Urban Foundation, Johannesburg, August 1992.

Seekings, J. "Quiescence and the Transition to Confrontation: South African Townships, 1978-1984." Ph.D. diss., Oxford University, Oxford, England, 1990.

——. "South Africa's Townships 1980-1991: An Annotated Bibliography." Department of Sociology Occasional Paper No. 16. Stellenbosch: University of Stellenbosch Research Unit for Sociology of Development, 1992.

——. "Civic Organization in South African Townships." *South African Review* 6, edited by G. Moss and I. Obery. Johannesburg: Ravan Press, 1992.

——. *Heroes or Villains?* Braamfontein: Ravan Press, 1993.

Shubane, K. "Civil Society in Apartheid and Post-apartheid South Africa." *Theoria*, no. 79 (May 1992).

——. "The Changing Urban Environment." *Strategic Planning for Civics*. Report on Workshop of Civic Associations of Johannesburg and the Urban Foundation Development Strategy and Policy Unit, Urban Foundation, Johannesburg, August 1992.

—— and Madiba, P. "The Struggle Continues? Civic Associations in the Transition." *CPS Transition Series*, Research Report No. 25. Johannesburg: University of the Witwatersrand Centre for Policy Studies, October 1992.

Shuman, M. *Toward a Global Village*. London: Pluto, 1994.

South African Communist Party. "The Role of the SACP in the Transition to Democracy and Socialism." *African Communist*, no. 132 (First Quarter 1993).

South African Government. *White Paper on Reconstruction and Development*. Capetown: Office of the President, November 1994.

South African National Civic Organization (SANCO). "Bank Capital Flight: SA's Next Economic Catastrophe?" Paper issued in conjunction with Eltsa (London), Johannesburg, 23 February 1993.

——. *Making People-Driven Development Work*. Johannesburg, April 1994.

Stadler, A. "A Strong State Civilises Society: A Response to Louw." *Work in Progress* (December 1992).

Swilling, M. "Socialism, Democracy and Civil Society: The Case for Associational Socialism." *Work in Progress* (July/August 1991).

——. "Quixote at the Windmills: Another Conspiracy Thesis from Steven Friedman." *Theoria*, no. 79 (May 1992).

——. *Roots of Transition*. Berkeley: University of California Press, forthcoming.

Tourikis, P. "The 'Political Economy' of Alexandra Township: 1905-1958." BA thesis, University of the Witwatersrand, Johannesburg, South Africa, 1981.

Tsenoli, L. and Mgidlana, S. "SANCO Has a Key Role in Economic Policy Making." *Business Day*, 17 November 1994.

Tshandu, Z. "The State of Health Care Services in South Africa: A Case Study."
BA thesis, University of the Witwatersrand, Johannesburg, South Africa,
1986.

Tucker, B. and Scott, B., eds. *South Africa: Prospects for Successful Transition,
Nedcor/Old Mutual Scenarios.* Johannesburg: Juta Press, 1992.

Urban Foundation. "Local Government Negotiating Initiatives in the PWV."
Unpublished paper, 1992.

Walton, J. and Seddon, D. *Free Markets and Food Riots.* Oxford: Basil Blackwell,
1994.

Wisner, B. *Power and Need in Africa.* London: Earthscan, 1988.

World Bank. "Effective Implementation: Key to Development Impact." Report of
the Portfolio Management Task Force. Washington, DC: World Bank, 1992.

Published articles by Mzwanele Mayekiso

"Carnage Comes to Alexandra." *Africa South* (May 1991).

"Hands Off the Civics and Civil Society!" *Work in Progress* (February 1992).

"Working-Class Civil Society: Why We Need It, and How We Get It." *African
Communist,* no. 129 (Second Quarter 1992).

"The Mood Is Changing…but Which Way?: A Departing View from Alexandra."
Africa South (August 1992).

"Civil Society and Local Government Negotiations: The Alexandra Experience."
Urban Forum 3, no.2 (1992).

"Harlem Trotting." *Africa South* (January/February 1993).

"Organizing Civics: We Need a Tight Federation." *Work in Progress* (April
1993).

"'Institutions that Themselves Need to Be Watched Over': A Review of Recent
Writings on the Civic Movement." *Urban Forum* 4, no.1 (1993).

"Heat, Light and Civil Society: Another Rejoinder to Nzimande and Sikhosana."
African Communist, no. 134 (Third Quarter 1993).

"Reinventing the Hammer and Sickle." *Work in Progress* (August 1993).

"I'm Black, So What's Bad?" *Africa South* (October 1993).

"The Legacy of Ungovernability." *Southern African Review of Books* (November/December 1993).

"ACO Presidential Address." *Alexandra Times* (December 1993).

"Civics Are Here to Stay." *Africa South and East* (January 1994).

"From the Trench to the Table." *Work in Progress* (February 1994).

"Report from the International Desk." *Umthunywa,* 21 March 1994.

"The 'Civics': Hope of the Townships." *Times Literary Supplement,* 1 April 1994.

"Charting a Future in South Africa." *Multinational Monitor* (May 1994).

"South Africa's Stepping Stone." *Red Pepper* (June 1994).

"The New Terms of Solidarity: A South African View." *Southern Africa Report*
(December 1994).

"Bell Curve, South African Style: Rewriting the Civics Movement." *Southern
Africa Report* (January 1995).